Leg Ulcers and Problems of the Lower Limb: An holistic approach

Other titles available from Wounds UK include:

Honey: A modern wound management product
edited by Richard White, Rose Cooper and Peter Molan

Essential Wound Management: An introduction for undergraduates
edited by David Gray, Pam Cooper and John Timmons

Wound Healing: A systematic approach to advanced wound healing and management edited by David Gray and Pam Cooper

Skin Care in Wound Management: Assessment, prevention and treatment
edited by Richard White

A Pocket Guide to Clinical Decision-making in Wound Management
edited by Sue Bale and David Gray

Paediatric Skin and Wound Care edited by Richard White
and Jacqueline Denyer

Trauma and Pain in Wound Care edited by Richard White
and Keith Harding

Advances in Wound Care, volume 1 edited by Richard White

Leg Ulcers and Problems of the Lower Limb: An holistic approach

edited by
Ellie Lindsay and Richard White

Wounds UK
Publishing

HealthComm UK Limited, trading as Wounds UK Limited, Suite 3.1,
36 Upperkirkgate, Aberdeen AB10 1BA

British Library Cataloguing-in-Publication Data
A catalogue record is available for this book

First published 2007
Reprinted 2008

ISBN-10 0-9555758-0-X
ISBN-13 978-0-9555758-0-8

Printed in the Malta by Gutenberg Press Limited, Tarxien, Malta

CONTENTS

Section II: The basics

Section III: Practical issues

CONTRIBUTORS

Anne-Marie Brown is Tissue Viability Service Lead, Tissue Viability Service, South West and South East Primary Care Trust

John Buchan is Associate Specialist in Age Care and Dermatology at Llandrindod Wells War Memorial Hospital, Llandrindod Wells, Powys, Wales

Janice Cameron is an Independent Nurse Advisor in Wound Care, Witney, Oxfordshire

Hildegard Charles is Lecturer and Consultant in Tissue Viability, Kensington and Chelsea Primary Care Trust, London

Louise Dalzell is District Nursing Sister and Leg Club lead at Combs Ford Surgery, Suffolk

Michael Clark is Senior Research Fellow, Wound Healing Research Unit, University of Wales, Cardiff

Mary Courtney is Professor of Nursing and Assistant Dean (Research), Faculty of Health, Queensland University of Technology, Institute of Health of Biomedical Innovation, Queensland, Australia

Keith Cutting is Principal Lecturer, Buckinghamshire New University, Chalfont St Giles, Buckinghamshire

Dr Leigh Davis is Lecturer in Nursing, School of Nursing, Faculty of Health, Institute of Health and Biomedical Innovation, Queensland University of Technology, Queensland, Australia

Julie Day is Leg Ulcer Specialist Nurse at Worcestershire Acute Hospitals NHS Trust, Worcester

Helen Edwards is Professor of Nursing and Head, School of Nursing, Queensland University of Technology and Institute of Health and Biomedical Innovation, Queensland, Australia

Kathleen Finlayson is Senior Research Assistant, Queensland University of Technology and Institute of Health and Biomedical Innovation, Queensland, Australia

Michelle Gibb is Project Coordinator, Australian Nurse Practitioner Project, Queensland University of Technology (QUT). At the time of writing her chapter for this book, she was Wound Care Clinical Nurse Consultant, Spiritus Care Services, Australia

Jenifer Hawkins is an Independent Health Psychologist/Clinical Supervisor and works part-time at Ipswich Hospital, Ipswich, Suffolk and The James Paget Hospital Gorlston, Great Yarmouth

Wendy Hayes is Nurse Consultant Vascular at Worcestershire Acute Hospitals NHS Trust, Worcester

Deborah Hofman is Clinical Nurse Specialist, Wound Healing, and Lead Nurse, Leg Ulcer Clinic, Department of Dermatology, Churchill Hospital, Oxford

Andrew Kingsley is Tissue Viability Nurse, Grampian Health Services, Aberdeen, and Clinical Manager, Wounds UK

Ellie Lindsay is Independent Specialist Practitioner and Associate Lecturer, Centre for Research and Implementation of Clinical Practice, Thames Valley University, London

Alistair McInnes is Senior Lecturer, University of Brighton, Eastbourne

Christine Moffatt is Professor of Nursing and Director of the Centre for Research and Implementation of Clinical Practice (CRICP) at Thames Valley University, London

Fiona Stephens is Head of Clinical Governance, Eastern and Coastal Kent Primary Care Trust

Joan Enric Torra i Bou is Clinical, Education and Prevention Manager, División Curación de Heridas, Advanced Wound Care, Smith & Nephew, Barcelona, Spain

Richard White is Professor of Tissue Viability, Institute of Health, Social Care and Psychology, University of Worcester, Worcester

FOREWORD

In the UK, wound care, especially the care of chronic wounds such as leg ulcers, has become a nurse-led discipline. This is entirely justified on the grounds that nurses are involved in much of the delivery of care, and, prominent nurses have been responsible for many of the major developments seen over the past 25 years. For example, the pioneering work of the Lothian and Forth Valley Leg ulcer group, the development of the four-layer bandaging system, the Cochrane Wounds collaboration, the Royal College of Nursing (RCN) guidelines for leg ulcers (1996), and, important books such as Cullum and Roe (1995). More recently, the establishment of the Leg Clubs also falls within this category of 'quantum leaps' in the care of patients with wounds and chronic leg conditions. All involved in health care will recognise the contribution of nurses; the unique combination of empathy, compassion and caring that addresses holistic and spiritual needs not met by surgery and medicines. Patient-centred care has always been at the heart of nursing. At the same time, even though the Leg Club has developed out of nursing/social philosophy, it can still be challenging for nurses to have equal partnerships with the Leg Club members. That is what the Government is supposedly wanting to promote at the moment — patient autonomy, partnership and participation. However, the balance of 'power' in health care is perceived as being threatened in the minds of some clinicians. This view is anachronistic. The therapeutic relationship between the nurse and the patient is at the heart of health care and that is what patients value most.

This book has been produced for all those involved in Leg Clubs and the Lindsay Leg Club Foundation, the charity that has been established to promote their work. All who have participated in its preparation have given freely of their time. The editors wish to acknowledge and thank the generosity and hard work of the following: all authors for their chapters, Binkie Mais for her care and diligence in preparation of the layout, and, the team at Wounds UK for undertaking the printing and distribution. Without their contributions, there would be no book.

Richard White
Professor of Tissue Viability
Institute of Health, Social Care and Psychology
University of Worcester

I am very pleased to be able to contribute to this foreword. Leg ulcers are a common problem and they cause an enormous amount of disability, which in some patients can last for many years. Their management spans several medical and surgical specialities but, at the end of the day, the bulk of the care of leg ulcers falls on the shoulders of community nurses.

I first met Ellie Lindsay, the founder of the Leg Club model, over 20 years ago. At that time I was able to teach her a few things she did not know about leg ulceration, and I always emphasised the point that a leg ulcer is a clinical sign and not a diagnosis in itself. Although over 75% of leg ulcers are due to venous malfunction, many other contributory co-morbidities need to be taken into account and investigated, especially diabetes, rheumatoid arthritis, anaemia and peripheral vascular disease. Thus, the care of the leg ulcer involves the care of the whole patient, and the treatment of the leg ulcer itself is often just the tip of the clinical iceberg. Ellie Lindsay understands this as well as anyone and has always taken a comprehensive approach to the care of her patients, which will be obvious from the chapters that follow in this book.

The management of leg ulcers is an advancing science. Venous surgery is playing a bigger part than it used to and peripheral ischaemia can often be improved by surgical techniques. The community nurse who manages leg ulcers needs to be aware of the multitude of medical conditions that can impact on leg ulcer wound healing and to be able to adapt her treatments at regular intervals to changing situations. She could not have a better tutor in Ellie Lindsay.

Dr Timothy Cutler
Consultant Dermatologist
Nuffield Hospital
Ipswich

The development of Leg Clubs has been an important development in the field of leg ulceration. Their approach is quite distinct from more traditional methods that focus on a medical model of care that frequently underestimates the psychological and social dimensions of this distressing condition. Leg Clubs embrace the potential for involving patients in their own treatment and of valuing the contribution that they can make to their own health. At the centre of this approach is recognising the shifting balance between professional and patient.

Patients attending Leg Clubs have been shown to have an improvement in their quality of life. While the effect of receiving appropriate care that results in ulcer healing is likely to be a major factor, other elements may also be influencing these changes. For many, the journey of leg ulceration is both distressing and lonely. Leg Clubs provide an important resource where patients can support each other and offer encouragement, while being encouraged to actively participate in their own treatment. Social isolation is a frequent problem for many patients with leg ulceration. Pain, poor mobility and a fear that people will notice their condition all compound this problem. This can frequently lead to a spiral of depression and hopelessness.

The success of the Leg Club relies on the partnership between professional and patient. The professionals involved in Leg Clubs must develop and maintain the skills required for assessment and management, as well as recognising and respecting the unique knowledge the patient has of their own condition.

Christine Moffatt CBE
Professor of Nursing and Director of the Centre for
Research and Implementation of Clinical Practice
Thames Valley University
London

References

Cullum N, Roe B, eds (1995) *Leg Ulcers, Nursing Management, A Research-based Guide.* Scutari Press, Middlesex

Royal College of Nursing (1996) *Clinical practice guidelines. The nursing management of patients with venous leg ulcers.* RCN, London

INTRODUCTION

The influence of Leg Clubs has been profound. The Leg Club is a new, socioeconomic model of care for chronic leg conditions. This is important when there has been significant pressure in a turbulent healthcare environment to balance quality of care with financial cost. This has been particularly pertinent in relation to leg ulcers. There is increasing interest in leg conditions among patients, carers, professionals, commissioners, managers and Members of Parliament. The care and prevention of leg ulcers is a complex issue requiring healthcare professionals to be educated and prepared in all aspects of tissue viability, and, while there have been significant advances in leg ulcer treatment, further research analysis is warranted. The provision of high-quality care is recognised as essential, but poses significant challenges to carers. One of the challenges is ensuring that clinical practice is based on the best available evidence. This challenge has created a demand for more evidence-based resources.

This book contributes to this demand, offering a comprehensive review of the literature relating to leg ulcers and other leg conditions. It contains a diverse range of topics and has been written by significant authors in the field. It represents a unique reading experience with text that informs and educates. Each chapter reviews the associated evidence. Practical aspects of care will be particularly relevant to clinicians. However, the implications of the collective work are far-reaching and are applicable to commissioners, providers and those receiving care.

The Lindsay Leg Club model is a unique approach to care delivery. It differentiates itself from conventional leg ulcer management in that:

- Treatment is carried out in a non-medical setting. Care and education are provided by local community and practice nursing staff. Staff are responsible for meeting the cost of the club sites with funds being raised through a number of fundraising activities.

- People are treated collectively. This helps meet the social needs of isolated people with leg conditions, by providing a mechanism for social interaction, empathy and peer support. It has been shown that Leg Clubs improve people's self-esteem and encourage the development of informal support networks. Collective treatment also encourages nurses to work to high standards in terms of infection control and evidence-based practice by encouraging constant peer review of practice.
- Leg Clubs operate on a drop-in basis and no appointment is required. This practice encourages attendance for information and advice, facilitating early diagnosis of problems and the provision of education and health promotion.
- Leg Clubs incorporate a 'well leg' check. Every person in the UK, whatever their age, has the right to self-refer to a Leg Club for assessment of their legs in order to prevent ulceration and other leg-related problems.

This book offers readers a comprehensive introduction to the Lindsay Leg Club model for those who are new to the concept. Those who are already familiar with the work of Ellie Lindsay, the founder of the Leg Club model, will still find each chapter enlightening. The book, in conjunction with the concept of Leg Clubs, challenges current thinking about care delivery. The reader should reflect on each chapter and carefully consider improvements that could be made to their practice or within their organisation. Those with a Leg Club in their area will find this book an invaluable resource.

It is a great pleasure to write this foreword not only because Ellie is a close personal friend, but because she is an entrepreneur, innovator and a leader who remains totally patient-focused. There is always a need for these attributes in nursing. Consequently, there is a real need for this work. It is very timely. Read, reflect, enjoy and let it influence your practice.

Jackie Stephen-Haynes
Consultant Nurse and Senior Lecturer in Tissue Viability for
Worcestershire Primary Care Trusts and
the University of Worcester
October 2007

Section I: The patient-centred approach

CHAPTER 1

LIVING WITH A LEG ULCER

Jenifer Hawkins and Ellie Lindsay

Patient stories have never formed an integral part of nursing research, as they are not considered to be academic enough. Once collected, they are usually divided up into themes and sub-themes for analysis. On rare occasions they may be presented as case studies or accounts, but never as evidence-based research in their own right.

This chapter presents a number of storytellers, all patients with leg wounds attending a social clinic. Such stories help us to understand the experience of being a patient and living with difficult and painful leg wounds (Hawkins and Lindsay, 2006). These evaluative patient stories add to nursing research and offer an everyday confirmation of the power of the storyteller. They also show how nurses can play a critical role in optimising the power of the story in the patient's journey towards physical and psychological healing.

According to the principles of hermeneutics, where things acquire meaning by being put into language, the very telling of a story gives it a deeper and clearer meaning for the teller, especially if the telling is assisted by skilled listening.

The Leg Club as a mode of clinical care gives both patients and staff the opportunity to develop and respond to complex narratives, often given in relatively short instalments, but over a sustained period of time.

Kirk and Kutchins (1997) claim:

We long since came to the conclusion that the various labels, classifications, categories and definitions which healthcare professionals conjure, obscure rather than illuminate the patient's story.

In telling their story, a patient in mental and or physical distress provides the healthcare professional with a wealth of evidence which can be used to help the patient on a journey of recovery. Their story is the heart of their human experience and, as such, should be the primary focus, embracing as it does everything of any significance for that person. Their experience of care and treatment represents critical chapters in their unique patient story.

Patients organise their experiences and even their memories primarily in the form of self-narratives, personal and family stories, myths about circumstances, reasons for doing or not doing something, in order to gain some sense of order, continuity and meaning in their lives. Participation in the 'Leg Club' encourages patients to be better informed and actively involved in their care, and, through narratives, to share with one another and the staff caring for them their experiences of living with a leg ulcer. Time spent at the club can include developing friendships, involvement in fundraising activities, or just sitting in the company of others and benefiting from the social interaction.

The first patient story recorded was obtained through an ethnographic study (Lindsay, 1996) and was told by Julie, one of the first patients to attend the original Leg Club which opened in a Suffolk village in 1995.

Julie's story

Julie had experienced living with bilateral leg ulcers following the birth of her third child. For over thirty years, despite weekly community nursing input, her leg ulcers had controlled her life. Julie self-treated and was subsequently treated for repeated infections and was labelled non-concordant by staff at the surgery. When informed that the community nursing service were introducing a social clinic she reluctantly agreed to attend. Julie went on to heal completely and, notwithstanding her personal journey of self-treatment, non-concordance, pain and poor self-esteem, she became an invaluable part of the Leg Club team. Julie advocated that being with and interacting with others who shared the same or similar condition helped her to overcome her own feelings of despair, discomfort and social isolation. Belief in the clinical and social benefits of the Leg Club and her consequent motivation to attend resulted in a positive attitude and improved health. This appeared to be strongly related to the support that she received and the friendships that developed during her attendance at the club. She claimed that attending the Leg

Club had given her confidence and control in the management of her care, empowering her to participate fully in its delivery.

James's story

A more recent story is that of James, a young professional man with a passion for football. It is primarily concerned with his physical well-being.

> The last few years of my grandfather's life were ruined by leg ulcers which rendered him immobile, in pain, malodorous and unhappy.
>
> I first remember being aware that I had protruding veins in my lower legs during a holiday to Greece when I was about sixteen years. I went with a group of mates and the whole holiday was spent on the beach wearing shorts and sandals trying to 'pull girls'. I remember being conscious of my legs and trying to walk at the back of the group whenever there were girls about so the legs would not be seen. The last time I was really conscious of my legs was my last beach holiday a few years ago, again I was with friends but this time there was female interest to raise my anxiety levels. Since then I have avoided beach holidays because I know how self-conscious I will feel. The only other time I am forced to expose my legs is when I play sport. I have taken to wearing tracksuit bottoms for the gym and to play squash, and when playing football I pull my socks up to cover my legs. Back in the changing room I am conscious of my legs but I can override it because it is an all-male environment. The only time a bloke has commented on my veins was after a football game, he pointed at the vein bulging from the inside of my thigh and said, 'ugh, look at that vein'. I remember doing my best to brush it aside by saying something along the lines that it always happened after I played sport.
>
> When trousers are just not practical or possible, for example, if it is just too hot or I go swimming, I have to do what I can to cover up by investing in long shorts, sitting and lying in positions calculated to hide the worst part of my legs.
>
> In private my girlfriend obviously sees my legs, she says she doesn't really notice veins and doesn't care at all. This has not been the case with other female friends where I have felt they found my varicosity pretty unpleasant.

After talking to a male friend who had had an operation to strip the veins from his leg I was encouraged to approach my GP. This I did three years ago, he examined my veins and told me there was nothing that could be done and ruled out any possibility of an operation. I was bitterly disappointed and became reconciled to just live with the varicosity.

Then, by chance, I encountered the collective Leg Club expertise. My legs were examined, I was booked in for a Doppler and given details of compression hosiery, which I was assured would help. Armed with this valuable information and advice I went back to the GP to demand an operation. This time I saw a different GP, initially he appeared indifferent to my problem until I explained the advice and information I had been given. He referred me to a consultant and a year later, in March 2006, I had an operation to remove the offending veins from my legs. I was massively pleased with the results. I booked a beach holiday to celebrate and was able, for the first time, to run around in my shorts on the beach without any anxieties about my appearance.

Both before and following his surgery, James was able to draw on the collective educational and clinical expertise of the Leg Club staff to improve his knowledge of his ongoing leg problem, thereby increasing not only his understanding, but also his physical and mental self-esteem.

As patients are treated collectively, nursing staff have access to a wide variety of leg wounds and treatment regimes, offering opportunities for learning and reflection on practice. The clubs can enhance the productivity of junior grade nurses by giving them a unique opportunity to observe a vast range of leg-related problems in one environment, while also enabling them to deliver, under supervision, a wide variety of clinical skills. The Leg Club Forum allows wound care nurses from the UK and overseas to meet and share best practice, as well as providing a support network to which they can refer for help and advice.

Nurse–patient relationship

Phenomenology offers a philosophical approach, valuing the importance of the person's lived and subjective experience above any interpretation, pre-judgement or preconceived theories or ideas (Morse, 1991). This has important implications for the way we view the assimilation of knowledge and develop our understanding of meaning. Meanings are socially constructed through ongoing relations between people, they are constructed by a dialectic process in everyday interactions. The main purpose of phenomenology is to describe the lived experience of individuals in such a way that it is true to the lives of the people described. Phenomenology fits particularly closely to the person-centred, humanistic, holistic approach to health care, which forms the basis of, and informs the nurse–patient relationship.

The establishment of the therapeutic relationship between nurse and patient is well-documented (Hawkins, 2003; Foster and Hawkins, 2005). The nurse is encouraged to develop a relationship with the patient characterised by respect and empathy; once the patient is able to perceive and appreciate these qualities the relationship is established. Only then will the patient feel safe enough to begin to disclose aspects of themselves and how they experience their life. When this disclosure comes with an understanding by the patient that their life experiences are inextricably linked with how they think and how their physical body feels, the patient's narrative really begins to unfold. How, when and if the patient shares this story, happens only if s/he feels engaged in the relationship with the nurse, and is completely dependent upon the listener's responses. Reverence for the storyteller is the oldest form of empowerment, and nurses play a critical role in optimising the power of the story in the patient's journey towards empowerment and self-healing (Barker *et al*, 2004). Virginia Henderson's work in the seventies suggests that the nurse who values nursing and its personal, individualised care, gives holistic rather than disease-centred care, treating the whole person, not just the ulcer.

Marion's story

Marion's story is particularly moving, she was able to share it with a large audience of healthcare and non-healthcare professionals in the distinguished environment of the House of Lords. It was August 2004 when she was diagnosed with a leg ulcer.

> I was in a lot of pain and was very frightened. I was frightened because the only person I had known with leg ulcers was my mother who had had them for more than ten years without them successfully healing. I was visiting my practice nurse twice a week for dressing changes and my general practitioner for pain relief and sick notes, while feeling very

sorry for myself. All the time my ulcer was getting larger and more painful. Although the practice nurses were kind, they seemed to have little understanding of the impact my leg ulcer was having on my life. They tried so many different types of dressing, none of which seemed to suit my wound and I seemed to get conflicting advice. No one explained anything to me or seemed to understand how I was feeling. In the end, the nurses were at a loss as to what to try next, and while all this was going on my ulcer was still growing and I was going mad with pain and started to feel depressed.

She went on to explain seeing an advertisement in a local paper for the Evesham Leg Club being held in a local church hall.

I mentioned it to the practice nurse and she suggested I went along. So the 1st November last year I went along, very sceptical at first. I really could not see how going to a church hall to have my leg dressed was going to make any difference, but boy was I wrong. The first person I met was the leader of the club, she made me feel very welcome, she was so positive, listened to me and reassured me that she would get my ulcer healed. All the nurses were so friendly and knowledgeable, they did not mind if I laughed or cried, they always managed to put a smile on my face. Every month my wound was measured and photographed, so that I had a true record of how my ulcer was progressing, at its worst it measured 5.5 cm x 3.5 cm. The whole atmosphere at the club was upbeat and positive, all the members had a cup of tea and a good laugh or moan, we no longer felt alone, those to benefit the most were elderly and housebound who no longer had to suffer alone.

Marion's conclusion showed real success and patient empowerment.

I am no longer depressed, my ulcer has healed, and I have returned to full-time employment. I feel as though I have been given my life back and an added bonus is that with the support of the staff and club members I have given up smoking… after 30 years.

We do not need to analyse Marion's story, but rather to reflect and identify in its telling the health benefits which are far and beyond the healing of a leg ulcer. The story illustrates a move from ignorance and a depressive state to one of health and well-being, and from confusion to clarity. The patient benefited from appropriate, accurate, evidence-based information and education on the management of her leg ulcer.

Psychological and social support from her interactions with both staff and fellow patients not only empowered her through the treatment of her leg ulcer, but also encouraged her to stop smoking. The patient does not stand alone, but is part of a web of influences emanating from the nurses and other patients.

That our patients are intimately involved in the construction of their stories, trying to make sense of what is happening to them, what it means to them, what part they may or may not have played in generating such experiences, illustrates precisely why we should hear their stories, without analysis, and learn directly from their telling.

Similarly, practitioners only truly know the patient is making progress or getting better when they are able to shape their own story of what has been said, noticed, observed, felt, and evidenced throughout the health journey. How listeners position themselves in relation to stories is crucial; one needs to help patients elaborate their stories, to hear them out fully and help them hear each other, and, as the story-teller engages with the story-hearer, a co-created story emerges which belongs to neither alone, but to both as a shared experience (Barker, 2002). This offers additional and perhaps a more profound dimension to phenomenological principles within a research context.

The purpose of research in nursing is to ask questions, the resultant answers refine existing knowledge or add to our existing body of knowledge. Patient stories and narratives add a further, profound dimension to that knowledge.

Patient stories and narratives are about individuals, about how they think and feel, rather than about what they do or have done to them. The choice of what to tell and what to omit lies entirely with the patient, they are memorable, grounded in personal experience and enforce reflection on practice by the professionals caring for them. They provide new and important information and encourage holism and a move to a more therapeutic approach to care. James and Marion both advocated that being with and interacting with others sharing the same or a similar condition helped them to overcome their own feelings of distress, uncertainty, and social isolation. Belief in the clinical and social benefits of the Leg Club provided the motivation to attend, which is clearly related to the support and friendship that develops between the members. In time, this leads to a more positive attitude towards health care.

Plummer (1995) claims that there is a fundamental shift in storytelling, the personal becomes public, then collective and, finally, political. Although every story is unique, there is a generic pattern that emerges, holding them together by certain, common experiences. The cement which holds our stories together is membership of the Leg Club. The physical and social environment of the Leg Club facilitates the sharing of lived experiences and the telling of patient narratives. It is through this process of sharing and telling that the patient stories provide robust evidence of good practice, on-going health promotion and qualitative nursing research

As nurses we need to recognise that every patient in our care has a story to tell — the fact that we may not hear their stories is due only to our extremely poor hearing skills.

References

Barker P (2002) The philosophy of empowerment. *Mental Health Nurs* **20**(9): 8–12

Barker P, Buchanan-Barker P (2004) Beyond empowerment: revering the story teller. *Mental Health Practice* 7(5): 18–20

Foster T, Hawkins J (2005) The therapeutic relationship: dead or merely impeded by technology? Br J Nurs **13**(13): 698–702

Hawkins J (2003) Task to talking in wound care. *Nurs Standard* **17**(31): 63–6

Hawkins J, Lindsay E (2006) We listen but do we hear? The importance of patient stories. *Br J Community Nurs* **11**(9): 6–14

Kirk SA, Kutchins H (1997) *Making us Crazy: the psychiatric bible and the creation of mental disorders*. Free Press, New York

Lindsay E (1996) *What are patients' views of leg ulcer management in a social community clinic?* BSc dissertation, University of Suffolk (unpublished)

Morse JM (1991) *Qualitative Nursing Research: A contemporary dialogue*. Sage, London

Plummer K (1995) *Telling Sexual Stories: power, change and social worlds*. Routledge, London

CHAPTER 2

PSYCHOLOGICAL SUPPORT OF PATIENTS WITH WOUNDS

Jenifer Hawkins

Psychology attempts to explain and understand the uniqueness of an individual's thoughts and behaviours in relation to specific situations. It emphasises this uniqueness by not expecting a commonality of thoughts or behaviours and by not making generalisations or placing people into defined boxes. Over the years there has been a major growth in the sector of psychology related specifically to health and illness, resulting in the discipline of health psychology.

Health psychology is concerned with the application of specific psychological knowledge and techniques to illness and health promotion. Its primary objective is to understand and to help improve the physical well-being of individuals, improve the quality of health care and to prevent illness and disease. Health psychologists are concerned with the stresses and strains of everyday life, effective communication with patients, and establishing why some patients find it so difficult to comply with medical advice. Kulik and Mahler (1993) claim:

> *Well supported patients are more likely to comply with treatments… emotional support reduces emotional distress which can itself impair treatment and recovery.*

The emphasis is on developing preventative programmes of health care and improving the quality of life of patients by supporting them through sometimes extremely difficult and traumatic procedures, while also facilitating them to make the necessary lifestyle adjustments which often accompany long-term ill-health and encouraging effective coping with the ever present problems of stress, pain and depression.

It is common for patients with wounds to experience a myriad of strong emotions, for example, they may have difficulties with mobility, body image and sexuality. The appearance and sometimes the smell of the wound is a constant reminder of their poor health status. All these factors identified by Hawkins and Foster (2005) further serve to exacerbate the patient's abilities to cope with their wound and often lead to distress and social withdrawal. Furthermore, wound care can impose particularly severe challenges and the stress that patients are under can sometimes negatively affect their interaction with those caring for them and with the prescribed treatment pathway, consequently impeding the expected healing process.

It is well established that social interaction and attitude can influence the impact of stress on the immune system This, taken together with a substantial body of well-designed research suggests that the mind has the power to heal the body (Kiecolt-Glaser *et al*, 1995).

Salmon (2000) claimed a psychological approach to health identifies four major points:

- body and mind are not separate
- patients do not just accept challenges but can actively manage them
- patients think about what happens to them
- psychological processes affect nurses as well as patients.

It is the belief of many that psychological principles are best incorporated into routine clinical practice rather than being added on as an 'optional extra'

Throughout clinical practice, I have observed how frequently nurses suffering from overwork show less empathy towards patients, adopting a depersonalising approach to care, minimising patient contact and seeking refuge in routine tasks (Hawkins, 2003). Sadly, many nurses do not know enough about what their patients think and worry about, and this is essentially because they neither ask nor let patients tell them. Research (Hollinworth and Hawkins, 2003) found that nurses identified 'chatting with' and 'observing strong feelings' in patients while caring for them, but did not take the opportunity to talk through these feelings with the patients concerned. Nurses need to learn to facilitate and enable patients to talk to them, to tell them what is bothering them (*Chapter 1*). Learning to really listen to the patient is the first and possibly the most important skill in offering psychological support.

Lack of time is one of the most frequently given reasons for not listening to patients. Hawkins (2003) asked a group of pre-registration nursing students undertaking a module based on psychological helping skills to complete a pie chart of the daily activities which they considered important in relation to their nurse training while on clinical placement. It was both a surprise and a disappointment that not one, of a group of 40 student nurses, listed talking to or listening to patients as a priority. When questioned it transpired that none of the student nurses listed talking and/or listening to patients as a unique or separate activity because it was felt that it could be undertaken more usefully when accompanied by a nursing task. The examples given included, while bathing patients or accompanying them to treatments, toileting and during drug rounds.

As said, time or lack of it was given as the reason for not engaging in communication as a separate activity with patients. Evidence is available to refute this on a daily basis in both our personal and professional lives: how many times do we mishear or totally misunderstand something which we have been told while busy with another activity? In clinical practice, patients who are given information during routine nursing tasks remember the details of the task but have little or no recall of what has been said to them by the nurse.

The focus must be on how best time can be used to deliver an effective and empowering interaction for both the patient and nurse.

Task to Talking model

The five-minute 'Task to Talking model' was devised by Hawkins (2003) to address the compelling need of patients to be given specific time to talk and for the nurse to listen, while addressing the serious lack of time available to both for this important activity.

The model relies heavily on developing the nurse/patient relationship and emphasises that through the use of a structured skills model, in a short time the nurse can gain access to the patient's subjective life by accurately exploring:

- what the patient is thinking
- what the patient's beliefs and desires are
- what sensations the patient is experiencing.

The Task to Talking model was based on a simple modification of the Three-stage Skill model of helping (Egan, 1982). The first of his stages, 'exploration', was reduced to just three distinct skills; listening and observing, clarifying, and communicating empathy. When used in a structured way, these skills facilitate the nurse in really listening to, and hearing the patient talking through their thoughts and feelings in relation to their wound and the impact it is having on their lifestyle.

Good emotional support will enable the patient to express anxieties, doubts and fears comfortably. No matter how nonsensical and irrational these may be, they should not be dismissed and neither should the time spent listening to them be regarded as wasted.

The Task to Talking model highlights the importance of separating and timing the part of the nurse/patient intervention devoted to listening and talking. No time limit is imposed on the nursing task or talking during the task, however, on completion of the nursing task, the nurse is required to sit with the patient and offer a minimum of five minutes devoted to listening and talking. As patients continue to claim that no one listens to them (Myerscough, 1992; Hawkins, 2003), this 'task-free' five minutes will enable the patient to be heard. It also links with the Government's agenda of patient involvement in decision-making (Nursing and Midwifery Council [NMC], 2002).

The model must take place within a specific timescale, which is a minimum of five minutes. If further time is available it must be stated at the beginning of the interaction, For example, on completion of the nursing task, the patient is told that the nurse has an additional five minutes to listen to the patient's concerns. Alternatively, the nurse may say to the patient 'I have ten minutes to listen to you now, or we can have twenty minutes once I have completed the drugs round'. The emphasis is on time, giving the patient a clear indication of how long they will have to talk.

Nearly 40 years ago, Asher (1972) stated:

To give a patient the impression you could spare him an hour, and yet to make him satisfied with five minutes, is an invaluable gift.

In today's task-centred climate, it is one that nurses need to perfect.

Listening and observation

Listening is an extremely active process; it requires effort, energy commitment and attention to be focused fully on the patient, many of whom may have a history of not being heard. Beckham and Frankel

(1984) in their seminal study found that the average patient is interrupted within 18 seconds of starting to tell his or her story. Some patients will tell their story without too much prompting; it comes gushing out, often because it has been suppressed for so long. Others will be more reticent, guarded, maybe afraid to put into words what will then have to be faced. Good listening skills enable the patient to feel valued, respected and encouraged to talk. Through the use of effective body language and facial expressions, the nurse should communicate 'I am with you'. Minimal prompts, for example, head nods, saying 'tell me more', can be useful reinforcements to help patients complete their story. Listening means learning not to reassure too quickly or inappropriately, allowing pain, worry and fear to be fully explored. Listening without distraction is not easy and can be uncomfortable for the nurse but, once attempted in this structured and timed way, can prove to be positive and rewarding for both patient and nurse.

Observation skills can help the nurse identify how the patient is feeling. Every emotion has a physical reaction and awareness can be heightened to recognise fear, embarrassment, confusion, anxiety and vulnerability through facial expressions and body language to help establish empathy with the client.

Seeking through observation to determine how the patient is feeling shows that there is an extremely close link between how we feel and how we look. As nurses we can clearly identify when a patient is anxious, afraid, depressed; we see it in their facial expressions and body language and hear it in the tone of their voice. A basic guide to keep in mind is the statistic which claims that 55% of how we feel is in our facial expression, 38% is in the tone of our voice and only 7% in the spoken word (Egan, 1986). By learning to read the patient's non-verbal behaviours, ie. posture, facial expressions, movement and tone of voice, the nurse will gain a clearer understanding of how the patient is feeling.

Immediacy and clarification

One further point, again drawn from the work of Egan (1985) and crucial to the success of the time-limited model, is that of immediacy, often referred to as 'the here and now'. This is the nurse's ability to discuss with the patient what is happening between them in the 'here and now' of any given interaction. Immediacy can be a difficult and demanding skill, nurses more readily point to the future often presenting the patient with inappropriate future responses to treatment. 'You will feel better once your dressing has been changed,' rather than addressing the patient's immediate concerns of discomfort or pain. The nurse who does not read and comment on cues indicating that the patient feels anxious, or does not notice and comment when the patient is in pain, is ignoring a major aspect of psychological support which recognises and highlights what is happening in the here and now. An acknowledgement such as, 'I can see you are in pain and worried about the dressing change' allows the nurse to affirm both the patient's physical and mental state at that moment.

Clarification of what has been said is important for both patient and nurse. The patient will recognise that they have been heard and understood, while the nurse, in clarifying what has been said through simple repetition of the patient's words back to them, demonstrates her ability to really hear the patient's concerns. This is an important skill to learn; we rarely check our understanding of what has been said to us, but usually just respond to what we assume we have heard. For patients this may be the only opportunity to share how they are feeling or coping with their health problem. This, combined with an observed feeling, demonstrates the depth of the nurse's hearing and observation skills. For example, 'You say your wound smells and is weeping, it makes you wary of being near people, you find that embarrassing, let's see what dressing we might use to help remove the smell'.

Empathy

The next skill in the model is that of empathy: placing what has been said and seen into the larger picture of the patient's life. It is perhaps one of the most important of the skills for the nurse to learn, with the nurse communicating a deeper empathetic understanding of the patient's experience. The larger empathetic picture has been gained from the nurse's concentrated listening and observation of the patient. It is done by putting the patient's wound into the context of his or her lifestyle, for example, 'It sounds as if this wound is really frightening you, you feel it will never heal and that you will not be able to continue to meet your friends for bridge and days out'. Here, the nurse demonstrates a strong empathetic understanding of the patient's day-to-day existence.

Unfortunately, nurses regularly fail to check or clarify their understanding of what the patient has said. The importance of this cannot be underestimated, as it alone allows the patient to recognise that they have been heard and understood. Combined with the skill of observation, it shows the depth of empathy and support given by the nurse.

'Feelings vocabulary'

Another important skill to develop is your 'feelings vocabulary'. We experience a wide range of feelings on a daily basis which, placed on a continuum, would stretch from happy to sad, with possibly the more difficult ones hidden or camouflaged underneath the umbrella feeling of anger. Most of us find it easy to admit to feeling happy or sad, and variations of intensity of these feelings can often be shared with another person, a friend or colleague. However, some feelings are more difficult to admit, for example, it is extremely difficult for patients to own up to feelings of embarrassment, vulnerability, or powerlessness during the course of their treatment. Yet, these are the very feelings that may cause the patient the most stress, thereby impeding their recovery. The Terence Higgins Trust produced a list of 500 feelings drawn from those experienced by their clients, which we will have all felt ourselves at one point or another in our lives, no matter how old or young we are. The more we move around in the world of feelings, the more likely we are to be able to begin to identify what our patients are feeling (Hawkins and Foster, 2005). Kelly (1985) produced an emotive account based on his diary entries of his feelings both before and following traumatic surgery: 'psychological turmoil, shame, desperation and panic shrouded my life… pain and discomfort were my constant companions'.

What the patient discloses is unique to them, it relates to how they are feeling, what is happening to them, and, more importantly, it determines their current and future health behaviour. Salmon (2000) summed this up when he claimed that, 'The benefits of good emotional support to patients are more extensive and more powerful than many physical treatments'. If we needed any additional evidence for the importance of psychological support for patients we have that given by Pennebaker (1993) who claimed that 'merely being enabled to express feelings about upsetting or traumatic challenges reduces physiological arousal and helps reduce damaging physiological effects'

The skill of giving accurate and appropriate information in such a way that the patient can accept, understand and remember cannot be minimised. Research demonstrates (Hawkins and Hollinworth, 2003) that information given on completion of listening to the patient's concerns is more readily accepted and adhered to. It is clear that an increased understanding of the patient and the patient's real needs will enable the nurse to have a better understanding of what the patient really wants and needs. Such understanding of the patient's situation enables the nurse to move to the skill of information-giving, which involves drawing on all their professional knowledge and expertise to give appropriate, accurate and detailed information to the patient. The patient, feeling satisfied with an interaction that acknowledged the uniqueness of his or her individual situation, will be more concordant with the nurses' requests relating to health promotion, for example, rest, keeping legs elevated, exercise and diet.

Reflection and evaluation

Reflection and evaluation are the final two skills that together form a continuous internal process for both the patient and the nurse. They allow both to reflect individually on their interaction and to evaluate its overall effectiveness. If a patient believes it has been a good interaction, one in which they have been enabled to talk through their concerns and have felt truly heard, they will be empowered to continue working through their concerns, fears, etc. A study examining the changes in professional practice of nurses who had attended a workshop on psychological helping skills found an increase in reflective practice alongside a growing awareness of the holistic needs of patients, and the value of supporting patients psychologically. Hawkins and Hollinworth (2003) found that nurses who had been taught psychological helping skills used reflection to question, modify, clarify, and sometimes even change their values, leading to a re-evaluation of their clinical practice. The skills of reflection and evaluation also allow nurses, as part of continuous professional development, to consider possible ways of implementing this model into their clinical practice to enhance the holistic care of all patients.

All models are likely to have some limitations when viewed objectively. However, the psychological helping skills used in this model have a core place in nursing practice today. The use of sensitive listening and active observing, together with clarifying what you believe you have heard the patient say to demonstrate your understanding are essential in building nurse/patient relationships, based on trust and respect, which facilitate good care (Hawkins and Foster 2005). It is clear that a five-minute time slot specifically for listening and talking to the patient is not going to suit every patient or every nurse. The model's timed approach could be considered too restrictive to enable a useful interaction and might be viewed by some as an insensitive approach. Five minutes will not be long enough for a patient to work through sensitive emotional concerns, however, five minutes will highlight for the nurse that the patient is in need of additional time to work through difficult or painful issues, and will encourage them to set aside a longer time in the near future when they will be able to talk together without interruption. Being able to say to an anxious patient, 'I have five minutes now, but if you prefer we can have an hour together later in the day to talk through the things which are bothering you' demonstrates a sensitive, empathetic response to a patient's concerns.

The skills in the model require practice and experimentation until it feels natural and comfortable to sit with the patient, maintain eye contact, shut out the world around you and concentrate on what is being said and seen.

The Task to Talking model is a specific reaction to the acknowledged pressure of the workplace and the ever-increasing need for patients to have interaction of this kind to improve the quality of care that they receive.

References

Asher R (1972) *Richard Asher Talking Sense*. Pitman Medical, London

Beckham H, Frankel R (1984) The effect of physician behaviour on the collection of data. *Ann Intern Med* **101**(5): 692–6

Egan G (1986) *The Skilled Helper: a systematic approach to effective helping*. Brooks/Cole, California

Hawkins J (2003) Task to Talking in wound care. *Nurs Standard* **17**(31): 63–6

Hawkins J, Foster T(2005) *Thinking Healing: the psychological aspects of wound care*. Wound Care Society Booklet, Huntingdon

Hawkins J, Hollinworth H (2003) Living theory: enhancing the psychological support of patients. *Br J Nurs* **12**(9): 543–8

Hollinworth H, Hawkins J (2003) Teaching nurses psychological support of patients with wounds. *Br J Nurs* (Tissue Viability Supplement) **11**(20): 8–18

Kelly M (1987) Managing radical surgery; notes from the patient's viewpoint. *Gut* **28**: 81–7

Kulik JA, Mahler HIM (1993) Emotional support as a moderator of adjustment and compliance after coronary bypass surgery; a longitudinal study. *J Behav Med* **16**: 45–64

Kiecolt-Glaser J, Marucha P, Malarky W, Mercado A, Glaser R (1995) Slowing of wound healing by psychological stress: *Lancet* **264**: 1194–96

Myerscroft P (1992) *Talking to Patients.* Oxford University Press, Oxford

Pennebaker JW (1993) Putting stress into words: health, linguistic sand therapeutic implications. *Behav Res Ther* **31**: 539–48

Salmon P (2000) *Psychology of Medicine and Surgery: A guide for psychologists counsellors, nurses and doctors.* Wiley, Chichester

Chapter 3

Body image and leg ulceration

Julie Day and Wendy Hayes

Leg ulceration is a chronic condition that affects 1–2% of the population (Callam *et al*, 1985), and these patients have much in common with patients with other chronic diseases (Royal College of Nursing [RCN], 2006). There is a growing body of research on the impact of leg ulcers on the patient's quality of life (Walshe, 1995). The RCN (2006) advise that healthcare professionals involved in the care of patients with leg ulcers should be sensitive to the issues surrounding changes in their quality of life. However, there is little consideration given to the impact of leg ulceration on the patient's body image, a significant factor when considering a patient's quality of life.

Body image is a person's perception of his or her own physical appearance, including what a person sees in a mirror and the manner in which people experience their own bodies (Atwater, 1983). Corey (1984) states that the concept of body image is related to the views of society and cultural values, and that a healthy body is culturally accepted as an ideal body image. Western society places great emphasis on body image in terms of perfecting that image and remaining attractive.

Body image is made up of three components (Price, 1990):

- body reality
- body ideal
- body presentation.

Body reality is the body as it really exists, 'warts and all', and changes in body reality are related to trauma, infection and malnutrition. Body ideal is the picture in our heads of how we would like the body to look and perform. Body presentation is how the body presents to the outside world and is linked to physical appearance. Body image affects our sense of self-worth and well-being, as well as our role in society and how we are perceived by others. It has an impact on our ability to socialise, seek employment and sustain financial stability.

A leg ulcer can change an individual's perception of their body image. It causes altered appearance not only in relation to the wound itself, but also with the presence of hyperkeratosis (a thickening of the surface layers, stratum corneum, in the skin or other stratified squamous epithelium which can have a scaly appearance). Other factors that alter appearance include exudate and odour, and changes in skin colour and the application of bandages and treatment therapies.

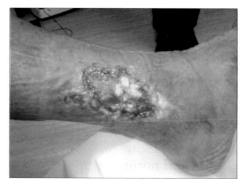

Figure 3.1: A typical leg ulcer

A wound (*Figure 3.1*) is a breach in the integrity of the skin. For patients this can be a disturbing site as they are confronted with an open wound which may contain sloughy tissue which would not normally be visible. Patients may feel incomplete now that they have a 'hole' in their skin and, as a result, may experience lowered self-esteem. Their ideal body image may no longer exist and they may feel unhappy with how their body has changed, and how these changes seem to others when treatment is ongoing.

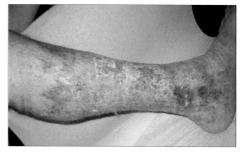

Figure 3.2: Hyperkeratosis (skin scales)

Many patients with leg ulcers have to cope with the unsightly appearance of hyperkeratosis (skin scales) (*Figure 3.2*), which is not a normal phenomena for the general population. The skin that is shed during dressing changes can cause embarrassment for the patient and also leave behind

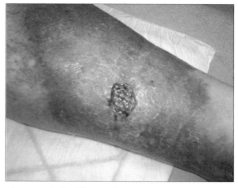

Figure 3.3: Skin changes, ie. haemosiderin and staining

loosened skin particles on the surrounding surfaces. Hyperkeratosis can also harbour fungal infections and have a distinct odour. The removal of skin scales is time-consuming, and so is an aspect of care that is frequently omitted. The presence of hyperkeratosis is, therefore, far from the 'body ideal'.

Changes in skin colour (*Figure 3.3*) are caused by the extravasation of erythrocytes into the skin (Grey *et al* 2006). Many patients find these changes distressing as they alter 'normal' body presentation. They are also permanent and difficult to disguise. Many female patients will try to conceal them by application of cosmetic products; a remedy that is not so readily accepted or undertaken by men. Patients will frequently adapt their clothing to hide their legs, thus altering how they would normally look.

For many patients with leg ulceration, the presence of exudate (*Figure 3.4*) and its strikethrough onto their outer bandages is their main concern (Hopkins, 2004). Body reality for most people does not include the

Figure 3.4: The presence of exudate is a concern for patients

leakage of large amounts of fluid from the leg. Some patients present with their legs wrapped in plastic bags with their foot bathed in a pool of exudate; again affecting how others view them. Many patients express concerns about the unsightly appearance of exudate and how it mars their activities of daily living. Leaving their familiar surroundings and socialising can cause immense distress due to concerns about exudate and how it can be disguised. It is not difficult to imagine how disturbing it would be to find that your legs have soiled upholstery, bedclothes and carpets. Therefore, it is not surprising that patients with leg ulceration can become socially isolated (Lindsay, 1999). Exudate is also associated with malodour.

Odour

Most of us would be concerned if we thought our body odour was causing offence to others, it would not be our ideal body presentation. Unpleasant odours are distressing to both the patient and to those in close proximity to them. We are all aware that there are some patients whose presence in the clinical setting is detected by odour even before they are seen. Healthcare professionals should refrain from making adverse comments such as 'your legs stink' (Rich and McLachlan, 2003) and should keep a professional attitude however offensive the odours may be

The appropriate use of wound care products, good skin hygiene and the removal of skin scales can all assist in the control of odour.

Bandages and treatment therapies

The gold standard treatment for venous leg ulceration is compression therapy (RCN, 2006). The following illustrations show some of the products that are currently available (*Figures 3.5–3.8*).

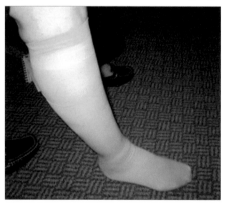

Figure 3.5: Short-stretch bandaging

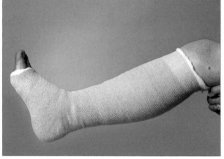

Figure 3.6: Multi-layer compression therapy. Courtesy of Urgo

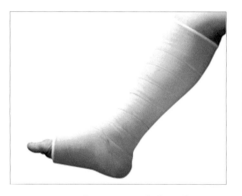

Figure 3.7: 2-layer hosiery system

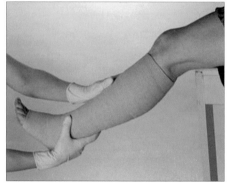

Figure 3.8: 3M™ Coban™ 2 layer compression system

Many patients experience difficulties with concordance, as compression therapy is reported to be uncomfortable, bulky, hot to wear, and fails to accommodate normal footwear (Annand *et al* 2002). It is evident from some of the more recent innovations in compression therapy, eg. Coban™ 2 Layer Compression System (3M), Actico short-stretch bandage (Activa Healthcare), and SurePress® Comfort™ Pro 2-layer

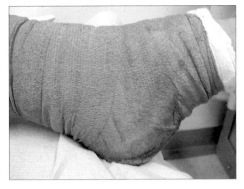

Figure 3.9: Bandage slippage as a result of poor application technique

hosiery system (ConvaTec) that attempts are being made to address some of the issues. However, for many patients the problems still remain. Poor application technique, as demonstrated in *Figure 3.9,* does little to address the patient's concerns regarding body image — imagine how difficult it would be to apply normal footwear over these bandages. Tissue damage and discomfort are also significant factors associated with poor application technique, which can further compromise body image.

The case reports overleaf demonstrate and contextualise how patients can feel about their bodies. The reports were selected from patients who presented at the authors' clinical practice. They represent a cross-section of the client group and serve to demonstrate that leg ulceration does not exclusively affect the elderly population.

Although the four patients featured were of different ages, with diverse needs, there were common themes that emerged concerning their body image. Hate is a strong word, but they all used it in relation to their ulceration and treatment therapies. Two male and two female patients were selected to highlight that these issues are germane to both. Drench (1994) identifies that body image is part of the self-concept pertaining to the body and has notions around masculinity and femininity, and that it is a product of social interaction. The limitations to footwear and clothing were an issue for all, as were the problems associated with management of exudate and the general appearance of the wound.

Clinical experience has confirmed our beliefs that individualised patient care considering issues relevant to body image is paramount to the provision of optimum care for patients with leg ulceration. We have found that this is an aspect of care that may be overlooked due to constraints upon resources.

Case study 1	
Mr A	• Aged 87 years • Married, main carer for wife • History of venous disease for over 70 years • Numerous surgical interventions over many years • Current ulceration the bilateral gaiter region, present for over two years
Body image issues	• 'I look like Nora Batty' • Concerned about visible exudate • Has to wear sandals in the winter whatever the weather, and is very conscious of his footwear • Was unable to comply with uniform requirements when serving in the army, due to bulky 'field dressings' in use at that time • He would ideally like to be bandage-free and wear normal footwear. He would even like to wear shorts in the summer • He has tried hosiery systems, which he found to be more aesthetically acceptable but, unfortunately, these did not have a positive benefit in terms of healing • He finds the discoloration caused by the untreated skin scales distressing

Case study 2	
Mrs B	• Aged 79 years • Widow • Leg ulceration for many years • Current ulcer present for two years
Body image issues	• Her body image is very important • Loves shoes • Hates the odour from her ulcer • Loves to socialise but does not like her visitors to see any exudate strikethrough • Has been known to remove the dressings before the arrival of her visitors to address this problem and therefore is seen as a non-concordant patient • 'The ulcer doesn't hurt but I hate the way it looks' • She hates the unglamorous footwear required to accommodate the bandages

Case study 3

Mr C	• Aged 34 years • Self-employed landscape gardener • Bohemian lifestyle • Recurrent ulceration (several episodes due to deep venous incompetence)
Body image issues	• Psychosexual issues causing relationship difficulties with his partner due to the appearance of the ulcer • Footwear a constant problem both socially and for the health and safety requirements of his job • Exudate an issue, especially as he frequently works away from home and has difficulty attending arranged appointments • The shedding of skin scales causes him anxiety especially when he is working away from home • 'I hate this leg, I don't wear shorts, it would frighten people'

Case study 4

Mrs D	• Aged 58 years • Married • Semi-retired shop worker • Many episodes of ulceration and varicose vein surgery
Body image issues	• Very conscious of her body image • Enjoys holidays but is severely limited in choice of location as she needs to attend practice nurse appointments on a regular basis due to exudate levels • Is desperate to remain independent • Hates the disruption to her normal hygiene regime • Wardrobe is determined by the need for bandages, as she wears trousers to disguise them • Hates the 'accommodating' footwear • 'I feel embarrassed to go out, I have to dress like a man and these shoes are awful'

The notion of 'one size fits all' cannot apply to this group of patients. Clinical knowledge and expertise is required to select the most appropriate treatment therapy for the individual patient, taking into account their particular body image needs and requirements. This is tempered with a duty to provide clinically effective care and, in order to achieve this, compromises may have to be made.

References

Annand SC, Dean C, Nettleton R, Praburaj DV (2002) Health-related quality of life tools for venous ulcerated patients. *Br J Nurs* **12**(1): 48–61

Atwater E (1983) *Psychology of Adjustment*. 2nd edn. Prentice Hall, New Jersey

Callam MJ, Ruckley CV, Harper DR, Dale JJ (1985) Chronic ulceration of the leg: extent of the problem and provision of care. *Br Med J* **290**: 1855–6

Corey G (1984) Body image. In: Corsini R, ed. *Encyclopedia of Psychology*. volume 1. Wiley, New York

Drench M (1994) Changes in body image secondary to disease and injury. *Rehabilitation Nurs* **19**(1): 31–6

Grey JE, Harding KG, Enoch S (2006) Venous and arterial leg ulcers. *Br Med J* **332**: 347–50

Hopkins A (2004) Disrupted lives: investigating coping strategies for non-healing leg ulcers. *Br J Nurs* **13**(9): 556–63

Lindsay E (1999) Show a leg. *Nurs Times* **95**(11): 67, 70, 73

Price R (1990) A model for body image care. *J Adv Nurs* **15**(5): 585–93

Royal College of Nursing (2006) *The Nursing Management of Patients with Venous Leg Ulcers*. RCN, London

Rich A, McLachlan L (2003) How living with a leg ulcer affects peoples daily life: a nurse led study. *J Wound Care* **12**(2): 52–4

Walshe C (1995) Living with a venous leg ulcer: a descriptive study of patients' experiences. *J Adv Nurs* **22**: 1092–100

CHAPTER 4

QUALITY OF LIFE

Hildegard Charles

Wound management therapies are invariably assessed and focused in terms of healing rates and cost-effectiveness, rather than quality of life. However, patients have described living with a venous leg ulcer as a forever healing process, with pain being a constant irritation and their ability to lead a normal life affected by numerous and significant restrictions. Some authors have suggested that leg ulcers have a wide-ranging impact on patients' lives, which can be described as physical, social, psychological and/or financial, while others have emphasised the effects on specific aspects, such as their inability to work or interact with others (Charles, 2004).

When health-outcomes research, including quality of life (QoL), is compared to traditional clinical and physiological research, health-outcome research is more comprehensive, has a greater focus on the patient, and measures what is often of greatest concern for the patient. For example, when the efficacy of two treatments in a clinical trial are found to be equivalent; the treatment associated with a better QoL score is more likely to be adopted for clinical practice (Marlow, 1999). On a regular basis, healthcare professionals make decisions about cost-effective treatment methods such as practitioner time and effort. They also need to consider QoL as an important factor in the treatment and management of an holistic process (Marlow, 1999).

The majority of studies investigating the effect of leg ulceration on the sufferers' QoL have used the quantitative paradigm. The measuring instruments employed have been either generic or disease-specific and may be presented as an index score or as a profile. The World Health Organization QoL group (WHOQOL-BREF, 1993) is a 26-item version of the WHOQOL-100 assessment. Results from the WHOQOL indicate a sound, cross-culturally valid assessment of QOL, as reflected by its four domains:

- physical
- psychological
- social
- environmental (Skevington *et al*, 2004).

These domains should be included in a generic quality of life instrument. Generic instruments cover a broad range of dimensions and allow comparisons between different groups of patients. Disease-specific instruments, on the other hand, are specially designed for a particular disease, patient group or areas of function.

Qualitative studies have employed various interview techniques and, subsequently, provide a richness of patient data which often graphically describes what it is like to live with leg ulceration on a daily basis.

A literature search on the studies investigating quality of life with leg ulceration was undertaken using internet searches on OVID, CINAHL, MEDLINE, *Journal of Wound Care*, *British Journal of Nursing*, Cochrane systematic reviews and the British Nursing Index databases. The search words associated with leg ulcers and quality of life were used to find studies and methods evaluating treatment and assessing quality of life.

Definition of quality of life (QoL)

The debate on quality of life is millennia-old, with Aristotle giving it much thought in his *Nicomachean Ethics*. He eventually settled on the notion of *eudaimonia*, a Greek term often translated as happiness being central. Quality of life is a broad term, meaning different things to different people. The WHO has defined health as a state of complete physical, mental and social well-being, not merely the absence of disease (WHO, 1984). In the context of clinical trials evaluating intervention on patients, researchers interpret this broader term as the impact of the disease on the normal functioning of a patient in addition to the effect of treatment on the patient's health (Fayers and Machin, 2000). This can also be referred to as health-related quality of life (HRQoL).

The study of HRQoL is a relatively recent development in the field of health services research. Though it is difficult to place an exact date on its origin, researchers began shifting their attention to health outcomes approximately 30 years ago. Historically, clinicians relied on traditional physiological measures to determine if a health intervention was needed and whether or not that intervention was successful.

Tools to investigate quality of life

A variety of tools have been employed to investigate QoL, these are generic, disease-specific tools and a variety of interview techniques.

Generic tools used at one point

Nottingham health profile (NHP) (Hunt *et al*, 1984/5)
This consists of two parts:

- Part I includes 38 questions in six sub-areas relating to energy level (3), pain (8), emotional reaction (9), sleep (5), social isolation (5) and physical abilities (8)
- Part II includes seven questions relating to life areas affected, namely: work, social life, home life, sex life, interests, hobbies and vacations.

Lindholm *et al* (1993) used the short version of NHP on 125 patients (74 females and 51 males) suffering from venous ulcers for more than six months. They reported significant poorer perceived health in men in the domains of pain, emotional reactions, social isolation and physical restrictions compared with women. They did find that the duration of the ulcer did not appear to influence quality of life, suggesting that patients use adaptive mechanisms to deal with long-term ulceration.

Franks and Moffatt (1998) used the NHP on 758 leg ulcer patients in six community trusts. They compared the scores with the age/sex matched with normal scores (normal scores are the standard scores obtained from healthy participants studied nationwide). These results were obtained from a previous study by Hunt *et al* (1985) that used the above questionnaire on patients. All the leg ulcer patients (both male and female) reported poorer HRQoL in all domains, which are: energy, pain, emotional reactions, sleep, social isolation and physical mobility. The researchers reported that the younger age group (age less than 65 years) had poorer QoL scores. Men also had poorer QoL scores than women in the domains of body pain, sleep and social isolation.

The authors also reported that patients who were treated in their home and not at the clinic had poorer energy, higher bodily pain, poorer sleep and mobility compared with those patients being treated in leg ulcer clinics.

Hamer *et al* (1994) using the NHP on 88 patients also reported pain restricted mobility and loss of social contacts. These findings are similar to the two previous studies.

Short-form health profile SF-36 (Ware and Sherbourne, 1992)

The SF-36 originated in the USA and is used with patients suffering from various diseases. The questionnaire consists of 36 items covering: physical functioning (10), social functioning (2), physical role limitation (4), emotional role limitation (3), body pain (2), mental health (5), vitality (4), general health (5) and one question about general health that compares current health with that one year ago (health transition). The sub-class are scored on a scale from 0 as worst possible health state and 100 as best possible health state.

Price and Harding (1996) used the short-form survey (SF-36) questionnaire to measure the quality of life of 55 patients who attended a specialist wound healing clinic and compared the results with UK norms. The norm data was previously obtained on health controls in people with an age range of 70–74 years (Jenkinsons *et al*, 1993). They reported that the patients rated themselves significantly less on seven of the eight sub-scales compared to the control group (age equivalent norm), and thus concluded that leg ulceration has an enormous impact on quality of life. They reported significantly poorer perceived health in women suffering in the domains of physical functioning, vitality, and social functioning, with a poorer but non-significant difference in general health. This is different to Lindholm's study which reported that men had poorer health.

Semi-structured questionnaire and rating scale for pain

Hofman *et al* (1997) investigated the QoL of patients suffering with leg ulcers (mixed aetiology) on 140 patients with a semi-structured questionnaire and a pain rating scale. In this study, 69% of patients reported pain to be the worst thing, 38% had continuous pain, and 64% reported sleep disturbance as a consequence of their pain.

These studies demonstrate that people suffering from leg ulceration have a poorer QoL than those without. The most dominant affected areas are pain, immobility, sleep disturbance and social isolation.

Disease-specific tools

More recently, several disease-specific tools have been developed for patients to reflect their views about a particular disease. Disease-specific measures are more sensitive to change and contain items that are more relevant to the patient's perspective to a particular disease, namely, leg ulcers (Patrick and Deyo, 1999).

Cardiff wound impact schedule (CWIS) (Price and Harding, 1997)

This tool has been developed for patients with wounds and is divided into four key sections:

- physical symptoms and daily living (12 items)
- social life (seven items)
- well-being (seven items)
- overall quality of life (two items).

This tool has also been translated into French, German and adapted for use in the USA. Price and Harding (1997) reported on 20 patients with acute wounds and 32 with leg ulceration. The tool was found to be reliable and sensitive across wound types, making it a unique evaluation tool (Acquadro *et al*, 2005).

The authors found that patients with leg ulceration reported a greater impact on bathing, mobility, sleep, pain, odour than those with acute wounds. These findings reflect those with the generic tools.

Charing Cross venous leg ulcer questionnaire (Smith *et al*, 2000)

This tool consists of 22 items which cover a range from social function, domestic activities, cosmesis, eg. bodily beauty and surgical correction and emotional status. It was validated against the SF-36 and identified the adverse effects of venous ulceration. The tool needs to show its effectiveness in clinical trials to enhance its usefulness further.

Freiburger Lebensqualitäts assessment questionnaire (FLQA) (Augustin *et al*, 1997)

This instrument consists of 83 items and was piloted on 246 patients to test its acceptance and consistency. It was compared with the NHP and Questionnaire Alltagsleben scores. The authors concluded that it is valid, obtaining high correlation with the above questionnaires, ie. NHP and QA. There are no other available studies.

Qualitative research

Phenomenology
Qualitative research has often been investigated with the phenomenological paradigm, which was first described by Husserl (1962) and focuses on an individual's interpretation of his/her experience. This approach has been used by several nurse researchers to explore leg ulcer sufferers' experiences. Tape-recorded interviews are mostly used to obtain the patient's experience. Various methods can be used to analyse the content of the interviews. The transcripts from the interviews need to be read several times so the researcher becomes familiar with them. By using this approach, the transcripts can be organised into categories and these can be colour-coded into different themes and sub-themes (Field and Morse, 1985). Another method is by use of computer programme analysis that organises the transcript into words or phrases. This has been described by Ford *et al* (2000).

Interviews
Hopkins (2004) carried out unstructured interviews using hermeneutic phenomenology to explore the lived experience of five people who had non-healing venous leg ulcers. Interpretative phenomenological analysis was utilised to identify themes and patterns. The core themes identified were biographical disruption and the loss of self, which could mean the change from an active to a sedentary life where nothing much happens, ie. 'just hobble around in the flat'. Another theme was 'ways of coping'. This was expressed as pure acceptance of the situation. Social implications were identified when the patient's private life becomes public, eg. the smelly discharge could be recognised in public. The author also identified therapeutic relationships that the patient developed with the healthcare professionals, eg. a longstanding positive relationship.

Rich and McLachlan (2003) used descriptive phenomenological and in-depth, semi-structured interviews involving eight patients and reported pain as a primary issue. Other problems included lack of consistent care, discomfort, feeling self-conscious about the smell and look of the ulcer, difficulties with clothes and shoes and fear of further injury when moving about.

Douglas (2001) used a qualitative grounded theory and interviewed eight patients. The author reported five major categories that emerged:

1. The relationship between healthcare professionals and patients;

patients felt that there was a lack of understanding from practitioners about the leg ulcer and different practitioners were giving conflicting advice.

2. The physical experience was expressed as a sort of 'going-on-and-on' pain. Pain also caused sleepless nights. Leakage and odour were particularly distressing, along with impaired mobility and a restricted lifestyle.

3. Patients expressed a loss of control since they had to rely on other people all the time which they hated.

4. Feelings about the future were expressed pessimistically as the typical cycle of leg ulceration which was 'going-on-and-on'.

5. The fifth category was from the carers' perspective. Again, they said that they were given conflicting advice from different healthcare professionals.

Chase *et al* (1997) used a phenomenological approach by participant observation, interviews, field notes, pain and activity logs involving 37 patients and identified four major themes:

1. A forever healing process, which refers to the extended time over which healing occurs. They also reported that leg ulcer pain was a constant irritation and found that patients reported pain of varying intensity.

2. Limits and accommodations related to mobility and activity restrictions due to pain and disfigurement. Some patients felt that they couldn't go out and others were unable to work.

3. Patients felt powerless and had resigned themselves to the inevitability of wound recurrence.

4. Some patients believed that nobody cared. In addition, they felt that when they tried to get professional help it was delayed until the condition worsened and the ulcer became large and infected.

Mayfield (1992) interviewed eight patients and explored the hypothesis of whether patients gained from non-healing ulcers, eg. social contact with practitioners. She reported that patients suffered from pain, sleeplessness, immobility and lifestyle restriction and concluded that patients did not gain from non-healing ulcers.

Charles (1995) used the phenomenological approach and interviewed four patients who each suffered from leg ulceration for over five years. She identified themes in the physical, psychological and social areas (*Table 4.1*). The themes in the physical area were pain, sleeplessness, impaired mobility, and that no one listened or explained. The themes in the psychological area were identified as hopelessness, helplessness and a lack of control. In the social area, patients reported that their working life was altered and human interaction was diminished.

These studies have highlighted the daily problems and restrictions patients are forced to endure. The hopelessness of the ongoing and prolonged healing process were expressed by many patients

Table 4.1: Areas relating to QoL among patients with leg ulcers
• Conflicting advice
• Depression, hopelessness
• Loss of independence
• Immobility
• Impaired social life
• Pain
• Sleeplessness
• Wound leakage — odour

(Douglas, 2001; Chase *et al*, 1997). The imposed change from an active to a sedentary life and being dependent on other people produces a state of patient powerlessness (Hopkins, 2004; Charles, 1995). It is not surprising that patients become depressed and feel in a hopeless state. All of the reductions in quality of life have to be endured with pain and, in some cases, with the non-listening or non-understanding healthcare professionals. This is further compounded when conflicting advice is given by practitioners. On a positive side, there are some patients who developed coping mechanisms and therapeutic relationships with their healthcare professionals (Hopkins, 2004).

Studies investigating quality of life before and after intervention

These studies include:

- patients telling their stories (Hawkins and Lindsay, 2006; *Chapters 1* and 2)
- Rand medical outcomes study pain measures (Edwards *et al*, 2005)
- short-form health survey SF-36
- short-form McGill pain questionnaire (Melzack, 1975)
- questionnaires used to investigate patients activities.

Patients telling their stories

Hawkins and Lindsay (2006) recorded stories from patients (four) who attended a Leg Club (*Chapter 1*). They described the suffering and areas of hardship that were caused by their leg ulcers, eg. a patient had suffered for 30 years and the ulcers controlled her life; a young man suffered embarrassment for many years; another patient endured very painful ulcers and ineffective treatment. Patients told how the attendance at the Leg Club changed their lives. It was the effective treatment in combination with interacting with others, ie. sharing the same or a similar condition that helped them to overcome their own feelings of distress, uncertainty and social isolation. Once they attended the Leg Club they fully understood the treatment options and they got involved in the treatment discussions and decisions and felt they were in control of their condition and its treatment.

Rand medical outcomes study pain measures

Edwards *et al* (2005) used the Rand medical outcome pain measures questionnaire in an Australian community Leg Club to investigate pain and quality of life on 33 patients, 16 in the intervention and 17 in the control group. The questionnaire consists of 12 items covering the amount, frequency and duration of pain and how it affects daily lives.

At the start of the study there were no significant differences between the intervention and control groups. After 12 weeks of treatment, significant reductions were found in the intervention group, ie. those treated within a Leg Club setting, in the amount of pain experienced, ie. mean pain scores, degree in which pain affected mood and sleep and the degree to which pain interfered with normal work. The authors concluded that healing rates and quality of life of patients might be improved through a community Leg Club environment.

Short-form health survey SF-36

Charles (2004) administered the short-form SF-36 questionnaire to 65 patients suffering from venous leg ulceration at the beginning of treatment and at 12 weeks of treatment or earlier if the wound had healed. The research was carried out in a leg ulcer clinic or in the patient's home if the patient could not attend the clinic. The data were also compared to a population without leg ulceration. At the start, patients with leg ulceration reported poorer health than patients without leg ulceration in six of the SF-36's eight domains. After 12 weeks of treatment, patients with leg ulceration showed measurable improvements in all of the eight domains and in health transition based upon the previous year. Statistically significant improvements were noted in bodily pain, social functioning, mental health and health transition.

Short-form McGill pain questionnaire

The McGill Pain questionnaire consists of 78 adjectives that describe pain. They are grouped into 20 sub-groups. These are further classified into four groups:

1. The sensation experienced.
2. The attitude of the patient to the pain (affective).
3. The impact the pain has on the patient (evaluative).
4. Other salient aspects of the pain experience. Pain intensity is assessed using a score from 0 (no pain) to 10 (most severe pain).

Charles (2002) used the McGill pain questionnaire to investigate the pain experience of 65 patients suffering with venous leg ulceration before and after 12 weeks of treatment, or earlier if the wound had healed. At the first interview, over 30% of patients described pain sensation in terms of throbbing, sharp, itchy, sore and tender. In the affective sub-class, the most used descriptor was tiring and in the evaluative sub-class annoying, which was followed by nagging in the miscellaneous sub-class. Pain intensity at the beginning was reported by 70% of patients with a mean score of 4.5 (out of a total score of 10); this intensity was dramatically reduced after just two weeks of treatment to an average of 1.5 and at 12 weeks to 0.4.

Questionnaires to investigate patients' activities

Liew *et al* (2000) in Tasmania/Australia employed questionnaires on the effects of sleep, appetite, social activities, mobility and clothing worn on patients who attended a leg ulcer clinic. The questionnaire was completed at the first visit to a leg ulcer clinic and, on average, eight weeks later to 57 patients.

The most frequent pain types that were reported were burning, aching and throbbing. Mobility showed a significant improvement between the two interviews. Sleep patterns improved markedly once treatment began. In contrast, there were no significant changes in appetite levels, social activities or clothing worn.

These qualitative studies demonstrate that there is no need for patients to endure pain and reduced quality of life on a 'forever-and-ever basis'. Healthcare professionals must take these findings seriously and aim to provide effective leg ulcer management and QoL in whichever setting, eg. the patient's home, leg ulcer clinic or Leg Club. In addition, managers need to support their staff to achieve this goal and this is especially true for research-based training.

Discussion

Over recent years there has been an increasing interest among healthcare professionals to investigate the experience of patients suffering from wounds, especially leg ulceration. Various research studies using quantitative research either with generic or disease-specific tools, and qualitative research interview methods have been conducted. These research studies have shown that there is no doubt that leg ulceration affects patients' quality of life in many aspects and to varying degrees in their daily activities. Quantitative research gives an overall insight into reduced quality of life compared to patients without leg ulcers. Qualitative research studies demonstrate in detail how patients are affected on a daily and long-term basis when living with leg ulceration. The studies also demonstrate the relationship between patients and professionals, which is often not as supportive as patients would expect it to be.

A number of research studies have shown the positive impact effective treatment has on QoL (Edwards *et al*, 2005; Hawkins and Lindsay, 2006; Charles, 2002, 2004; Liew *et al*, 2000). These studies should be seen by professionals not only as a challenge, but as a requirement to improve leg ulcer management and, thus, patient quality of life.

The way forward

Assessment/standardised effective care

At the initial assessment when demographic data is recorded, pain and QoL must become part of the assessment. Some local guidelines/documentation have taken this on board and record it as routine. This being the situation, the treatment and management process must not only focus on healing but aspects of the individual's QoL. Consistent, standardised and continued care should be promoted through care pathways, audit on patient's satisfaction, healing rates, and benchmarking.

There is also a need to investigate the quality of care in different settings, ie. home setting, leg ulcer clinic, Leg Club and hospital out-patient clinics to ensure standards of care are consistent throughout the services for all patients.

Education for professionals

It is well-recognised that a registered nurse or specialist community nurse must maintain their professional knowledge and competence and act to identify and minimise the risk to patients and clients (Nursing and Midwifery Council [NMC] Code of Professional Conduct). It seems that since the nursing profession has become comfortable with nurse specialists the knowledge in each subject has increased, resulting in a knowledge gap among the generalist nurses. This gap needs to be closed with appropriate education.

Many patients said that they obtained conflicting information from different healthcare professionals. To address any confusion about care, clear standardised care pathways between nurses is essential. This is especially important when nurses work on their own, or do not have the time to seek advice from colleagues (Lindsay and Hawkins, 2003).

Patient education

Conflicting advice by healthcare professionals can lead to non-concordance. It is of great importance to remember that patient education with subsequent understanding can be linked to concordance

(Cameron and Gregor, 1987; Harker, 2000). Lindsay (2006) identified social isolation needs of patients and pioneered Leg Clubs which address social interaction, participation, empathy and peer support to ease loneliness in surroundings where old friends can meet and new friendships are formed. These surroundings facilitate patient empowerment, build up the low self-esteem of sufferers and create a support network to address the educational, social and psychological needs of those living with an ulcer (Edwards *et al*, 2005).

Conclusion

It has been recognised by healthcare professionals that there is a need for an holistic approach to leg ulcer treatment. Both quantitative and qualitative research have demonstrated the suffering of patients. Recent research has shown that effective treatment and management can improve patients' quality of life. Clear pathways, standardised treatment by well-educated professionals, who will link theory to practice and apply critical reasoning and a problem-solving approach, will hopefully achieve this goal in whatever setting best fits the patient–practitioner relationship (Flanagan, 2000).

References

Augustin M, Dieterle, W, Zschocke I, *et al* (1997) Development and validation of a disease-specific questionnaire on the quality of life of patients with chronic venous insufficiency. *J Vasc Dis* **26**: 291–301

Acquadro C, Price P, Wollina U (2005) Linguistic validation of the Cardiff Wound Impact Schedule into French, German and US English. *J Wound Care* **14**(1): 14–17

Cameron K, Gregor F (1987) Chronic illness and compliance. *J Adv Nurs* **12**(6): 671–6

Chase S, Melloni M, Savage A (1997) A forever healing: The lived experience of venous ulcer disease. *J Vasc Nurs* **10**(2): 73–8

Charles H (2004) Does leg ulcer treatment improve patients' quality of life? *J Wound Care* **13**(6): 209–13

Charles H (2002) Venous leg ulcer pain and its characteristics. *J Tissue Viability* **12**(4): 154–8

Charles H (1995) The impact of leg ulcers on patients' quality of life. *Prof Nurse* **10**(9): 571–4

Douglas V (2001) Living with a chronic leg ulcer: an insight into patients' experiences and feelings. *J Wound Care* 10: 355–60

Edwards H, Courtney M, Finlayson K, Lindsay E, Lewis C, Shuter P, Chang A (2005) Chronic venous leg ulcers: effect of a community nursing intervention on pain and healing. *Nurs Standard* 19(52): 747–54

Fayers P, Machin D (2000) *Quality of Life Assessment, Analysis and Interpretation.* John Wiley and Son, Chichester

Field P, Morse J (1985) *Nursing Research: The application of qualitative approaches.* Aspen, Rockville, MD

Flanagan M (2000) The responsibility is yours. *J Wound Care* 9(8): 357

Ford K, Oberski I, Higgins S (2000) *The Qualitative Report* 4: 3–4. Available online at: www.nova.edu/ssss/QR/QR4-3/oberski.html

Franks PJ, Moffat CJ (1998) Who suffers most from leg ulceration? *J Wound Care* 7(8): 383–5

Hamer C, Cullum N, Roe B (1994) Patients perception of chronic leg ulcers. *J Wound Care* 3: 299–101

Harker J (2000) Influences on patient adherence with compression hosiery. *J Wound Care* 9(8): 379–82

Hawkins J, Lindsay E (2006) We listen but do we hear? The importance of patient stories. *Br J Community Nurs* 11(9): 6–14

Hofman D, Ryan TJ, Arnold F, *et al* (1997) Pain in venous leg ulcers. *J Wound Care* 6(5): 222–4

Hopkins A (2004) Disruptive lives: investigating coping strategies for non-healing leg ulcers. *Br J Nursing* 13(9): 556–63

Hunt SM, McEven J, McKenna SP (1985) Measuring health status: a new tool for clinicians and epidemiologists. *J R Col Gen Pract* 35: 185–8

Hunt SM, McEwen J, McKenna SP (1984) Perceived health: age and sex comparisons in the community. *J Epidemiol Community Health* 38: 156–60

Husserl E (1962) *Ideas: General Introduction to Pure Phenomenology.* Collier, New York

Jenkinson C, Coulter A, Wright L (1993) Short form (SF-36) health survey questionnaire; normative data for adults of working age. *Br Med J* 306: 1437–40

Liew U, Kaw J, Sinha S (2000) Do leg ulcer clinics improve patients' quality of life? *J Wound Care* 9(9): 423–6

Lindholm C, Bjellerup M, Christensen OB, *et al* (1993) Quality of life in chronic leg ulcers. *Acta Derm Venerol* 73: 440–3

Lindsay E, Hawkins J (2003) Care Study: The Leg Club model and the sharing of knowledge. *Br J Nurs* 12(13): 784–90

Lindsay E (2006) Leg Clubs: giving patients a voice in leg ulcer management. *Community Practitioner* 79(7): 44–5

Marlow S (1999) System 4: the four-layer bandage system from SSL International. *Br J Nurs* 8(16): 1104–7

Mayfield S (1992) *An exploration of elderly women's experience of chronic venous ulceration.* Unpublished BSc dissertation. University of Surrey, Guildford

Melzack R (1975) The McGill pain questionnaire, major properties and scoring methods. *Pain* 1: 277–99

Patrick D, Deyo R (1999) Generic and disease-specific measures in assessing health status and quality of life. *Med Care* 27(suppl): 217–32

Price PE, Harding K (1997) *The suitability of a wound-specific QoL measure (CWIS) for patients with diabetes-related foot ulcers.* Presentation to ETRS, Cologne, Germany (available from the British Library, Boston Spa, Wetherby, West Yorkshire, UK)

Price P, Harding K (1996) Measuring health-related quality of life in patients with chronic leg ulcers. *Wounds* 8(3): 139–40

Rich A, McLachlan L (2003) How living with a leg ulcer affects people's daily life: a nurse-led study. *J Wound Care* 12(2): 51–4

Skevington SM, Lofty M, O'Connell KA, WHOQOL Group (2004) The World Health Organizations' WHOQOL-BREF quality of life assessment: psychometric properties and results of the international field trial. A report from the WHOQOL group. *Qual Life Res* 13(2): 299–310

Smith JJ, Guest MG, Greenhalgh MA, Davies AH (2000) Measuring the quality of life in patients with venous ulcers. *J Vasc Surg* 31: 642–9

Ware JJ, Sherbourne CD (1992) The MOS 36-item short-form health survey (SF-36), conceptual framework and item selection. *J Med Care* 30: 473–84

World Health Organization (1984) *Uses of Epidemiology in Ageing, Report of Scientific Group, 1983.* Technical Report Series. WHO, Geneva: 706

Chapter 5

The Lindsay Leg Club® model

Ellie Lindsay

This chapter discusses the introduction of a new service delivery for leg ulcer management based on patient empowerment, health promotion and education, and its implication for clinical practice. It focuses on an initiative that provides a patient-centred resource for the prevention, treatment and management of leg ulcers and associated conditions.

The author introduced the concept and opened her first Leg Club in 1995. As a district nursing sister serving a rural community, she sought to provide a framework for holistic care that, in addition to clinical treatment, would address the psychosocial and economic factors influencing concordance with treatment, healing and recurrence. The success of the concept quickly led to the establishment of a second Leg Club in a neighbouring location and interest from the wider nursing community. In 2005, the Lindsay Leg Club Foundation was formed as a registered charity to facilitate and support nurses wishing to set up leg clubs.

The Lindsay Leg Club model

The Leg Club® model was developed to address the limitations of existing mechanisms, such as home visits and leg ulcer clinics, in meeting patients' needs (Hawkins and Lindsay, 2006). It provides a cost-effective framework in which members are educated and empowered to take ownership of their care and make informed decisions regarding treatment, a departure from the traditional nurse dominant/patient passive relationship. The model unites the primary care organisation (PCO), nurses, patients (known as members) and the community in the common objective of improving patients' health and well-being through significant improvements in patients' quality of life. By informing and empowering members to participate in their treatment, Leg Clubs implement the core themes of the Government's healthcare policy, as outlined in the *National Health Service Plan* (DoH, 2000), National Service Framework for Older People (DoH, 2001), *Creating a Patient-led NHS: Delivering the NHS Improvement Plan* (DoH, 2005) and the recent Government White Paper, *Our health, our care, our say: a new direction for community services* (DoH, 2006). They have also proved to be cost-effective in the use of nursing resources by reducing travel costs and the need for the duplication of equipment, simplifying planning and administration, and eliminating wasted home visits.

Background and rationale

For many elderly people living in the community loneliness is a significant issue. Retirement, poor mobility, the death of family or friends or the effects of demographic change on the cohesiveness of the family unit can all create an environment of social isolation. For people suffering from leg ulcers, the correlation between social isolation, poor compliance to treatment and low healing rates is well documented (Lindsay, 2000). Pain, odour, obtrusive bandages may exacerbate feelings of low self-esteem, depression and social stigma. Home visits by community nurses do not address the social and psychological needs of these individuals. In the author's experience, a problem faced by many district nurses is poor concordance to treatment. It is vital that the nurse works with the patient to achieve concordance to help prevent further leg ulcers developing. The nurse must consider the individual's beliefs, attitude, motivation and social behaviour. Becker (1974) asserts that, even when an individual recognises personal susceptibility, action will not occur unless he or she also believes that becoming ill will bring organic or social repercussions. Becker also identifies salience, a factor that enables the individual to experience the feeling of doing something about the nature of the problem. Beliefs, attitudes and values may be cultural in origin. People often need help in clarifying their own beliefs about aspects of their health and this is an important component of the self-empowerment approach, as self-awareness is necessary to facilitate the decision-making process.

As a district nurse in Suffolk, the author was aware of anecdotal evidence that social factors and isolation could significantly influence patients' response to treatment. From the examination of available literature (Wise, 1986; Charles, 1995), it is evident that patients who are treated for leg ulcers experience lack of motivation, loneliness, family and social isolation. These are areas that may not be best addressed by medically-based clinics. Further enquiry via literature review (Callam *et al*, 1985), examination of demographic factors and patients' daily circumstances, and a study of established leg ulcer clinics led the author to the conclusion that a new type of clinic could help to address these issues. The author's theory included the idea that, were patients fully informed of effective research-based treatment, they could make rational decisions that would lead to concordance with treatment. The conceptual framework for this new approach was a health belief model (Becker and Maiman, 1975) for obtaining and assessing the patient's views and perception of health and well-being.

In the field of leg ulcer management, the Leg Club model delivers an environment for truly patient-centred holistic care through a synergistic combination of four binding principles:

- a non-medical setting – community/church/village hall
- collective treatment – people sharing their experiences
- open access, no appointment required – opportunistic attendance
- integrated 'well leg' regime – maintenance and health promotion.

The principal aims of the Leg Club are to:

- empower members to become stakeholders in their own treatment, promoting a sense of ownership and involvement
- facilitate an informal support network
- achieve concordance to treatment through informed beliefs and modified behaviour
- provide continuity of care and a co-ordinated team approach to its delivery
- minimise recurrence by systematic post-treatment monitoring and 'well leg' checks
- adopt a simple, flexible 'drop-in' approach that encourages attendance to obtain information and advice.

The ethos of the Leg Club model seeks to encourage 'wellness' rather than treat 'illness' in all age groups, an alternative approach to the traditional management of leg conditions. One facet of the model is the 'well leg' programme, aimed at prophylaxis, education and advice, and prevention and maintenance of further leg-related problems once the ulcer has healed. According to McAllister and Farquhar (1992) health beliefs have important implications for nursing, given the role of the nurse in health promotion and patient teaching.

In accordance with Leg Club guidelines, every Leg Club offers members the option of receiving treatment in private (ie. they are not treated in view of other members). However, internal data show that, in practice, less than 1% elect to do so, and that members overwhelmingly favour collective treatment (ie. in a communal treatment area).

Health and safety and infection control are primary considerations for Leg Clubs, which have been covered in their guidelines and risk assessment. Working practices and lifting protocols have been audited and approved by occupational healthcare representatives.

Leg Clubs continue to develop and improve through the reflective practice and shared experiences of the members. The Leg Club Forum provides a support network to which members and nurses can refer for help and advice. Collaborative working is the foundation of Leg Club culture. Members and nurses work together in an open environment, where interactive learning is paramount. Shared knowledge allows an open forum where excellence in practice can be observed, recognised, critically evaluated and mirrored by all the nursing staff (Lindsay and Hawkins, 2003).

Application of theory into practice

At the invitation of a member of a primary care organisation (PCO) who has read about the Leg Club model, the author attends a meeting to present the concept and to take questions from staff. With the support of their managers and director of clinical services, community nurses and their colleagues who decide to set up a Leg Club are encouraged to visit existing Leg Clubs to see the model in action and liaise with volunteers, the committee, members and staff, and observe the organisational structure of the Club. A mentorship programme has been established where experienced Leg Club leads play a pivotal role in supporting and advising new team members.

Leg Clubs belong to the members (patients) and the local community, who meet the costs of premises and equipment through fundraising. Volunteers provide transport, clerical services, refreshments, etc. Nursing staff and direct treatment costs are provided by the PCO. From the outset, the team involves the local community and works with their current patients, informing them of the proposed changes and inviting them to participate in setting up and running the Club. A health promotion fundraising coffee morning may be held at, for example, the local community hall where members of the public are invited to attend for advice and information on the proposed plans. Funds generated from the event contribute towards the purchase of equipment such as a hand-held Doppler ultrasound monitor and a treatment couch.

Through advertising in the local paper and direct contact with patients and the local community, a volunteer committee is recruited, comprising chairman, secretary and treasurer. Once the committee is formed, a bank account is opened and funds are generated from a variety of local and European Community grants, coffee mornings and general fundraising events involving the whole local community. Another interesting facet of the Leg Club model has been the development of roles within the local community volunteer group. In many parts of the world, people who have retired are seen as extremely active individuals who participate in neighbourhood committees, educational activities, welfare work, and serving their neighbourhood in various ways. It is interesting to note that the majority of the Leg Club teams have community volunteers from this group who have come out of their retirement status and become extremely active in contributing to their community. Far from categorising retirees as a frail, incapacitated or dependent group, the Leg Club model provides a framework in which older members of the community have an opportunity to provide a valued and fulfilling role and remain as active as possible. Their enthusiasm and boundless energy has resulted in the creation of friendship clubs and peer groups, where support and advice is offered to volunteers involved in newly-formed Leg Clubs. The role of the volunteer receptionist has evolved to include news letters, questionnaires, general information, fundraising letters and information leaflets, organisation of fundraising events, maintenance of patient register and documentation.

In practice

As the umbrella organisation for Leg Clubs, The Lindsay Leg Club Foundation provides guidance, support and training during the setting-up phase. Although the model has its own documentation, guidelines and referral pathways, the team ensures that local PCO protocols and procedures are followed. To ensure all aspects are covered, the staff may liaise with their tissue viability nurse specialist, infection control specialist and clinical governance coordinator, as changes in the working culture and practice have to be fully supported by the PCO, a factor critical to the success of any innovation.

Within the already existing clubs, the community nursing teams are receptive and have adopted a positive approach to the change, acknowledging the benefits for club members. The attitude of members and the local community to their own health has changed significantly. Data collected since the model's inception illustrates dramatic reductions in both non-concordance and prescription costs (Gordon *et al*, 2006). Apart from housebound patients, home visits for leg ulcer management have been virtually eliminated, yielding significant savings.

Some nursing teams, who had previously never undertaken such activities, have presented the model and demonstrated cost savings to fellow healthcare professionals, the PCO and the professional executive committee (PEC) board (*Figure 5.1*). They have created posters and literature to enable them to provide ongoing support and information to their practice population, and have been invited to present to a public audience within other areas of the PCO/health board. In a process of continuous improvement, a few of the teams have evaluated the services currently provided and have identified a need for the consultant vascular surgeon and tissue viability nurse to hold outreach clinics within their Leg Club.

Many of the Clubs have an educational display area that includes sections on leg health, skin care, compression hosiery and the provision of health promotion and education materials. Local community volunteer group information is also presented, such as Age Concern and other community and national agencies, as well as local grants for older people.

Discussion

The benefits of patient empowerment have been widely promoted in such documents as the *National Health Service Plan* (DoH, 2000) and *Our health, our care, our say* (DoH, 2006), where the emphasis is on individuals being listened to and encouraged to make informed choices regarding their treatment and care. However, while the ideals of patient empowerment are widely embraced in principle, in the author's experience they are rarely implemented in practice successfully.

The concept of the Leg Club has been embraced by many forward thinking PCOs and in Australia, where the value of individualised care and socialisation has been recognised as contributing to quality of life and increased healing (*Chapter 7*). It must be acknowledged, however, that patient empowerment is not an easy concept, and it is inevitable that some nurses and nurse managers are uncomfortable with the notion of moving from a 'nurse dominant/patient passive' relationship to one of an equal partnership in care.

By having the courage and motivation to implement change, engaging with their local community, exposing their practice to peer review, and empowering their members to participate in care delivery, the nurses who have opened Leg Clubs have responded to core themes of NHS policy, providing cost-effective care and enhancing patient quality of life. As healthcare professionals, their commitment and motivation to the management of leg ulcers within their area demonstrates the imagination and energy needed to drive positive change forward to benefit the local community.

However, the advent of commissioned services for leg ulcer management in the community presents new challenges to this patient-centred approach. For example, there are indications that many leg ulcer services may become assimilated within the existing GP surgery framework, in which clinics conventionally focus on clinical need, the treatment of 'sickness' and the alleviation of symptoms. The

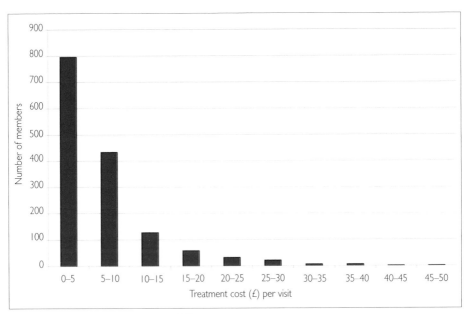

Figure 5.1: Treatment costs (£) per visit

formal clinical environment reinforces 'sick role' behaviour, in which patients attend when they believe they require treatment and in which they assume a passive role in their care delivery. This culture is further encouraged when clinics are incentivised on patient contacts and procedures, rather than the ongoing management of 'well legs' within the practice population.

By engaging the community and empowering members to become stakeholders in their care, the Lindsay Leg Club model encapsulates current national strategies for health care. The author's goal is to determine a strategy for the Leg Club model to continue to make a significant contribution to best practice within a commissioning environment.

Conclusion

Today's healthcare world is increasingly focused on value for money, faster throughputs, measurable outcomes and cost-effectiveness. In this environment, it is all too easy to lose sight of the importance of the caring ethos and the quality of patients' lives. The Leg Club model of care shows that these two seemingly incompatible aims can be united. The people who attend Leg Clubs experience companionship, develop friendships and, once again, become fully integrated into their communities, thereby bringing new meaning to their lives.

In successfully implementing the Leg Club model, the nursing teams have demonstrated true patient empowerment, enabling their members to become expert partners in the process of their care, destigmatising their condition, encouraging informed behaviours and facilitating the sharing of sensitive and/or emotional concerns in a supportive empathic environment. Meanwhile, the nurses themselves have forged ties with their local community, gained skills and confidence and become empowered to foster change within their profession. The Lindsay Leg Club model serves as an excellent example of how the model unites the PCO, nurses, patients and community in the common objective of improving patient quality of life.

References

Becker M (1974) The health belief model and sick role behaviour. Workshop/Symposium on Compliance with Therapeutic Regimes. McMaster University, Hamilton, Ontario, Canada

Becker M, Maiman L (1975) Sociobehavioural determinants of compliance with health and medical care recommendations. *Med Care* **13**(1): 10–25

Callam H, Ruckley C, Harper D, Dale J (1985) Chronic ulceration of the leg: Extent of the problem and provision of care. *Br Med J* **290**: 1855–56

Charles H (1995) The impact of leg ulcers on patients' quality of life. *Professional Nurse* **10**(9): 571–4

Department of Health (2000) *The NHS Plan: a plan for investment, a plan for reform*. DoH, London

Department of Health (2001) *National Service Framework for Older People*. DoH, London

Department of Health (2005) *A Patient-led NHS*. DoH, London

Department of Health (2006) *Our health, our care, our say: a new direction for community services*. DoH, London

Edwards H, Courtney M, Finlayson K, Lindsay E, Lewis C, Shuter P, *et al* (2005) Chronic venous leg ulcers: effect of a community nursing intervention on pain and healing. *Nurs Standard* **19**(52): 47–54

Gordon LG, Edwards H, Courtney M,Finlayson K, Shuter P, Lindsay E (2006) A cost-effective analysis of two community models of care for patients with venous leg ulcers. *J Wound Care* **15**(8): 348–53

Hawkins J, Lindsay E (2006) We listen but do we hear? The importance of patient stories. *Br J Community Nurs* **11**(9): 6–14

Kemm J, Close A (1995) *Health Promotion. Theory and Practice*. Macmillan Press Ltd, London

Lindsay E (2000) Leg Clubs: a new approach to patient-centred leg ulcer management. *Nurs Health Sci* **2**(3): 139–41

Lindsay E, Hawkins J (2003) Care study: The Leg Club model and the sharing of knowledge. *Br J Nurs* **12**(13): 784–90

McAllister G, Farquhar (1992) Health beliefs: a cultural division. *J Adv Nurs* **17**: 1447–54

Wise G (1986) The social ulcer. *Nurs Times* May: 47–9

CHAPTER 6

DELIVERING WOUND MANAGEMENT IN A SOCIAL ENVIRONMENT

Louise Dalzell

As a district nursing sister based at a small village surgery, this is a personal account of my experiences introducing a new approach for delivering holistic wound management to my patients. It deals with the practical and emotional challenges of overcoming barriers to change and forging new working relationships, both within the nursing team and with the patients and wider community.

With the encouragement and support of Ellie Lindsay, originator of the Lindsay Leg Club model, Combs Ford Leg Club was set up in 2000 to provide leg ulcer management in an empowered and stigma-free environment. Through the commitment and efforts of nurses, volunteers and patients working together, difficulties and resistance have been confronted and overcome, and Combs Ford Leg Club today is a thriving and vibrant resource, treating, supporting and educating those experiencing leg ulcers or other leg-related conditions.

The author has been working in community nursing for 12 years, for the past nine years as a district nursing sister at Combs Ford, a village surgery with a practice population of 9 200. Leg ulcer management has always taken up a significant proportion of my nursing caseload. This can be an acute and often chronic condition afflicting all ages, but especially the elderly and those who suffer with other complex conditions such as diabetes. Historically, leg ulcerations have been extremely difficult to heal and it is a hard task to prevent recurrence.

Approximately five years ago, I attended a presentation by Ellie Lindsay, a fellow district nursing sister. Her concept, 'The social dimension in leg ulcer management' (Lindsay, 2001), although perhaps difficult to grasp at first, seemed to offer the 'missing link' between the treatment and healing of leg ulcers and the prevention of recurrence. The 'link' was the birth of a Leg Club which can be described as a meeting of people with a common condition in convivial, informal surroundings where management of their condition can take place in a supportive carefully controlled environment.

Ellie Lindsay's work inspired me to adopt the Leg Club concept and gave me an entirely new perspective on leg ulcer care. For the first time in my career in community nursing, I became excited about the prospect of healing and, above all, keeping these ulcers healed, through careful monitoring and health promotion.

Setting up

I wanted to incorporate the 'social dimension' of the Leg Club model into my own surgery. I therefore invited Ellie Lindsay to present her concept to the general practitioners and the practice manager. I quickly realised that running a Leg Club clinic there would not be possible, as it did not meet one of the primary criteria of the Leg Club model, the social aspect that requires care to be delivered in a non-medical setting. I felt that this was the most important element of the scheme, since it offered the opportunity to meet community residents and to gain a better understanding of their needs.

Following the initial presentation, the general practitioners and the practice manager were impressed with the concept and felt it would be an appropriate service for their clients. Their only stipulation was that the new service was to be called 'The Combs Ford Leg Club' and that only their practice patients were to be treated. Since I manage a relatively small team, I felt this was a manageable and realistic goal, rather than trying to recruit from a wider base.

I next organised a community nurse team meeting. This was comprised of a community staff nurse, a healthcare assistant and myself. They felt that setting up a Leg Club would be possible in principle and we agreed to start the project in 2000. Ellie Lindsay was invited back to discuss the holistic assessment documentation with the community nurse team. She helped us to complete the necessary data demonstrating cost-effectiveness of the Leg Club, and emphasised to the team that all record-keeping and data collection must be to the highest standard. This would highlight any shortfall in training and knowledge regarding leg ulcer management. The data collection should take place on a three-month cycle.

We had to find a suitable venue for club meetings, essentially a site not too far from the surgery in Combs Ford. Having consulted patients on the caseload and members of staff in the surgery, they recommended the local community centre (previously the local primary school). I visited and assessed the venue for kitchen and toilet facilities and found that several rooms were available. I finally chose the centre's assembly hall, as it could be divided into the necessary areas:

- a social area
- a treatment area
- an area to carry out regular Doppler ultrasound assessments.

I then spoke to the local council that owned this building and explained my needs. Having set the rental, the Council agreed to lease the centre to the Leg Club.

Equipment for the Leg Club was the next obstacle to overcome. I was at this time taking a diploma in aromatherapy and body massage for which I had bought a couch. Realising that it could also be made available to Leg Club members, I donated it to the Leg Club. I initially transported this couch by car every week, until the Council offered us a large storage cupboard at the centre. We were then able to store all the equipment required for the Leg Club on site, instead of transporting everything in cars.

Other substantial pieces of equipment were acquired with the help of the local NHS central equipment stores as they had old stock items available. Smaller items like plastic buckets and containers for first dressings were purchased at a local warehouse store. Equipment for repeated use was all made of plastic for ease of frequent cleaning and to reduce cross-infection (_Chapter 18_).

A Leg Club handbook was supplied to the club that included important risk assessments on subjects such as infection control, safe management of water, environmental issues and the safety of our volunteers.

Staffing Leg Club sessions so that important tasks could be undertaken safely was a vital issue to resolve. Creating the right relaxed atmosphere is an essential element to the social dimension of the scheme. We needed firstly a volunteer to make teas, so I asked at my surgery if anyone was interested in this role and we were lucky to find a recently bereaved lady who was free when the club met on Tuesday afternoons. The club secretary is an ex-patient from the caseload and she has also enrolled the help of her husband, who is now our volunteer driver. A member of the reception team at the surgery who already had bookkeeping skills became our treasurer.

Once the premises, volunteers and equipment were secured, posters advertising the Combs Ford Leg Club were placed in the surgery, the local post office, the council offices and community centre. Our patients, termed club members, initially came from a variety of sources, including the existing caseload and referrals from GPs and practice nurses. As the club developed we received an increasing number of self-referrals as well as referrals from relatives (*Figure 6.1*).

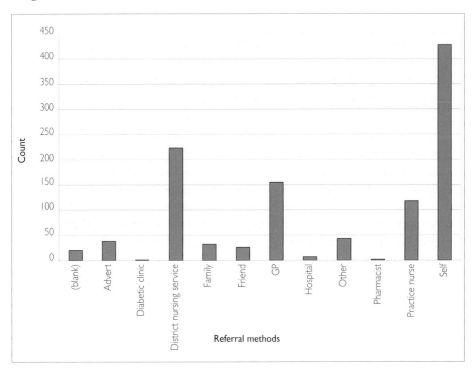

Figure 6.1: Referral methods for all Leg Clubs

Fundraising

Successful fundraising for the club was essential but proved a difficult task because the Leg Club team had little experience in this sphere. I resolved these difficulties after contacting the secretary of the already well-established Grundisburgh Leg Club, who gave me some excellent ideas, like coffee mornings and weekly raffles.

I also discussed fundraising ideas with the practice nursing team and we came up with a 12-week sponsored slim involving the entire staff at the surgery. This proved a great success; I lost 18 pounds altogether, coming joint first with our female GP. This raised £170 and the profile of the Leg Club within the locality.

The Leg Club received a letter in October 2000 from the then primary care group (PCG), which employs the community nursing team, inviting bids for financial assistance up to £88000 for innovative local community services. Bids were considered at PCG fundholder meetings of GPs, patient support group members, PCG members and our own practice manager. I spoke at one of these meetings to explain the concept of the Leg Club, emphasising the need for help with our single biggest outgoing, the monthly rental charge for premises. It was agreed that a grant of £500 would be made available and ultimately paid into the Combs Ford Leg Club account.

Since decreasing prescription costs and nurses' working time and mileage was to be encouraged, any sister/charge nurse wanting to set up their own Leg Club would be offered the same amount.

It would be more appropriate for Leg Club equipment to be financed by other fundraising schemes. In 2004, the current primary care trust (PCT) contributed £290 towards a replacement Doppler ultrasound machine to enable necessary assessments to be carried out. Invitations to visit the Leg Club have sadly so far not been taken up by the PCT.

Adhering to the Nursing and Midwifery Council (NMC) code, I identified representatives from healthcare companies as potential sources of assistance and wrote letters to them explaining the Leg Club concept and outlining its needs. Consequently, several were able to donate small amounts, which enabled us to purchase much-needed screens for our members' personal dignity and to provide a division of the different working areas. Company representatives have proved an invaluable educational resource of research data on their products. Their knowledge on how products can be used in wound healing and prevention has been of great benefit to the club.

Leg Club members are now also coming up with their own fundraising proposals.

Running the club

Successful wound care and leg ulcer management is dependent upon each team member's knowledge and skills gained both by 'in house' study days and my own ENB N18 Leg Ulcer Management qualification. In early 2001, two original members of staff left the Leg Club team through job-change and retirement. I subsequently employed both a new healthcare assistant (who was very enthusiastic about the concept of the Leg Club) and a staff nurse, who had some initial apprehensions but was prepared to try the experience.

Nurses have a responsibility to provide the most effective research-based care for their patients and they must be given the resources and training to achieve this Moffatt (1992). The new Leg Club team required initial training in documentation, data collection and especially the high standard of wound care needed. Other staff changes came about within the volunteer group. Our treasurer was unable to continue due to other commitments but a past Leg Club member, whose leg ulceration had healed, offered us his assistance instead. His assertiveness and connections with our surgery GPs and fundraising groups subsequently proved invaluable. His support for the club was rewarded as he found a companion in our volunteer tea lady; so blossomed our first Leg Club romance!

Through volunteers and staff both working hard at evaluation, assessment, treatment and monitoring, our healing rates have been excellent, approximately 90%. The staff have found that the time spent with the member is constructive; discussions can take place privately or in the treatment area without the constraints of an appointment time. Issues not related to 'leg problems' can be dealt with and it has improved and hastened the healing rates of ulceration. My staff and I have experienced and shared with the members issues of bereavement, house burglary, the loss of their pets and the happy occasions they have had with families. As a team we have been able to be advocates for our members, ie. speaking to the local council officer for home improvements and the local police force regarding home safety. Within this 'social concept', our members are also given a 'social support' network, which can 'buffer' people against stress, vulnerability to illness and increase chances of recovery (Sarason *et al*, 1990; Duck and Silver, 1990).

Another aspect of the treatment offered in the Leg Club environment is the washing of legs and feet at each visit. The members have often commented how good it feels when they are able to put their feet into warm water and how much better their skin feels after simple cleansing, something they cannot always do for themselves. The application of emollients has also been reported as beneficial, being 'psychologically' uplifting to the members' mood:

Touch is not only a biological need, but a communication tool.
(Davis, 1999)

The time and attention given during this procedure allows the staff to listen to any problems that might be imparted and also encourages good eye contact which indicates to the member the staff's empathy towards them. Several cases of long-term ulceration have come on to become 'well leg members'.

Following discussions, the Leg Club team decided to extend membership by inviting some of our more housebound patients to join. Transportation to and from the venue was our immediate concern. We researched a service called 'DIAL-A-RIDE', which would cost the club £5 a year and up to £2 for each journey within the Stowmarket area and its outlying villages. This was approximately a five-mile radius.

Our secretary's husband wanted to contribute more to the club and offered to transport our more local members to and from the community centre. Following careful thought about health and safety issues, insurance and liability, the team agreed to accept this proposal. We added a further risk assessment to the *Leg Club Handbook* both for our members' safety and for our new volunteer driver.

The Leg Club today

The Leg Club concept allows an open forum for practice because the nursing team is not working in isolation, but together with the patients. Open discussion about treatment between team and Leg Club members is common, with all treatment decisions being reached through dialogue.

Continuing education, developing skills and sharing knowledge in wound care and leg ulcer management is an essential team goal. Sharing of journals and articles is undertaken regularly and a non-product led formulary (Morgan, 2004) is used. Students are frequent visitors to the Leg Club. They have reported that the social environment is a unique learning experience. They are able to learn anatomy and physiology of the circulation and the effects of a poor circulation, and how this is improved by consistent skin care and evidence-based wound care practice. They are given an invaluable insight into how psychological and emotional issues can have a huge bearing on the healing rate of a leg ulcer. They have commented that in the Leg Club we give holistic care and do not just 'pay lip service to the concept'. One student commented that the way in which the Leg Club concept works underpins the true meaning of 'the art of nursing', working holistically to a framework and referral on to other healthcare professionals when it is necessary.

There is now established a Leg Club Forum, arranged for all those involved in running Leg Clubs. Forum meetings are held to discuss and share experiences, helping us continuously to enhance our own care and practice.

The social dimension concept creates a rewarding environment in which to work. Of particular importance is our ability to monitor our members' progress after ulcers have healed, using the 'well leg' process. Members and staff have the time and space to discuss new developments and information, so that management of the condition becomes routine and, through a higher level of understanding, a way to prevent further ulceration in the future.

Leg Clubs have heightened my awareness of the high risk of leg ulceration and leg problems during and after pregnancy. Many of our members' problems started when they became pregnant. In view of this I looked into their assessment after referral from the community midwife, namely, what type of assessment was done and if compression was prescribed with leg care advice, ie. hydration of skin and elevation of limbs.

After discussions with the community midwife and looking at the assessment documentation, we agreed pregnancy should remain as normal as possible and that the DN service would receive referrals from the community midwife, and that assessment and skin care advice would be given to those pregnant women with circulation and leg problems.

Joint assessment with the community midwife in one instance led to an urgent vascular referral for one lady. I was also able to give telephone advice to a new mother, sending out leg care information and arranging a Doppler assessment. This partnership is in its embryonic stages, but there is certainly a valuable role for the district and community nursing services to play by embracing healthcare education and promotion, to help prevent leg ulceration in the future with this high risk group.

Another high risk group was identified while attending a motor cyclists meeting in Suffolk. By chance, I was able to give a considerable number of men leg care advice and general healthcare education regarding their blood pressures in a comparatively short space of time. I was also able to discuss the importance of the use of compression hosiery to prevent circulatory damage which can take place during lengthy motorcycle rides. These examples illustrate how the Leg Club concept can be used in a variety of different environments.

The social and holistic components of the concept were looked upon favourably by the audit commission after their visit to the Combs Ford and Thetford Leg Clubs two years ago. They believed that the utilisation of these components would be a help in reaching national service framework (NSF) targets in a social, rather than a medical environment. Their visit resulted in an award of 'Best Practice' for holistic care given in a social environment.

Members continue to support the Leg Club long after their own active leg ulcer has healed. I would like to illustrate this with excerpts of a letter written by one of our members:

I have attended the Combs Ford Leg Club regularly over the past two years. In that time the care I have received has been excellent, and I have been fortunate enough to make new friendships. I cannot praise too highly, the dedication and care from the nurses... and the volunteers who give their time willingly, cheerfully and voluntarily.

To illustrate a typical Leg Club success, one member (in his late forties) had suffered bilateral recurrent ulcers for nearly 20 years. He received quick, appropriate referrals from the Leg Club to the vascular surgeon and a dermatologist together with copies of our documentation. This gentleman subsequently received vascular surgery to his legs and with weekly, consistent leg ulcer management, his ulcer has virtually healed. He has now introduced his wife to the Leg Club for prevention and 'well leg' monitoring.

The Leg Club environment has brought in patient educators, sometimes from the least expected sources. These 'educators' are members who have experienced having a leg ulcer, receiving appropriate treatment, advice and support throughout that treatment and their leg ulcer healing. They continue to attend, offering support and advice to other members with leg ulcers and those within the 'well leg' process.

Our healthcare assistant has created a Leg Club newsletter that includes local information for the members and reports on what the club has to offer. A recent letter sent to us by a member said:

I would like to congratulate you on the launch of the first 'Leg Club Newsletter'. This is a wonderful achievement and something that I am sure we will all appreciate. We have a very dedicated team of nurses to care for our needs and we need to give thanks that we have an established, friendly environment, where we can socialise with each other.

Events at the Combs Ford Leg Club are reported and edited into a national Leg Club Newsletter.

We are now receiving many and varied visitors to the Leg Club, whom our members welcome as a chance to share their personal experiences at the Club. These visitors have included:

- an Australian Professor whose own research has demonstrated Leg Club benefits for patients and clinical effectiveness (Finlayson *et al*, 2004)
- a district nurse tutor from Portsmouth, who spent one day with me to experience my role in the Leg Club environment and the wider community
- a research member of the Royal College of Nursing (RCN) involved in 'The Audit of Leg Ulceration 2004', validated by the Commission of Health Improvements
- the editor of a well-known nursing journal, who subsequently wrote an editorial article about the Leg Club concept
- healthcare professionals from Italy and France, where the Leg Club concept is being explored and (hopefully) adopted.

Finally, among the most rewarding visitors to the Leg Club was a district nurse degree student. She was sufficiently enthusiastic about our work that she has since gone on to open a Leg Club of her own. I shared with her the caseload management structure that enables me to accommodate the Leg Club in my daily work.

Our club has often been subject to arm's length scrutiny from peers and colleagues, whose support has at times seemed less than complete. I can only offer in response the club's achievements since its inception. My team of staff and volunteers and our club members continue to work hard to keep up a happy and empowered momentum. The experience has been a huge learning curve for us all, and one that still continues daily to unfold. I have found it all a rewarding and satisfying time in my professional life and I am looking forward to the new journey it is taking me on with great anticipation.

This chapter is modified from an article that was originally published in the *British Journal of Nursing* 2005, **14**(17).

References

Davis PK PhD (1999) *The Power of Touch*. Revised edn. Hay House Inc, USA

Duck S, Silver R (1990) *Personal Relationships and Social Support*. Sage, London

Finlayson K, Edwards H, Courtney M, Lindsay E, Lewis C, Dumble J (2004) *Chronic leg ulcers: Effectiveness of a community nursing intervention on healing and quality of life*. Australian Wound Management Association 5th National Conference Proceedings, Hobart, Tasmania, 17–20 March 2004: 71

Lindsay E (2001) The social dimension in leg ulcer management. *Primary Intention* 9(1): 31–3

Moffatt C (1992) Compression bandaging — the state of the art. *J Wound Care* 1(1): 45–50

Morgan D (2004) *Formulary of Wound Management Products. A Guide for Healthcare Staff*. Ninth edn. Euromed Communications Ltd, Haslemere

Nursing and Midwifery Council (2002) *Code of Professional Conduct*. NMC, London

Sarason BR, Pierce GR (1990) *Social Support: A transactional view*. Wiley: New York

CHAPTER 7

A COMMUNITY NURSING MODEL OF CARE FOR PEOPLE WITH CHRONIC LEG ULCERS

Helen Edwards, Kathleen Finlayson and Mary Courtney

Chronic leg ulcers affect approximately 1–3% of the population aged over 60 years in the UK, Europe, USA and Australia (Briggs and Closs, 2003; Margolis *et al*, 2002). Prevalence increases with age (Margolis *et al*, 2002), rising from around 0.6% of the general adult population up to 2–5.6% of those aged over 65 years (Bergqvist *et al*, 1999). With today's ageing societies (Parker, 2005), this condition will become an increasing problem in the future. Leg ulcers often take months or years to heal and frequently recur, becoming a lifelong chronic condition associated with prolonged ill-health, pain, restricted mobility and decreased quality of life (Chase *et al*, 2000; Walshe, 1995).

When planning care for people with chronic leg ulcers, a healthcare model is required, which not only addresses the need for evidence-based wound care, but also pain management, symptom management and quality of life issues associated with the condition. Prevalence of pain associated with leg ulcers is reported as ranging from around 50% (Nemeth *et al*, 2003) to 80% (Hareendran, 2005), and leg ulcer pain is reported to decrease energy levels (Persoon *et al*, 2004), interrupt sleep (Edwards *et al*, 2005a), affect mood (Edwards *et al*, 2005a) and restrict mobility (Brown, 2005) and ability to manage normal work (Edwards *et al*, 2005a). Mobility is often further constrained by the need to wear bulky, multilayered bandages, limiting the type of footwear and clothing able to be worn. Reduced mobility impacts on independence in activities of daily living and productivity. For example, Abbade *et al* (2005) found that 49.2% of patients had a functional disability impacting on daily activities and work and Persoon *et al*'s (2004) review of 37 studies found restraints in work and leisure activities were one of the major limitations imposed by leg ulcers.

Pain, limited mobility and embarrassment associated with leg ulcers often leads to social isolation (Ebbeskog and Ekman, 2001; Persoon _et al_, 2004). The combination of pain, restricted mobility and social isolation in turn contributes to a negative impact on psychological health (Ebbeskog and Ekman, 2001; Persoon _et al_, 2004); such as depression and anxiety (Jones _et al_, 2006). In addition, the long-term nature of the disease can lead to uncertainty, disappointment, loss of hope, or despair (Ebbeskog and Ekman, 2001). Problems with poor understanding of the cause and treatment of the condition have been noted (Chase _et al_, 2000), leading to feelings of powerlessness, lack of ownership and apathy with regard to management strategies. Not surprisingly, measures of quality of life in people with chronic leg ulcers have generally found significantly lower quality of life scores than in the general population (Franks _et al_, 2003; Jull _et al_, 2004).

In today's healthcare environment, models of care must address client needs in a resource-efficient and cost-effective manner. Significant amounts of time and resources are invested in managing chronic venous leg ulcers. The long-term nature of the disease and extensive wound care requirements result in substantial costs to healthcare systems, with developed countries estimated to spend approximately 1–2.5% of total health costs on care for chronic leg ulcers (Abbade and Lastoria, 2005). Treatment in the UK is reported to cost £400 million each year (Ruckley, 1997) and in the USA over $US3 billion/year and the loss of over two million workdays each year (McGuckin _et al_, 2002). In addition to the costs associated with long-term supplies of wound dressings and compression bandages, it is reported that up to 22–50% of community nurses' time is spent managing the problem (Hampton, 2003; Simon _et al_, 2004).

As well as direct costs to the healthcare system, chronic leg ulcers are associated with many hidden financial burdens on the community. The pain, ill-health and extensive bandaging associated with the condition commonly results in loss of mobility, decreased independence in activities of daily living and loss of participation in the workforce and society (Husband, 2001; Wissing _et al_, 2002). Additional costs are thus associated with lost productivity, provision of social support systems necessary for people with limited mobility and health complications resulting from prolonged immobility.

Caring for this group of people represents a challenge to healthcare professionals and the healthcare system. In Australia, many people with chronic leg ulcers are cared for in the community by community registered nurses who visit the clients individually in their own homes, particularly those who are unable to attend metropolitan hospital clinics due to poor health and limited mobility. However, this system is not always able to meet their needs for social and peer support and is resource intensive, involving significant amounts of registered nurses' time in travel. Reports on the development of alternative models of care, such as the Lindsay Leg Club model (Lindsay, 2000), prompted the desire to trial a similar service in Queensland, Australia, to address this group's specialised needs. Implementing a new model of care represents a significant investment by healthcare agencies and limited evidence was available on the effectiveness of this model at the time. Therefore, an investigation into the effectiveness of the new model of care in comparison to the usual individual community home care was planned, with regard to both client outcomes (healing, pain and quality of life outcomes) and health service outcomes (cost-effectiveness measures).

Planning the study

A review of published studies found that a number of evaluations of varying types of community leg ulcer clinics had previously been undertaken with generally positive results (Ghauri *et al*, 2000; Morrell *et al*, 1998; Simon *et al*, 1996). However, these trials were limited to non-randomised samples, thus excluding people living in the community who were unable to attend the clinics. It is possible that this excluded group may have been less mobile and in poorer health than those who were able to attend the clinics, thus biasing the results. In addition, the trials compared outcomes from clinic patient groups who received consistent care following best practice treatment guidelines by expert clinicians, to community patient groups who received a variety of 'usual care' treatments. A randomised controlled trial was therefore chosen for this study to provide evidence on the effectiveness of the new model in the Australian setting, where participants were randomised to receive either 'individual care' in their own homes, or to attend a Leg Club for care.

To determine the effectiveness of the different models of care, rather than specific wound treatments, participants in both the control and the intervention groups were required to receive consistent wound care following the same treatment guidelines, provided by staff who were skilled in application of these guidelines. To meet this challenge, a project steering group was formed to develop study protocols on management of venous leg ulcers for the purpose of the research study; and to plan for the skills assessment and update of a small team of nurses who cared for people in the areas involved in the study.

To develop the study treatment protocols, a review of current evidence on venous leg ulcer care was undertaken and results discussed with the steering group, which included experienced wound care clinicians from the specific branches of the healthcare agency involved in the study. The local clinicians provided advice on the types of compression systems the nurses were familiar with and skilled in applying, and those which were readily available in the study areas. Importantly, they also provided advice on types of compression systems which were more likely to be tolerated in the hot and humid Queensland environment and were affordable by the participants, who are required to pay for their own dressings and bandages in the local healthcare system. Based on the evidence review, clinical guidelines (listed in _Table 7.1_) and input on local requirements, it was decided to choose a non-medicated simple dressing and a short-stretch compression system for the study protocols.

A number of strategies were implemented to ensure wound care was provided in a consistent manner to participants in both the control and intervention groups. A small team (approximately

Table 7.1: Guidelines consulted to develop study protocols

Royal College of Nursing (1998, 2006) _Clinical practice guidelines: The management of patients with venous leg ulcers._ RCN Institute, Centre for Evidence-based Nursing, University of York, www.rcn.org.uk/publications/pdf/guidelines/venous_leg_ulcers.pdf

Registered Nurses' Association of Ontario (RNAO) (2004) _Assessment and Management of Venous Leg Ulcers._ RNAO, Toronto, Ontario, www.rnao.org/bestpractices/PDF/BPG_venous_leg_ulcer.pdf

Stacey MC, Falanga V, Marston W, et al (2002) The use of compression therapy in the treatment of venous leg ulcers: a recommended management pathway. _EWMA Journal_ 2(1): 3–7, www.ewma.org/pdf/spring02/03-CompressionTherapyInTheTreatmentOfVenousLegUlcers.pdf

Scottish Intercollegiate Guidelines Network (SIGN) (1998) _The Management of Patients with Chronic Leg Ulcers: A National Clinical Guideline._ SIGN Publication No 26, www.sign.ac.uk/pdf/sign26.pdf

Jull A, Arroll B, Bourchier R, et al (1999) Care of people with chronic leg ulcers: An evidence-based guideline. New Zealand Guidelines Group, www.nzgg.org.nz/guidelines/0008/ACF672.pdf

10) of registered nurses who were interested in wound care were provided with education sessions on the research project, the Leg Club concepts, and research procedures and protocols. Workshops and practice sessions on updating skills in leg ulcer assessment, Doppler assessments, wound care and compression bandaging were provided prior to the commencement of the study. These workshops and education sessions were repeated approximately every six months during the two-year recruitment and data collection time period. The same team of nurses who treated participants in the Leg Clubs once/ week also provided the treatment for control group participants in the home environment. Research staff attended nursing staff meetings regularly to provide information about the study.

The establishment of the Spiritus (previously St Luke's Nursing Service), South Brisbane and Gold Coast Leg Clubs occurred simultaneously with the commencement of the research project in mid-2002, with the official Leg Club openings celebrated in June 2002. Setting up the study and assisting with the establishment of the Leg Clubs involved integration and adaptation of the UK Leg Club clinical documentation processes with local Australian requirements, and the necessary documentation requirements for the research project.

Ethical approval for the study was obtained from the Spiritus Ethics Committee and the Queensland University of Technology Human Research Ethics Committee, which conforms to the NH and MRC Statement on Human Experimentation and complies with the Declaration of Helsinki rules for human experimentation.

Setting

The branches of the community nursing service involved in the study served the southern Brisbane and Gold Coast suburbs, an area of approximately 11 000 square kilometres with a population around 1 500 000 in south-east Queensland, Australia. The distances involved were quite large, and some participants travelled up to 25 km to attend a Leg Club. The two Leg Clubs involved in the study were established in: 1) an old house in the grounds of a church, which was also used as a respite centre in an older suburb of Brisbane (*Figure 7.1*); and 2) a respite centre attached to a church in a relatively new area of the Gold Coast. The distances involved were one of the greatest challenges in setting up the Leg Clubs. The majority of participants were unable to travel independently and were too frail to access public transport options. A volunteer transport network was established and trained by the community nursing agency, which provided vehicles for the volunteers to pick up and transport the clients to a Leg Club. Due to time and resource constraints, participants who lived further than 20 km from the closest Leg Club had to be excluded from the volunteer transport offer, although some

Figure 7.1: Queensland house: setting for the South Brisbane Leg Club

enthusiastic participants were able to travel via trains and buses to a near-by station, where they were then picked up by the volunteers.

Procedures

After providing informed consent and collection of baseline data, participants were randomised to either a 'usual care' group or an intervention group using a computer-generated random number table. The usual care group received treatment individually in their own homes following the study protocols. The intervention group were invited to attend a local Leg Club once/week to receive their treatment following the study protocols. Participants who were unable to travel to the Leg Club independently were provided with a volunteer transport service. If more frequent visits were required for either group, these were provided in their homes.

All participants, whether in the control or intervention group, received:

- a comprehensive health assessment including ankle brachial pressure index (ABPI) measurement
- referral for more extensive circulatory assessment when indicated from the initial assessment
- venous ulcer treatment based on evidence-based guidelines and study protocols, primarily relying on a short-stretch compression bandaging system
- advice and support about venous leg ulcers
- follow-up management: once participants' venous leg ulcers were

healed, they were reviewed and reassessed every 12 weeks for preventative care and management.

In addition, participants in the intervention group who attended a community Leg Club received:

- *Peer support and social interaction:* participants attending Leg Clubs were invited to join in morning/afternoon tea and social activities with other Leg Club members before and after their wound treatment. Peer support and information-sharing was encouraged through collective treatment in a friendly, non-clinical environment.
- *Goal setting:* this was to encourage self-management of the chronic condition and treatment, functional and social activities and adoption of coping strategies. Goal setting is commonly used to increase motivation as well as improve self-esteem and control. Participants attending the community Leg Clubs were assisted to identify individualised strategies for modifying daily activities and setting goals to achieve improvements. Staff, volunteers and healed Leg Club members encouraged clients to gain more control of their condition and treatment.

Participants

All clients with chronic leg ulcers who had been referred to the community nursing service were assessed for suitability using the inclusion and exclusion criteria (*Table 7.2*). If fitting the criteria, they were provided with an information package and invited to participate in the study. The clients were referred either from community nurses, medical practitioners, or self-referred in response to local newspaper advertisements and articles. During the study period a total of 146 clients with chronic leg ulcers were referred for possible inclusion in the study. However, a large number of these were ineligible due to the following reasons:

- the leg ulcers were of non-venous origin
- the clients lived over 20 km from the nearest Leg Club and were unable to find transport
- the clients were under the age of 60 years and not eligible for classification as 'young disabled' and were, therefore, ineligible for

subsidised funding from a community health agency
- the clients were unable to leave their homes as they were full-time carers for another member of the household
- the clients were unwilling to be randomised for the site of care
- the clients were hospitalised before the start of the intervention.

Table 7.2: Inclusion and exclusion criteria

Inclusion criteria:

- Presence of a leg ulcer below the knee of primarily venous origin
- Ankle brachial pressure index (ABPI) of >0.8 and <1.3

Exclusion criteria:

- Ulcers of primarily non-venous origin, eg. arterial or neuropathic
- ABPI ≤0.8 or ≥1.3
- Diabetes mellitus
- Totally immobile clients, ie. unable to sit in a wheelchair for an hour to be transported to a Leg Club

---

Evaluation measures

The model was evaluated for its effectiveness on outcome measures of ulcer healing, symptom control, pain, functional ability, quality of life, depression, morale, self-esteem and cost-effectiveness.

Data were collected from all participants at recruitment time and prior to commencement of the intervention, at 12 weeks from the initial assessment, and at 24 weeks from the initial assessment. Data included demographic information, general health status, ulcer status, functional ability, levels of pain, quality of life indicators and data related to cost-effectiveness.

Progress in ulcer healing was evaluated in a number of ways:

- regular photographs and tracings of the ulcer area, which was then calculated using the dot point planimetry method (Bahmer, 1999)
- regular evaluation of lower limb oedema and skin assessment
- calculation of the number of participants healed in each group following 12 weeks and 24 weeks of treatment
- use of the Pressure Ulcer Scale for Healing (PUSH). This scale was developed in 1997 and revised by Stotts _et al_ (2001) and includes three dimensions of ulcer healing (area, tissue type and exudate),

providing a more sensitive measure of healing than examining changes in ulcer area alone. Testing for validation of the use of the scale in the venous leg ulcer population has commenced (Ratliff and Rodeheaver, 2005).

Data related to pain, functional ability and quality of life were collected via self-administered questionnaires containing the instruments listed in *Table 7.3.*

Table 7.3: Outcome measures	
Pain	Medical Outcomes Study Pain Measures (Sherbourne, 1992)
Quality of life	Spitzer's Quality of Life scale (Spitzer et al, 1981)
Depression	Geriatric Depression scale (Brink and Yesavage, 1982)
Morale	Philadelphia Geriatric Centre Morale scale (Lawton, 1972)
Self-esteem	Rosenberg's Self-esteem scale (Bowling, 1997)
Social support	Medical Outcomes Study Social Support scale (Sherbourne and Stewart, 1991)
Functional ability	Activities of Daily Living scale (Katz and Akpom, 1976)

Data related to general health status, comorbidities, venous history, leg ulcer history and current ulcer status were collected from participants' medical history and clinical assessments undertaken by the community nurses.

A cost-effectiveness analysis was conducted to assess the two models of care (ie. the Leg Club model received by the intervention group or the standard community nursing model of care with individual home visits). A broad perspective was taken to analyse cost-effectiveness including not only costs to the health system, but also to the clients and the community (Gordon et al, 2006).

Two health outcomes were used in the cost-effectiveness analysis, numbers of completely healed ulcers in each group and numbers of clinically significant reductions in pain measures. Reduction in pain is believed to be a major influence in improving client quality of life through increased function, mobility and comfort. A score reduction of at least three points on the six-point scale was considered significant (ie. going from moderate or severe to none at all or very mild) and has implications for carrying out normal activities/work, eg. shopping and housework (Gordon *et al*, 2006).

Types of resources included in the analysis were those directly borne by the healthcare system and the community (eg. personnel, medical and office equipment, consumables, and operating expenses, etc) and those borne by the clients (eg. travel expenses, dressings and bandages, etc). Operating costs included vehicle leasing, medical consumables, production of resource and educational materials, printing, office administration support, telephone, and other incidentals. Volunteers were involved in running the Leg Clubs and the value of their time was estimated using the market replacement cost method (Australian Bureau of Statistics, 1997).

Findings

Sample characteristics are displayed in *Table 7.4*.

Table 7.4: Sample characteristics (n = 67)

- 46% were female, 54% male

- 10% were aged <60 years, 22% between 60 and 69 years, 33% between 70 and 79 years, 33% between 80 and 89 years and 2% were 90 years or older

- 28% were married, 29% were single and 43% were widowed

- 57% lived alone

- 17% were the primary caregiver for another member of the household

- 64% had two or more comorbidities, most commonly hypertension (54%) and osteoarthritis (43%)

- 55% were unable to mobilise without a walking aid

- 70% had a history of varicose veins, 23% a previous deep vein thrombosis and 32% had previous venous surgery

- 75% of participants had a history of previous venous leg ulcers

- There were no significant differences found in these variables between the intervention and control groups

Ulcer healing

On recruitment to the study, the average ulcer size was 8.97 cm²
(Edwards *et al*, 2005a), and the median duration was 26 weeks.
Analysis of data found a significantly greater reduction in mean ulcer
size in the group attending Leg Clubs in comparison to the control
group by 12 weeks (Edwards *et al*, 2005a). The group attending Leg
Clubs also had a significantly greater reduction in their mean PUSH
scores in comparison to the group receiving home care (Edwards *et
al*, 2005a), indicating improvements in area reduction, tissue type
and exudate level. When examining percent reduction in size, 74%
of the intervention group's ulcers had reduced by over 50% in size,
in comparison to 59% of the control group following 12 weeks of
treatment (Edwards *et al*, 2005a). By this time, 46% of the intervention
group were completely healed compared to 26% of the control group
(Edwards *et al*, 2005a). Although a 20% difference in healing rates
between groups is of clinical significance, the small sample size meant
this measure was not a statistically significant difference. Significant
improvements were found in the Leg Club group in comparison to the
home care group in levels of lower leg oedema, exudate and presence
of venous eczema (Finlayson *et al*, 2005).

Pain, functional ability and indicators of quality of life

In comparison to the control group, the intervention group attending
Leg Clubs were found to have significantly decreased levels of pain,
including reductions in:

* overall pain scores
* severity of pain scores
* effects of pain on the participants' mood, enjoyment of life and
  ability to mobilise, sleep, undertake normal work activities and
  recreational activities (Edwards *et al*, 2005a; Edwards *et al*,
  2005b; Finlayson *et al*, 2006).

Clients attending the Leg Club were also found to have significantly greater
improvements in quality of life, functional ability, morale and self-esteem
when compared to the control group (Edwards *et al*, 2005b; Finlayson *et
al*, 2006). No significant differences were found between groups in the
measure of social support or depression (Edwards *et al*, 2005b).

Cost-effectiveness

From the perspective of the health service provider, the Leg Club incurred overall lower costs by $3,464 AUD (€2 139) over six months (65% of the home care cost), mostly because of lower personnel and vehicle leasing costs in comparison to home nursing care (Gordon et al, 2006). The home nursing cost per healed ulcer was three times that for the Leg Club at 0–3 months, and

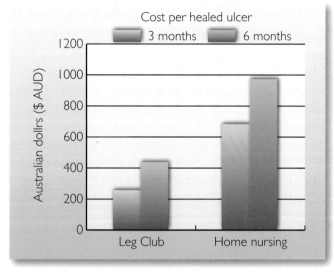

Figure 7.2: Cost per healed ulcer

twice that for the Leg Club at 0–6 months (Gordon et al, 2006), as shown in *Figure 7.2*.

When looking at costs to the clients and community, total costs for the Leg Club were slightly higher than the home nursing option, due to the additional community volunteer support and client out-of-pocket expenses for travel. In comparison to health system resources, the financial and in-kind contributions from both clients and the local community were substantial (Gordon et al, 2006).

Discussion

Findings from this study suggest that implementation of this model of care was effective in improving client outcomes and care was provided in a cost-effective manner. Results indicate that the intervention group receiving care at a community Leg Club have significantly improved outcomes in ulcer healing, pain levels, morale, self-esteem, activities of daily living and quality of life. Although the small size of our sample limits the generalisation of the findings, the positive findings support further introduction and evaluation of this model of care.

From the perspective of the health system, the Leg Club is an economically efficient option over the traditional or usual home nursing practice, although additional costs are transferred to the clients and community for items such as transport and volunteer labour. However in this study, the health and social benefits of the Leg Club model of care encouraged the active participation of the community in supporting the Leg Clubs as a worthwhile investment in optimal health care. This cost-effectiveness analysis was based only on healing rates and pain levels. Potential benefits of Leg Clubs for clients in terms of improved quality of life, improved functional ability, reduced need of external home-help services, greater socialisation, respite care relief and other downstream effects are some advantages over home nursing not included in this cost-effectiveness analysis. Hence this study may have underestimated the true beneficial impact of Leg Clubs. The Leg Club model of care also fosters opportunities for nurses' professional development and learning in a group environment that home nursing cannot offer. Further studies are recommended, as this study highlighted the potential of Leg Clubs as an alternative model of care for chronic leg conditions.

This study was a joint Spiritus and Queensland University of Technology research project. The study was supported by a grant from the Queensland Nursing Council, Australia. The views expressed do not necessarily represent the views of the Council or the members, Executive Officer or staff of the Council. Support for the study was also provided by Smith and Nephew and Jobst.

References

Abbade LPF, Lastoria S (2005) Venous ulcer: epidemiology, physiopathology, diagnosis and treatment. *Int J Dermatol* **44**(6): 449–56

Abbade LPF, Lastoria S, Rollo HD, Stolf HO (2005) A sociodemographic, clinical study of patients with venous ulcer. *Int J Dermatol* **44**(12): 989–92

Australian Bureau of Statistics (1997) *Unpaid Work and the Australian Economy*. Australian Bureau of Statistics, Canberra

Bahmer FA (1999) Wound measurement made truly simple by point counting. *Arch Dermatol* **135**(8): 991–2

Bergqvist D, Lindholm C, Nelzen O (1999) Chronic leg ulcers: the impact of venous disease. *J Vasc Surg* **29**(4): 752–5

Bowling A (1997) _Measuring Health: A review of the quality of life measurement scales._ 2nd edn. Open University Press, Buckingham

Briggs M, Closs SJ (2003) The prevalence of leg ulceration: a review of the literature. _EWMA J_ 3(2): 14–20

Brink T, Yesavage J (1982) Screening tests for geriatric depression. _Clin Gerontol_ 1: 37–43

Brown A (2005) Leg ulcers. Chronic leg ulcers, part 2: do they affect a patient's social life? Br J Nurs 14(18): 986–9

Chase S, Whittemore R, Crosby N, Freney D, Howes P, Phillips T (2000) Living with chronic venous leg ulcers: a descriptive study of knowledge and functional health status. _J Community Health Nurs_ 17(1): 1–13

Ebbeskog B, Ekman S (2001) Elderly persons' experiences of living with venous leg ulcers: living in a dialectal relationship between freedom and imprisonment. _Scand J Caring Sci_ 15(3): 235–43

Edwards H, Courtney M, Finlayson K, Lindsay E, Lewis C, Shuter P, _et al_ (2005a) Chronic venous leg ulcers: effect of a community nursing intervention on pain and healing. _Nurs Standard_ 19(52): 47–54

Edwards H, Courtney M, Lindsay E, Lewis C, Finlayson K (2005b) _A Randomised Controlled Trial of Nursing Interventions for Managing Patients with Chronic Venous Leg Ulcers: Final Report._ Queensland University of Technology, Brisbane

Finlayson K, Edwards H, Courtney M, Lewis C, Lindsay E (2005) _Improved symptom management for clients with chronic leg ulcers._ Proceedings of International Council of Nurses 23rd Quadrennial Congress, Taiwan, CD-ROM, C.0135B

Finlayson K, Shuter P, Edwards H, Courtney M, Lewis C, Lindsay E (2006) _Improved quality of life for clients with chronic venous leg ulcers: Results from a randomised controlled trial._ Australian Wound Management Association 6th National Conference, 'Matrix of Wound Care' Conference Proceedings, Canberra: 58

Franks PJ, McCullagh L, Moffat C (2003) Assessing quality of life in patients with chronic leg ulceration using the Medical Outcomes Short Form-36 questionnaire. _Ostomy/Wound Management_ 49(2): 26–37

Ghauri ASK, Taylor MC, Deacon JE, Whyman MR, Earnshaw JJ, Heather BP, _et al_ (2000) Influence of a specialized leg ulcer service on management and outcome. _Br J Surg_ 87(8): 1048–56

Gordon LG, Edwards H, Courtney M, Finlayson K, Shuter P, Lindsay E (2006) A cost-effectiveness analysis of two community models of nursing care for managing chronic venous leg ulcers. _J Wound Care_ 15(8): 348–53

Hampton S (2003) Jobst Ulcercare compression hosiery for venous leg ulcers. *Br J Community Nurs* 8(6): 279

Hareendran A (2005) Measuring the impact of venous leg ulcers on quality of life. *J Wound Care* 14(2): 53–7

Husband LL (2001) Venous ulceration: the pattern of pain and the paradox. *Clin Effectiveness Nurs* 5(1): 35–40

Jones J, Barr W, Robinson J, Carlisle C (2006) Depression in patients with chronic venous ulceration. *Br J Nurs* 15(11): S17-S23.

Jull A, Walker N, Hackett M, Jones M, Rodgers A, Birchall N, *et al* (2004). Leg ulceration and perceived health: a population based case-control study. *Age Ageing* 33(3): 236–41

Katz S, Akpom C (1976) Index of ADL. *Med Care* 14: 116–18

Lawton M (1972) The dimensions of morale. In: Kent D, Kastenbaum R, Sherwood S, *et al*, eds. *Research Planning and Action for the Elderly: the power and potential of social science*. Behavioral Publications, New York: 144–65

Lindsay E (2000) Leg clubs: A new approach to patient-centred leg ulcer management. *Nurs Health Sci* 2: 139–41

Margolis DJ, Bilker W, Santanna J, Baumgarten M (2002) Venous leg ulcer: incidence and prevalence in the elderly. *J Am Acad Dermatol* 46(3): 381–6

McGuckin M, Waterman R, Brooks J, Cherry G, Porten L, Hurley S, *et al* (2002) Validation of venous leg ulcer guidelines in the United States and United Kingdom. *Am J Surg* 183(2): 132–7

Morrell CJ, Walters SJ, Dixon S, Collins KA, Brereton LM, Peters J, *et al* (1998) Cost effectiveness of community leg ulcer clinics: randomised controlled trial. *Br Med J* 316(7143): 1487

Nemeth KA, Harrison MB, Graham ID, Burke S (2003) Pain in pure and mixed aetiology venous leg ulcers: a three-phase point prevalence study. *J Wound Care* 12(9): 336–40

Parker SG (2005) *Do current discharge arrangements from inpatient hospital care for the elderly reduce readmission rates, the length of inpatient stay or mortality, or improve health status?* WHO Regional Office for Europe, Copenhagen. Health Evidence Network Report; www.euro.who.int/Document/E87542.pdf, accessed 27 March 2007

Persoon A, Heinen MM, van der Vleuten CJM, de Rooij MJ, van de Kerkhof, PCM, van Achterberg T (2004) Leg ulcers: a review of their impact on daily life. *J Clin Nurs* 13(3): 341–54

Ratliff CR, Rodeheaver GT (2005) Use of the PUSH tool to measure venous ulcer healing. *Ostomy/Wound Management* 51(5): 58–60, 62–53

Ruckley C (1997) Socioeconomic impact of chronic venous insufficiency and leg ulcers. *Angiology* 48: 679

Sherbourne C (1992) Pain measures. In: Stewart A Ware J, eds. *Measuring Functioning and Well-being: The Medical Outcomes Study Approach.* Duke University Press, Durham, North Carolina: 220–34

Sherbourne C, Stewart A (1991) The MOS Social Support Survey. *Soc Sci Med* **32**: 705–14

Simon DA, Dix FP, McCollum CN (2004) Management of venous leg ulcers. *Br Med J* **328**(7452): 1358–62

Simon DA, Freak L, Kinsella A, Walsh J, Lane C, Groarke L, *et al* (1996) Community leg ulcer clinics: a comparative study in two health authorities. *Br Med J* **312**: 1648–51

Spitzer WO, Dobson AJ, Hall J, Chesterman E, Levi J, Shepherd R, *et al* (1981) Measuring quality of life of cancer patients: a concise QL-index for use by physicians. *J Chronic Dis* **34**: 585–97

Stotts NA, Rodeheaver GT, Thomas DR, Frantz RA, Bartolucci AA, Sussman C, *et al* (2001) An instrument to measure healing in pressure ulcers: Development and validation of the Pressure Ulcer Scale for Healing (PUSH). *J Gerontology Series A: Biological Sciences and Medical Sciences* **56**(12): M795–99

Walshe C (1995) Living with a venous leg ulcer: a descriptive study of patients' experiences. *J Adv Nurs* **22**(6): 1092–100

Wissing U, Ek A, Unosson M (2002) Life situation and function in elderly people with and without leg ulcers. *Scand J Caring Sci* **16**(1): 59–65

Chapter 8

An educational journey

Michelle Gibb

I was first introduced to the Leg Club concept twelve months ago when I started work with Spiritus Care Services as the wound care clinical nurse consultant. I was intrigued by this model but did not think that it would be any different from the traditional leg ulcer clinic where I had worked for the last six years. The last twelve months has shown me that it is indeed very different. The purpose of this chapter is to share with you the journey that I have taken to grow and establish further Leg Clubs with Spiritus Care Services in Australia, and some of the challenges that I have faced and the ways that I have sought to overcome them.

Community-based leg ulcer clinics

Undertaking my Masters in Wound Management has enabled me to explore the theoretical concepts underpinning the Leg Club model in more detail, and helped me to identify and develop strategies that could be implemented in clinical practice to enhance Leg Club functioning in Australia.

Firstly, I needed to find out what this Leg Club concept was all about and how it differs from traditional community-based leg ulcer clinics. Community-based leg ulcer clinics have three main characteristics:

- nurse-led specialist practice
- evidence-based treatments
- a community setting (Thorne, 1998).

A search through the literature revealed that community-based leg ulcer clinics improve wound healing rates and are more effective than traditional home nursing (Simon *et al*, 1996).

Evaluations on the effectiveness of community-based leg ulcer clinics have demonstrated significant improvements in leg ulcer healing rates. A randomised controlled trial by Edwards *et al* (2005) demonstrated that there were significantly higher healing rates at 12 weeks, following the introduction of a community-based 'Leg Club'. These results were supported by numerous other authors who also compared healing rates in community-based leg ulcer clinics to home-based nursing (Moffatt *et al*, 1992; Ghauri *et al*, 2000; Thurlby and Griffiths, 2002; Thorne, 1998; Simon *et al*, 1996; Musgrove *et al*, 1998). The community leg ulcer clinic model has been supported in two separate comparative studies to have significantly higher healing rates (Ghauri *et al*, 2000; Simon *et al*, 2004).

Literature on the area of community-based leg ulcer clinics also provided evidence that approximately 50% of a community nurse's time is spent caring for this client group (Simon *et al*, 2004); care which takes place in the person's own home and is often the only social contact that they receive (Musgrove *et al*, 1998; Thorne, 1998). The community nurses operate in an isolated, autonomous and distinct role, supported by managers within a hierarchical structure (Lindsay, 2005). The practice of treating patients in isolation restricts the opportunity for peer support and peer education (Lindsay, 2005).

A number of the articles investigated the reasons why community-based leg ulcer clinics were more effective than traditional home nursing. There was general consensus that community-based leg ulcer clinics improve access to resources (such as compression bandaging which is not always available to community nurses providing home-based care), improved access to specialist nursing staff skilled in both wound management and application of compression bandaging (Edwards *et al*, 2005; Musgrove *et al*, 1998; Ghauri *et al*, 2000; Simon *et al*, 1996; Lindsay, 2005; Thurlby and Griffiths, 2002; Thorne, 1998).

Community-based leg ulcer clinics also have associated benefits such as decreasing social isolation on the individual, improving quality of life and providing an avenue for peer support and empathy (Edwards *et al*, 2005; Lindsay 2005). Literature suggests that community-based leg ulcer clinics can improve a clients' level of enthusiasm, motivation and concordance with treatment, and improve knowledge and understanding (Edwards *et al*, 2005; Lindsay, 2005; Thorne, 1998). These clinics are less formal than other types of care (Lindsay, 2005). Clients are encouraged to attend for preventive care and treatment because prevention and health promotion is a key feature of a community-based model (Edwards *et al*, 2005; Lindsay, 2005).

The Leg Club model is the most frequently cited example of a community-based leg ulcer clinic that addresses or incorporates the social aspect of care. This model was established in response to the literature that suggested that social factors and isolation can significantly influence a patient's response to treatment (Edwards *et al*, 2005; Lindsay, 2005).

This model of care is a cost-effective, innovative approach for community-based leg ulcer management with positive benefits for clients, nurses and care providers. Research indicates that Leg Clubs have enhanced patient quality of life through a combination of improved healing rates, low recurrence rates and positive health benefits, and that the costs are significantly reduced when compared to conventional home-based treatments (Edwards *et al*, 2005; Lindsay, 2005).

There is an increasing trend towards community-based leg ulcer treatment because of the shift in emphasis from care in the acute sector to community care (Edwards *et al*, 2005; Thorne, 1998). The relationship between leg ulcers and age means that the number of older people in the community needing treatment will increase (Edwards *et al*, 2005; Thorne, 1998).

How the Leg Club model of care was established

Spiritus Care Services, formerly St Luke's Nursing Service, was established in 1904 and is the oldest community nursing organisation in Australia. Spiritus Care Services provides community nursing, social services and aged care residential services throughout Queensland and in Sydney, New South Wales.

After hearing about the benefits of Leg Clubs in the United Kingdom, Spiritus Care Services decided to establish Leg Clubs in Queensland. The South Brisbane and Gold Coast Leg Clubs have been running for over four years. After much preparation we now have another two Leg Clubs, one located in south-east Brisbane and the other at Redlands Bay. It is anticipated that another two Leg Clubs will be opened in Queensland within the next twelve months in response to a growing community need for specialist wound management services.

Theory into practice — barriers to change

Once I had a good understanding of the theoretical concepts underpinning the Leg Club model and became more involved with the day-to-day operation, it soon became apparent that there were several barriers that were affecting the long-term sustainability of the Leg Club model.

One of the biggest barriers was the educational level and experience of the nurses involved with the Leg Clubs. Similar to other healthcare organisations globally, Spiritus Care Services was experiencing a period of significant change as a result of internal restructuring and there had been a great deal of staff turnover in recent months. Consequently, I found that the nurses' knowledge of basic wound and leg ulcer assessment was lacking and their practical skills, particularly in the application of compression bandaging, was poor. The nursing practice was ritualistic and task-oriented. Cooper (2000) states that the environment of care, peer pressure, the power of nursing rituals and the skills, knowledge and attitudes of other staff are all factors that can impede the implementation of evidence-based clinical practice. It was certainly my experience that as I introduced training and education and questioned wound dressing practices and bandaging technique, the nursing staff became reluctant to attend the Leg Club because I was challenging their nursing practice and they were reluctant to embrace change.

Implementing change in nursing, like other healthcare professions, is widely recognised as a difficult process (Lindsay, 2005). Some nurses embrace the theoretical knowledge as it adds a new dimension to their clinical practice, while others are resistant. Leg Clubs offer an ideal environment to foster education, as theory and practice are closely interwoven (Lindsay, 2005). Education is a key feature of Leg Clubs, which aim to equip nurses with the skills, knowledge and attitudes so that they can improve their clinical practice (Cooper, 2001).

To address the theory-practice gap, skill-based assessments or clinical competencies based on best practice guidelines were developed, particularly in relation to leg ulcer assessment and compression bandaging, to enable nurses to identify their level of practice and areas for further professional development. In a competency-based framework, nurses are required to demonstrate a skill until they are considered to be competent. This framework teaches the nurse how to perform the skill but does not teach principles that allow the adaptation of the skill to other areas of clinical practice (Cooper, 2001). Using a competency-based framework is only part of the overall picture, as we also want the nurses to gain and possess knowledge, facts and information related to that skill. Knowledge is usually imparted through written information and lectures and is most commonly assessed by examinations and written assignments. However, the possession of knowledge and skills to inform practice does not necessarily mean that the practice will change. To implement changes into clinical practice, alongside the necessary skills and knowledge, nurses need to have appropriate attitudes. As Cooper (2001) states, attitudes cannot be taught and traditional education methods do not encourage nurses to explore attitudes and deeply held beliefs. Behavioural compliance to change practice does not automatically occur as a result of increased knowledge (Cooper, 2001). The nurse must possess the motivation to change practice (Cooper, 2001). It has been my experience that attitudes are a major barrier to clinical learning and exacerbate the theory-practice gap. Successful Leg Clubs are the product of competent, open-minded and motivated nursing teams working to best practice guidelines with management support (Lindsay, 2005).

As a wound care clinical nurse consultant working in a Leg Club, I am at the theory/practice interface, developing new initiatives and trying to push the boundaries of nursing into future dimensions, where nursing care is patient-centred, evidence-based, collaborative and responsive to changing patient and community needs. Through sharing knowledge, experience and leadership, I am able to support changes in culture — moving away from traditional practice to that supported by research evidence. I have found that self-awareness and leadership skills are required to support nurses in challenging the culture and dynamics of the work environment. I have learnt that it is important to address issues slowly, with diplomacy, and, while frustrating, will ultimately lead to a move away from tradition to an evidence-based approach where clinicians, aware of their accountability, will aim to deliver clinically effective care.

Growing and expanding

When I first took on the Leg Club 12 months ago, the number of members attending was generally quite poor and nursing staff were reluctant to participate. To address this problem, educational strategies were developed that promote the use of evidence-based practice by sharing knowledge and experiences, through critical analysis and direct participation in all aspects of Leg Club functioning, and by encouraging ongoing research at the Leg Club. Slowly, the number of members attending started to increase as nurses sent clients along for expert advice and assessment, recognising that they lacked knowledge and skills in leg ulcer assessment and management. The nursing staff really started to change their attitudes about the value of the Leg Club when several of their clients that had been treated at home for a long period of time showed signs of healing, or were healed within a matter of weeks.

Nurses in a Leg Club are encouraged to be involved in all decisions concerning wound management. They are encouraged to use a questioning approach and to reflect on their experiences and consider how holistic variables, such as nutritional status and motivation, will influence decision-making. Nursing staff and members are viewed as partners in the decision-making process. In a Leg Club environment, peer pressure, nursing rituals, the skills, knowledge and attitudes of other staff become very apparent and, if not managed, can impede the implementation of evidence-based treatment. An example of this was when nurses were filmed as part of a research study conducted by Queensland University of Technology investigating compression bandaging methods and nurses' interaction during this process. Video footage was collected over a four-week period and then replayed in a laboratory environment and the footage was analysed. It was interesting in that it revealed how some of the nurses demonstrated the ritualistic process of removing the bandage, washing the leg and then reapplication of the bandage with virtually no interaction with the member during this process. Footage taken a week following this interaction revealed that the member had removed the bandage as it was too tight and, unfortunately, there was a deterioration in wound status. This is opposed to other footage which demonstrated how other nurses engaged the member throughout the clinical intervention to arrive at a mutually agreeable plan of care with positive outcomes over the following weeks. Such video footage has the potential to become a valuable learning tool, as often we may not be aware that we are engaging in a certain behaviour until it is reflected upon.

The video footage also revealed other benefits to communal working. The Leg Club environment enables nurses to look over their shoulder and bounce questions off each other and to question 'why did you do that' or 'how did you do that' and to correct inappropriate practices in a timely manner. In the Leg Club, it is important that nurses are able to question their own and others' practice in an open, non-threatening manner which encourages discussion, role-play, and reflection on practice, and enhances skills in communication and negotiation.

Following the processes established in the UK, Leg Clubs in Australia incorporate strict criteria governing environment and clinical practice, defined in written guidelines and comprehensive documentation. Compliance with using this documentation and the processes involved has been a challenge, which is further exacerbated as the workload increases: the busier nurses become, the less likely they are to implement procedures they perceive to be time-consuming.

In response to growing consumer demand for access to specialist advice and treatment, a further two Leg Clubs have opened in recent months with further Leg Clubs planned. Similar to the UK, the establishment of Leg Clubs, their sustainability is threatened by the lack of a skilled, educated and motivated nursing workforce. In Australia, the geographical distance to cover, the shortage of funding and adequate venues, together with the lack of advocacy and management support, are all added obstacles to overcome.

Where to from here?

One thing that the Leg Club has taught me is that life-long learning is essential. True learning centres on self-discovery and through reflection and increasing self-awareness individuals can begin to understand their influence on others and their surroundings (Trudigan, 2000). Providing support to nurses through clinical supervision and enabling and empowering nurses to develop their skills and knowledge will ultimately benefit patient care.

Having been involved with research with the Leg Clubs I can also see how much more research needs to be done. There is also a need for the development of evaluation tools that are reliable and validated to obtain accurate data to enable benchmarking and comparisons to be made with Leg Clubs and other service delivery models both nationally and internationally. There is a clear need to perform continuous quality improvement and auditing to enable comparative benchmarking to be performed. This will help to:

- influence and advise nationally and internationally on leg ulcer management

- accurately assess and communicate the social cost of leg ulcers to the community so that funding can be allocated
- raise the priority of leg ulcer prevention and management in Australia (Lindsay, 2005).

Conclusion

My experience with the Leg Club has been a positive one, and, despite the seemingly insurmountable barriers that seem to face us at times, I believe that the value of the Leg Club and the impact that it has will ultimately win the day and make the hard work worthwhile. I look forward to the future and continuing to being a part of this innovative concept and expanding Leg Clubs throughout Australia.

References

Cooper T (2001) Educational theory into practice: development of an infection control link nurse programme. *Nurse Education in Practice* 1: 35–41

Edwards H, Courtney M, Finlayson K, *et al* (2005) Chronic venous leg ulcers: effect of a community nursing intervention on pain and healing. *Nurs Standard* 19(52): 47–54

Ghauri A, Taylor M, Deacon J, Whyman M, Earnshaw J, Heather B, Poskitt K (2000) Influence of a specialized leg ulcer service on management and outcome. *Br J Surg* 87(8): 1048–56

Lindsay, E. (2005) Leg clubs: personal reflection on implementing change. *J Clin Nurs* 19(8): 15–21

Moffatt C, Franks P, Oldroyd M, Bosanquet N, Brown P, Greenhalgh R, McCollum C (1992) Community clinics for leg ulcers and impact on healing. *Br Med J* 305(6866): 1389–92

Musgrove E, Woodham C, Dearie P (1998) Leg ulceration and clinical effectiveness: nurse-led clinics. *Nurs Standard* 12(28): 57–60

Simon D, Freak L, Kinsella A, Walsh J, Lane C, Groarke L, McCollum C (1996) Community leg ulcer clinics: a comparative study in two health authorities. *Br Med J* 312(7047): 1648–51

Thorne E (2007) Community leg ulcer clinics and the effectiveness of care (structured abstract). Database of Abstracts of Reviews of Effects, Issue 3. Available online at: www.mrw.interscience.wiley.com/cochrane/cldare/articles/DARE-978206/frame.html

Thurlby K, Griffiths P (2002) Community leg ulcer clinics vs home visits: which is more effective? (structured abstract) *Br J Community Nursing* 7(5): 260–4

Trudigan J (2000) The role of the clinical practice educator in tissue viability nursing. *Nurs Standard* **15**(11): 54, 59–60, 62

Simon D, Dix F, McCollum C (2004) Management of venous leg ulcers. *Br Med J* **328**(7452): 1358–62

Section II: The basics

CHAPTER 9

DELIVERING CARE IN THE NEW NHS

Fiona Stephens

The Labour Government proposed that by applying the National Health Service (NHS) principles outlined in the *NHS Plan* (Department of Health [DoH], 2000a), organisations would ensure the integrity and patient-centredness of NHS services. Robust clinical governance systems, patient involvement, the provision of suitably trained and educated practitioners, the necessary resources and evidence-based care were all seen as integral to this vision. Since the turn of the century, many policy documents have changed the way acute health services are both delivered and funded and, more recently, the focus has turned to primary care. The White Paper, *Our Health, Our Care, Our Say* (DoH, 2006a) described an ethos that delivers 'care closer to home'. The vision is that market forces will determine how healthcare services look, at a local and community level, the vision being not for national coordination but local commissioning.

The ways to achieve this are three-fold, through:

- choices of patients
- decisions of commissioners
- innovation of practitioners.

Choices of patients

This concept, central to the Government's programme of reform for the NHS, has so far been limited to 'choose and book' (DoH, 2004a). This system is intended to promote and develop local healthcare markets. To date, this has focused on acute services, requiring the patient needing elective surgery to choose between healthcare organisations. The focus is now on community care, which, together with the DoH policy of increasing the plurality of providers, will mean patients choosing between providers from a range of sectors. These are likely to be:

- primary care trusts (PCTs) — directly provided clinical services
- NHS community foundation trusts — still being planned, but a viable alternative to existing provision
- independent sector — clinic or primary care based services
- third sector organisations — charities or social enterprises. Both are being promoted by Government policy as viable alternatives to state provision of public services (Royal College of Nursing [RCN], 2007).

The DoH's intention is to have competition between both provider services and clinicians. This choice by patients would take commissioning to a micro level, and has the potential to increase opportunities for nurses and other healthcare professionals, replacing the traditional monopoly of doctors.

Decisions of commissioners

Commissioning is seen as one of the least efficient parts of NHS service management. The reform of Strategic Health Authorities (SHAs) and PCTs is focused on reducing that deficiency by identifying the decreasing role in the provision of services by PCTs, and the increasing role in commissioning of services (DoH, 2005, 2006b). The development of practice-based commissioning (DoH, 2004b) has increased both the scope and range of commissioners and general practice is central to the creation of the NHS market economy, making decisions on behalf of individuals and groups of patients.

The decisions of commissioners that will shape the services of the future must be reflective of the wishes and choices of the patients (DoH, 1999a). Historically, practitioners have taken a paternalistic approach and made decisions in the best interest of their patient; today, decisions have to be based on inclusive and equitable relationships with patients and must reflect their views and preferences (DoH, 2006a). However, in an NHS with finite resources, free at the point of delivery, there has to be control over the number and cost of services offered, just as there has to be control on the demands made on a service. The waiting list has been an historical control factor and bodies such as the National Institute for Health and Clinical Excellence (NICE) increasingly make recommendations that further control that demand. Demands have been made for robust methods, with emphasis being put on patients by the Government regarding responsibilities to counterbalance patients' rights to service ensuring that every patient makes a contribution to cost-effective and efficient use of resources. Examples of these thresholds of entitlement are based around lifestyle choices, including: exclusion based on an excess body mass index (BMI); smoking; and failure to comply with treatment regimes. More specific indicators for inclusion may be the level of sight loss prior to cataract surgery.

Innovations of practitioners

Practitioners should be challenged and reassured by the prospect of leading in developing new ways to deliver evidence-based practice in partnership with their patients and colleagues. However, the prospect of changing culture and practice can be daunting in the current business-oriented, market-driven economy of health care. Financial deficits have meant that short-term financial decisions have taken precedence over sustainable planning, leading to long-term consequences for both patients and services. For practitioners to innovate as part of a market-led, patient-focused economy of care, there is a need for continued investment in and development of high quality practice by clinically-based leaders, as well as opportunities to acquire the business acumen that is needed to be entrepreneurial and enterprising. Recent responses to offset financial deficits include cuts in training budgets and the freezing of posts by some NHS organisations. The priority for financial recovery identifies a potential lack of understanding or consideration for the need for innovation and continuous improvement.

Effective clinical engagement is essential in innovation, modernisation and commissioning to ensure quality improvement and patient-focused care continues to flourish. Commissioners need support to deliver robust services, effective management of payment by results and patient choice, and the assurance of sustainability. The clinical governance lead for the organisation, ideally a professional with a clinical background, is best placed to ensure that all aspects of the governance agenda are assured.

Clinical governance

Clinical governance became a buzz word in the new NHS with the publication of the Government White Paper (DoH, 1998a), and since that time the world in which clinicians practice has considerably developed and changed. Clinical governance mechanisms have been developed as part of an integrated governance system to ensure that clinical quality, staff development and patient involvement are appropriately addressed through practice-based commissioning, independent contractors and provider services, whether employed or commissioned.

The modernisation agenda increases the emphasis upon health improvement for the entire population, with a focus on long-term conditions, identifying primary care as the key area of delivery. Recognising the value of nurses and the importance of their contribution towards taking forward these policies, the Government has set out a new strategy for the development of new and existing nursing roles (DoH, 2002). The Government papers, *The new NHS: modern, dependable* (DoH, 1998b) and *Making a Difference* (DoH, 1999b) highlight the contribution made by nurses, midwives and health visitors to health care. However, to deliver on the plans outlined in Government policy, a change in culture, thinking and approach will be required (DoH, 2000b). *Creating a Patient-led NHS* (DoH, 2005) sets out the current phase in a managed approach to health care. It focuses on reconfiguration of healthcare systems, positions the role of practice-based commissioning and payment by results, and opens the field of service delivery to a wider range of potential providers. It is within the context of contestability that the nursing strategy is to be implemented. Nursing leadership and management structure have undergone extensive re-design in order to support the proposed development.

Underlying principles

The new strategic health authorities (SHAs) are much larger than previous organisations. As such, they are more remote and have had to develop a more strategic/overview role. They now have a strong focus on performance management. PCTs are also larger, enabling some to develop a greater critical mass of expertise and experience around clinical governance issues. One of the functions of creating a patient-led NHS

(DoH, 2005) is to develop organisations with robust commissioning functions. Commissioning for quality is an integral part of this: clinical governance and commissioning are inextricably linked.

Clinical governance is about relationships, and should be dealt with as close to the clinical interface as is feasible, acknowledging that there are economies of scale, a need for adequate expertise, statutory issues, and benefits in broad oversight in ensuring that there are lessons learnt, trends detected and good practice shared. Accountability for clinical governance, including clinical risk management, lies with trusts and their boards. It is envisaged that these new organisations will reduce bureaucracy, avoid duplication, and increase efficiency. With the increasing number of foundation trusts, independent and third sector providers, the systems that evolve must reflect this plurality.

Responsibilities of the new PCTs

PCTs are responsible for commissioning services and ensuring that there are effective systems to ensure quality. This requires effective performance management of clinical standards and governance arrangements in provider organisations. PCTs continue to have substantial responsibilities for service provision in the short and medium term. Provision and commissioning both require robust governance arrangements, but they are different and the difference in approach and management should be clear. Clinical governance is about the development of relationships and understanding of organisational processes. This promotes an ability to pick up and react to the softer signs of dysfunction than simple 'tick box exercises'. The new systems will foster open communication and encourage good working relations between organisations.

PCTs are responsible for much of the clinical governance function previously undertaken by the former SHAs, with specific focus on clinical risk management and the performance management of serious untoward incidents from provider organisations, a significant change. Closer links between clinical outcomes and financial and operational data need to be established through better indicators of clinical performance. Organisations need to be aware of both the financial and opportunity costs of serious untoward incidents, ensuring that effective systems are in place to learn from such incidents and ensure that effective changes are put in place to improve patient outcomes and experience (DoH, 2000c).

NHS organisations' relationships with regulators

The Healthcare Commission (HC) annual health check provides an important benchmark or baseline assessment for NHS trusts. The SHAs are responsible for performance management and ensuring that all organisations achieve compliance with core standards, and that progress towards developmental standards is adequate. SHAs will seek to extract maximum benefit from the process, and minimise duplication of work with the healthcare commission and PCTs. Clinical governance is central to healthcare commission standards. There are clear links to performance management systems and approaches to support the leadership of work on standards being located within clinical governance, ensuring a clear focal point and excellent communication across the organisation.

Developing relationships with external regulators, maintaining roles and responsibilities, as well as avoiding duplication, will be achieved through excellent communication. Relationships with other regulatory bodies such as the National Patient Safety Agency (NPSA), National Clinical Assessment Service (NCAS), the Mental Health Act Commission (MHAC) and Commission for Social Care Inspection (CSCI) should, in general, be led by clinical governance.

Networks

Clinical governance networks have been established across health economies and SHA areas; they have important roles in sharing learning and promoting good practice. They are supportive, developmental and provide a vehicle for the dissemination of relevant national and local information. They are particularly important in the new organisations, allowing sharing of experience, providing examples of good practice and a forum for sharing lessons learnt.

Research and audit

SHAs and PCTs must ensure adherence to research governance requirements and engage in networking within the SHA with national involvement. It is important to ensure that appropriate governance of research and development remains an SHA responsibility, and that there is adequate input by PCTs so that local context and knowledge are reflected. PCTs are responsible for ensuring that clinical audit is prioritised and performed by the provider services.

Ensuring service and practice development

To ensure robust clinical governance in practice and service development, the following are areas that need to be explored, developed and identified as being central to clinically- and cost-effective care delivery. They can also be used as part of the business planning process.

Education and training

All practitioners involved in the delivery of care to patients should have the necessary education and training to enable them to provide that care. While registered practitioners are required to have the necessary knowledge and skills to provide clinically- and cost-effective care to their patients, the healthcare organisation they work for needs to identify, through the knowledge and skills framework and training matrices, what training is expected for the post. Training should be sought from appropriate providers, be they local specialists, higher education institutions or colleagues in industry. Care must be taken to ensure that there is no potential bias, for example, product promotion.

Competency

All registered nurses, as with other registered practitioners, must ensure that they are competent and confident to deliver any care they provide for a patient (Nursing and Midwifery Council [NMC], 2004). If a practitioner identifies a deficit in their knowledge or skills, they must inform their line manager and together seek appropriate updating.

Initial and ongoing assessment is the responsibility of registered practitioners. The involvement of unregistered assistants in the delivery of patient care is increasing. Practitioners must ensure, before they delegate any aspect of patient care to an assistant, that she/he has the understanding and competency to undertake the task required. The registered healthcare professional remains responsible for the delivery of that delegated care.

Updating

Updating should be undertaken by practitioners when the evidence base changes in light of new products or treatment regimes, or as a result of audit or performance management recommendations. This should be documented and can take the form of a study session, literature search and subsequent reading, a piece of research, time with a specialist, or other identified route.

Risk management and infection control

Healthcare practitioners must have a good understanding of the risks and benefits to patients of the care they provide to enable the patient to make decisions and give informed consent. Some aspects of care may require documented and signed consent; these are mainly invasive procedures or involving children. The DoH has produced comprehensive guidance on consent (DoH, 2001b).

It is essential that infection control procedures are adhered to. Good hand decontamination practices before, during and after caring for patients (National Patient Safety Agency [NPSA], 2004), the use of sterile or clean, single-use gloves and aprons, and the safe disposal of contaminated waste will all reduce the risk of contamination and cross-infection. Reducing the risk of infection caused by bacterial contamination can help limit the incidence of morbidity and mortality in health care. Wound care practices can pose a significant infection risk.

Clinical audit

To promote clinical effectiveness, the audit cycle should be used as an ongoing process to ensure clinically- and cost-effective care, together with performance management, continuous review of the evidence and education provision. Results and recommendations from audit can be used to influence commissioning of education, documentation and ensure 'customer care'. NICE (www.nice.org. uk/page.aspx?o=tools) have a proforma for the identification of audit standards. This criteria is intended to make the process of developing clinical audit projects easier through the provision of ready-to-use criteria, including exceptions, definitions and data source suggestions. General information to help you carry out the audit is also included.

Utilising this, standards for future audit can be incorporated into clinical guidelines and protocols.

Independent, charitable and social enterprise providers

Identifying providers is a challenge for PCTs, however, the 'playing field' is much wider than ever before. The healthcare market is now attracting and encouraging commercial companies, independent healthcare and other providers, charities and social enterprise organisations.

Potential providers who fulfil predefined clinical, quality and financial requirements will be invited to tender for or develop business cases with practice-based commissioners to provide services to meet local healthcare needs.

An organisation with robust clinical governance arrangements, able to evidence positive outcomes for its client group, such as the model promoted by the Lindsay Leg Club Foundation, and with robust financial information must surely be a contender in this brave new world. Different models of delivery, closer to the patient's home, at a time and in a manner that is acceptable to patients, which are safe, clinically- and cost-effective, need to be explored.

This is a condensed update on the NHS and changes affecting care delivery. The process of change is ongoing and further developments will continue to happen, changing the NHS as we and our patients know it. It is vital that clinical governance should not be sidelined, but strengthened to protect patients and practitioners, especially as care will become much more fragmented as many more providers are commissioned to take over traditional care roles

References and further reading

Department of Health (1998a) *A First Class Service: Quality in the New NHS.* Stationery Office, London

Department of Health (1998b) *The new NHS modern and dependable a national framework for assessing performance consultation document — EL (98)4.* DoH, London

Department of Health (1999a) *Patient and public involvement in the new NHS.* DoH, London

Department of Health (1999b) *Making a difference. Strengthening the nursing, midwifery and health visiting contribution to health and health care.* Stationery Office, London

Department of Health (2000a) *The NHS Plan: A plan for investment. A plan for reform.* Stationery Office, London

Department of Health (2000b) *A health service of all the talents: developing the NHS workforce. Consultation document on the review of workforce planning.* DoH, London

Department of Health (2000c) *An organisation with a memory.* Stationery Office, London

Department of Health (2001a) *Building a safer NHS.* Stationery Office, London

Department of Health (2001b) HSC 2001/023: *Good practice in consent: achieving the NHS Plan commitment to patient-centred consent practice.* DoH, London. Available online at: www.dh.gov.uk/en/Publicationsandst atistics/Lettersandcirculars/Healthservicecirculars/DH_4003736

Department of Health (2002) *Liberating the talents: Helping primary care trusts and nurses to deliver the NHS Plan.* Stationery Office, London

Department of Health (2004a) *Choose and book: Patient's choice of hospital and booked appointment — policy framework. Choice and booking at point of referral.* DoH, London

Department of Health (2004b) *Practice-based commissioning: promoting clinical engagement.* DoH, London

Department of Health (2005) *Creating a Patient-Led NHS. Delivering the NHS Improvement Plan.* DoH, London

Department of Health (2006a) *Our health, Our care, Our say: a new direction for community services.* DoH, London

Department of Health (2006b) *Health reform in England: update and commissioning framework.* DoH, London

National Patient Safety Agency (2004) *Patient Safety Alert: Clean hands help save lives.* NPSA, London. Available online at: www.npsa.nhs.uk/site/ media/documents/644_cyh_alert.pdf

Nursing and Midwifery Council (2004) *The NMC Code of professional conduct: standards for conduct, performance and ethics.* NMC, London

Royal College of Nursing (2007) *NHS Reforms – Que Sera?* A Royal College of Nursing Policy Unit Discussion Paper. RCN, London

CHAPTER 10

WHAT IS EVIDENCE-BASED PRACTICE?

Leigh Davis and Mary Courtney

The critical application of evidence to practice is essential to the role of any professional. For healthcare professionals seeking to provide care that will deliver the best possible outcomes for patients, it is especially important to be able to assess current evidence to guide clinical decision-making. Evidence-based practice (EBP) has become synonymous with the move within healthcare organisations to shift away from a culture of authority-based practice, where decisions are based on opinion, past practice and ritual, towards a culture where healthcare decisions are based on the best available evidence.

This chapter will briefly outline the history of EBP, what is meant by evidence and where to find it. It will also cover the importance of critically appraising evidence before it is incorporated into practice. Finally, the importance of evaluating any changes to clinical practice is highlighted.

History of evidence-based practice

Evidence-based practice (EBP) is a term used to encompass the use of evidence in a wide range of healthcare settings. The original practice of evidence-based medicine (EBM) was devised as a strategy to promote clinical learning for doctors to justify medical practice (Sackett *et al*, 2001).

In 1979, one of the pioneers of the movement was Professor Archibald Leman Cochrane (1902–1988), a British epidemiologist who severely criticised physicians for their lack of critical appraisal and synthesis of research. He was the first person to recommend that practice should be based on evidence from research. In 1992, Cochrane's recommendations were formally implemented at Oxford

University and a year later the Cochrane collaboration was established (Krainovich-Miller and Gaber, 1993). Although it is not clear when the shift from EBM to EBP occurred, it is suggested that this was linked to the need to ensure the integration of all healthcare disciplines (Jennings and Loan, 2001).

What is evidence-based practice and why is it important?

While a number of definitions have been put forward, Sackett *et al* (2001) propose that evidence-based medicine (EBM) is about integrating the best research evidence with clinical expertise and patient values to achieve the best possible patient management. Similarly, Pearson agrees that EBP is about making clinical decisions based upon the best available scientific evidence but recognising patient preferences, the context of health care, and the judgement of the clinician (Pearson *et al*, 2005).

These definitions suggest that clinical practice should be based on sound research evidence about the effectiveness of healthcare procedures. However, evidence needs to be applied flexibly, depending on patient values, beliefs or treatment preferences, whether the evidence is appropriate to the healthcare context, and the expertise of the clinician. The assumption underlying evidence-based practice is that health care which is based on best available evidence will result in reduced variation in practice, eliminate ineffective and unnecessary practices, as well as achieve improved patient outcomes and cost savings (Haynes, 2002; Parahoo, 2006).

While EBP is not a new concept, in the early 1990s a number of factors combined which resulted in a surge of activity and interest. One of the most important reasons for the drive towards efficiency in health care is the increase in both private and public spending on health worldwide. Advances in technology have improved diagnostic and screening procedures, resulting in increased costs related to providing health care. This has forced governments to ensure that health expenditure is targeted to providing care that is effective with positive health benefits for the public and cost savings (Parahoo, 2006).

In addition, the volume of literature related to health care has, and continues to increase rapidly. However, the quality and appropriateness of research varies. It is important to appraise research findings critically before we can decide whether or not to use the evidence in our practice. Another factor which helped the evidence-based movement to thrive was a change in attitudes of consumers to health care. Since the advent of the personal computer and online access to information, there are a growing number of patients and family members who are seeking out the latest evidence about the most effective treatment, and who seem more willing to challenge decisions and actions of healthcare professionals (Parahoo, 2005). Since governmental policy has an emphasis on clinical effectiveness, nurses are increasingly being called upon by payers, accrediting bodies and patients themselves to be professionally accountable for their practice which is based on up-to-date evidence.

The importance of EBP has been underscored by findings from health services research which has consistently reported a gap between best practice (as determined by scientific evidence), and actual clinical care (Grol and Wensing, 2004). Studies from the United States and the Netherlands have suggested that at least 30–40% of patients do not receive care according to current scientific evidence, while 20% or more of the care provided is not required or potentially harmful to patients (Grol and Grimshaw, 2003). The value of transferring evidence of effective health care into practice and reducing the research-practice gap has been recognised by both government and professional bodies. Implicit to the debate is the belief that the implementation of good quality research is likely to lead to improved outcomes for patients and, therefore, important for quality of patient care (Kitson *et al*, 1998).

The process of EBP involves five main steps:

- formulation of a clear question related to a clinical practice issue
- search for relevant research studies
- critical appraisal of selected studies
- implementation of 'best' evidence
- evaluation of implemented evidence (Sackett *et al*, 2001).

As a profession, nurses are systematically curious and all EBP does is to provide an organised method for that exploration. However, this model is flexible and dynamic and not simply a matter of following these five steps.

What do we mean by evidence?

While few would disagree that providing patient care based on reliable information of what works is required, there remains significant challenges about what evidence is. A unifying theme in definitions of evidence is that, however the evidence is obtained, it needs to be independently observed and verified and subjected to scrutiny.

In the early 1990s when evidence-based medicine began to move forward, there was a common assumption that evidence meant research evidence and, specifically, evidence from randomised controlled trials, meta-analyses and systematic reviews (Sackett *et al*, 2001). This type of evidence was regarded as the 'gold standard' because it is less likely to produce misleading information about the effects of an intervention (Sackett *et al*, 2001). Current approaches to evaluating quantitative methodologies uses a hierarchy which grades study designs according to their perceived capacity to minimise or eliminate bias in the effect being measured. An example of one hierarchy of evidence from the National Institute for Clinical Excellence (NICE) is shown in *Table 10.1*.

However, the practice of nursing is mediated through contacts and relationships between a nurse and her patient. The centrality of this relationship complements the role of scientific evidence, but suggests that the nature of evidence needed for nursing practice is much broader than evidence derived from research. Traditionally, nurses have used a variety of evidence sources to inform their practice. For example, a decision made about a patient's clinical care can involve a diverse blend of personal and clinical experience, intuition, reasoning, expert reports, clinical practice guidelines, policies or recommendations. It has been suggested that evidence in EBP should be considered as knowledge that is derived from a variety of sources, including research evidence that has undergone testing and been found to be credible (Higgs and Jones, 2000). Therefore, all sources of evidence need to be evaluated to the same extent as that from trials for clinical experience and knowledge to be considered trustworthy as a source of evidence.

Where is the evidence and how do I find it?

While technology has developed with the information explosion and it is possible to store a great deal of information, effective retrieval systems to extract relevant information have not been developed (Lipman, 2000; Dawes, 2005). Clinicians have quickly realised that attempting a simple, quick and effective search of the popular databases is not always possible. The starting point for EBP is to convert the need for information about a clinical practice issue into a clearly defined

Table 10.1: Levels of evidence for intervention studies	
Hierarchy of evidence	Research method/study design
1++	High-quality meta-analyses, systematic reviews of RCTs, or RCTs with a very low risk of bias
1+	Well-conducted meta-analyses, systematic reviews of RCTs, or RCTs with a low risk of bias
1-	Meta-analyses, systematic reviews of RCTs, or RCTs with a high risk of bias*
2++	High-quality systematic reviews of case-control or cohort studies. High-quality case-control or cohort studies with a very low risk of confounding, bias or chance and a high probability that the relationship is causal
2+	Well-conducted case-control or cohort studies with a low risk of confounding, bias or chance and a moderate probability that the relationship is causal
2-	Case–control or cohort studies with a high risk of confounding bias, or chance and a significant risk that the relationship is not causal*
3	Non-analytic studies (for example, case reports, case series)
4	Expert opinion, formal consensus
* Studies with a level of evidence '-' should not be used as a basis for making a recommendation	

Adapted from the National Institute for Clinical Excellence (2005) *Guideline Development Methods*. www.nice.org.uk

searchable question. The advantages of taking a structured approach to searching for research evidence include:

• key elements of a focused question will guide the search strategy
• a clearly defined question will maximise the potential of finding relevant evidence that can be applied to a specific patient or context
• it will save you hours of non-focused literature reading which may or may not be relevant or applicable.

A research question will often guide the choice of study design, eg. a randomised controlled trial can investigate the effectiveness of a new intervention, whereas a qualitative design will be required to understand how patients feel about the effects of an intervention. Increasing attention has been directed toward the development of methods that can provide valid and reliable information about what works best in health care.

Systematic reviews

The systematic review process has been identified as one strategy to make it easier for clinicians to integrate evidence into practice. A systematic review is a method of summarising research and the systematic methods used in these reviews enable reviewers to determine studies of sufficient quality to provide clinicians with confidence to use the findings as the basis for their practice. Systematic reviews should be the first place to search when trying to find information on a clinical topic. Those authors who produce systematic reviews have often reduced and synthesised sizeable amounts of information on a given topic, so all the clinician needs to do is to read the review critically. Examples of websites containing libraries of systematic reviews are provided in *Box 10.1*.

Database of abstracts of effects

Also contained within the Cochrane library is another useful database, the 'Database of Abstracts of Reviews of Effects' or DARE. DARE contains

---

Box 10.1

Cochrane Library
Free of charge. There are four Cochrane Collaborative Review Groups related to: www3.interscience.wiley.com/cgi-bin/mrwhome/106568753/HOME

Joanna Briggs Institute (JBI)
This is an international research collaboration for the evaluation of research and integration into nursing practice. The JBI identify practice areas that require summarised evidence, conduct systematic reviews, and design, conduct, and promote broad dissemination activities.
www.joannabriggs.edu.au/about/home.php

summaries of systematic reviews which have met strict quality criteria and each summary provides a critical commentary on the quality of the review. The database covers a broad range of health and social care topics and can be used for answering questions about the effects of interventions, as well as for developing guidelines and policy-making.

Clinical guidelines

If no systematic review is available, then clinical guidelines are instruments of communication between synthesised research knowledge and the clinicians and patients who take advantage of the best treatment options. The underlying principle for developing evidence-based clinical practice guidelines is that their use will help to shape clinical practice and achieve better health outcomes for patients.

In principle, guidelines are based on the best available research evidence. Most organisations involved in the development of guidelines involve as many stakeholders as possible in the process. This means that not only healthcare professionals are involved, but also patients and carers and those from industry and academic institutions. Some examples of websites that contain libraries of clinical practice guidelines are presented in _Box 10.2_.

Computerised databases

If no clinical guidelines are available, then searching computerised databases such as the CINAHL (Cumulative Index of Nursing and

Box 10.2

US National Guidelines Clearing house
www.guideline.gov/

National Institute for Health and Clinical Excellence (NICE) UK
www.nice.org.uk/

Scottish Intercollegiate Guidelines Network Group (SIGN)
www.sign.ac.uk/index.html

Turning Research into Practice (TRIP)
www.tripdatabase.com/index.html

Allied Health Literature), Medline or PsycINFO is the next place to search for evidence. To undertake an effective search it is necessary to first of all formulate a searchable question.

Developing a searchable question

Using the patient/population, intervention, comparator and outcome (PICO) approach to formulate a searchable question will enable the search to be as specific and sensitive as possible. This format will guide a search, although not all four components are relevant to a search topic. How to develop an effective searchable question and from there construct a search strategy is illustrated in the following practice example.

Practice example
Figure 10.1 demonstrates how a research question from a clinical scenario can be changed depending on what we want to know.

Develop a search strategy using the PICO format

Electronic databases can be searched in a focused and precise way to find answers to clinical questions. These databases contain current research studies which are regularly updated. In this search, Cinahl (*Figure 10.2*) subject headings were used for bandages and dressings and compression therapy and patient compliance.

How do you know if the evidence is any good?

The second major problem facing a practitioner is knowing whether or not to believe the research information that is found. There is a clear need to appraise critically the information contained in primary research journals. It may therefore not be enough to accept the results of a trial at face value just because it appears in a reputable journal. There are a number of EBP online sites which provide information and tools which can assist healthcare professionals to appraise critically different research study designs. These tools provide a checklist of questions that a reviewer may wish to consider in determining whether the study findings are valid and applicable to practice. Some examples of websites containing tools for critical appraisal are presented in *Box 10.3*.

Clinical situation	A 70-year-old man presents with a large (6 cm x 8 cm) venous ulcer on the medial aspect of his lower leg. The wound is weeping copiously, the surrounding skin is inflamed and scaly and the wound bed is sloughy. The man is overweight and the ankle and lower limb is oedematous. Compression bandaging has been recommended and tried once in the past, but the patient found it uncomfortable and is reluctant to try again.
Informational need	Depending on the information we want to know, this scenario could be translated into different types of questions.

Question one	*What are the most effective therapies for the problem?*
Type of question	Intervention
Ideal study type	Randomised controlled trial or systematic review
PICO format	P = patients with venous leg ulcers I = compression bandaging C = no compression bandaging O = healing rates
Answerable question	For example: in patients suffering with venous leg ulcers (P) is treatment with a compression bandaging (I) compared to no bandaging (C) effective in healing the ulcer? (O)

Question two	*What factors do patients perceive affect their compliance with treatment in this situation?*
Type of question	Phenomena
Ideal study type	Qualitative
PICO format	P = patients with venous leg ulcers I = not applicable C = not applicable O = knowledge of what affects patient's compliance with treatment
Answerable question	What do patients with leg ulcers perceive affects their compliance with treatment?

Figure 10.1: Practice example

		Search statements
P	1	Leg ulcer* or venous ulcer*
I	2	Bandage* or dressing* or stocking*
	3	Compression therapy
	4	2 or 3
	5	1 and 4
C	6	1 and 4
O	7	Patient compliance
	8	5 and 7
	9	6 and 7
	10	Healing
	11	8 or 10
	12	9 and 10
Narrow search by limiting to specific studies	13	1 and 10 (limiters peer reviewed, research articles)
	14	13 and qualitative
	15	5 (limiters peer reviewed, research articles)
	16	5 (limiters peer reviewed, evidence-based practice)
	17	4 (limiters peer reviewed, research articles)
	18	4 (limiters peer reviewed, evidence-based practice)
	19	6 (limiters peer reviewed, research articles)
	20	6 (limiters peer reviewed, evidence-based practice)

*The authors are grateful to Lynn Evans, Liaison Librarian, Queensland University of Technology for developing this search strategy

Figure 10.2: Search strategy

How do you put the evidence into practice?

Incorporating evidence into recommendations, guidelines and protocols

While terms such as recommendations, guidelines and protocols are used interchangeably by some, for others, these terms have distinct meanings (Ilott *et al*, 2006).

A recommendation is a suggestion or endorsement of something that is worthy of acceptance or trial and, in health care, general recommendations are frequently made by professional organisations for the promotion of, for example, physical activity, healthy eating or smoking cessation (Rich and Newland, 2006). On the other hand, guidelines are official recommendations which outline a more prescribed approach to specific conditions. Protocols may be more specific than guidelines and have been defined as a detailed plan of a treatment or procedure that has been tailored to suit a specific population and practice situation (Rich and Newland, 2006). There is limited opportunity to deviate from protocol, therefore, less scope for clinicians to exercise their clinical judgement. As these definitions show, evidence may be incorporated into any of the above tools to get evidence into practice

Implementing the evidence into practice

Once a decision has been made about whether research evidence is rigorous and worthy of application in practice, plans need to be made about how best to go about introducing, managing and evaluating its implementation. It has been suggested that firstly piloting the evidence in practice by writing an evidence-based standard (eg. policy, procedure, or guideline) that is specific to the healthcare setting and using a rating system (eg. NICE guidelines in *Table 10.1*) is the first step (Everett and Titler, 2006). This rating system allows the nurse to see that practices are based on evidence and what type of evidence (eg. randomised controlled trial, expert opinion). Clinicians who adopt EBP are influenced by their perceived participation and opportunity

---

Box 10.3

NHS Public Health Resource Kit: Critical appraisal skills programme (CASP)
www.phru.nhs.uk/casp/appraisa.htm

Qualitative studies: Occupational therapy evidence-based practice research group
www-fhs.mcmaster.ca/rehab/ebp/

Clinical guidelines: The AGREE collaboration
Appraisal of Guidelines for Research and Evaluation (AGREE) instrument provides a framework for assessing the quality of clinical practice guidelines.
www.agreecollaboration.org

should be given to review and comment on the written standard. Focus groups may be a useful way to provide feedback and identify key areas that could be problematic in the implementation phase.

The implementation process goes beyond writing an evidence-based policy or protocol; it requires involvement of the direct care providers to champion and promote evidence acceptance, leadership support and system changes.

How do you know if the evidence was effective?

Evaluating the EBP change is a critical component of any implementation plan and will determine if the change should be retained, modified or eliminated. Evaluation of the process should include barriers that staff encountered in carrying out the practice, differences in opinion among nurses and any difficulty in carrying out the steps of the practice as originally designed. These data can be collected from staff or patient self-report or both, medical record audits, or observations of clinical practice (Everett and Titler, 2006). Outcome data are also important to the evaluation process to assess whether the expected patient, staff and economic outcomes have been achieved. Outcome variables are those which are proposed to change and, therefore, baseline data is measured before the change can be compared to data collected after implementation. This evaluation should be ongoing and data should be collected every 12 months thereafter (Everett and Titler, 2006).

Findings can then be communicated to clinicians to reinforce the impact of the change in practice. Feedback can include:

- verbal or written appreciation for the work
- visual presentation of progress in implementation
- improvement in patient outcomes.

The key to effective evaluation is to ensure that the change is warranted in improving patient outcomes and that it does not bring harm to patients.

Putting it all together

In this chapter we have looked briefly at the history of EBP as a movement whose purpose is to transform the basis on which health care and clinical decisions are made. The meaning of evidence and where to find it has been discussed. However, all evidence must be critically appraised before it can be incorporated into clinical policies and guidelines. Perhaps the most difficult step in the evidence-based process is implementing a change in practice which involves a series of steps over weeks and months, involving stages that are often non-linear. Incorporation of evidence into practice must also be evaluated to ensure that change has achieved its projected outcomes.

Evidence-based practice is not intended to replace individual clinical experience but attempts to augment nurses' clinical decision-making. Whether or not it reduces variation in practice, ineffective practice, and saves money on a significant scale, remains to be seen. It is likely that EBP will continue to develop as an important resource for nurses in their day-to-day work.

References

Dawes M (2005) Critically appraised topics and evidence-based medicine journals. *Singapore Med J* **46**(9): 442–9

Everett LQ, Titler MG (2006) Making EBP part of clinical practice: The Iowa model. In: Levin RF, Feldman HR, eds. *Teaching Evidence-based Practice in Nursing. A guide for academic and clinical settings*. Springer Publishing Company, Inc, New York: 295–324

Grol R, Wensing M (2004) What drives change? Barriers to and incentives for achieving evidence-based practice. *Med J Aust* **180**(6 Suppl): S57–60

Grol R, Grimshaw J (2003) From best evidence to best practice: effective implementation of change in patients' care. *Lancet* **362**(9391): 1225–30

Haynes RB (2002) What kind of evidence is it that evidence-based medicine advocates want health care providers and consumers to pay attention to? *BMC Health Serv Res* **2**(1): 3

Higgs J, Jones M (2000) *Will evidence-based practice take the reasoning out of practice? Clinical reasoning in the health professions*. Butterworth Heinemann, Oxford: 307–15

Ilott I, *et al* (2006) What is protocol-based care? A concept analysis. *J Nurs Management* **14**(7): 544–52

Jennings B, Loan L (2001) Misconceptions among nurses about evidence-based practice. *J Nurs Scholarship* **33**(2): 121–7

Kitson A, Harvey G, McCormack B (1998) Enabling the implementation of evidence-based practice: a conceptual framework. *Quality in Health Care* **7**(3): 149–58

Krainovich-Miller B, J Haber (2006) Transforming a graduate nursing curriculum to incorporate evidence-based practice: The New York University experience. In: Levin RF, Feldman HR, eds. *Teaching Evidence-based Practice in Nursing. A guide for academic and clinical settings.* Springer Publishing Company, Inc, New York

Lipman AG (2000) Evidence-based palliative care. In: Lipman AG, Jackson JC, II, Tyler LS, eds. *Evidence-based Symptom Control in Palliative Care: systematic reviews and validated clinical practice guidelines for 15 common problems in patients with life-limiting disease.* Haworth Press Inc, New York: 1–9

Parahoo K (2006) Evidence-based practice. In: Parahoo K, ed. *Nursing Research. Principles, process and issues.* 2nd edn. Macmillan, Basingstoke

Pearson A, Wiechula R, Court A, Lockwood C (2005) The JBI model of evidence-based healthcare. *Int J Evidenced-based Healthcare* **3**: 207–15

Rich ER, Newland JA (2006) Creating clinical protocols with an apgar of 10. In: Levin RF, Feldman HR, eds. *Teaching Evidence-based Practice in Nursing. A guide for academic and clinical settings.* Springer Publishing Company, Inc, New York: 121–32

Sackett DL, Straus S, Richardson WS, *et al* (2001) *Evidence-based medicine. How to practice and teach EBM.* Churchill Livingstone, London

CHAPTER 11

FROM THEORY TO PRACTICE

Anne-Marie Brown

Studies into the everyday lives of patients with chronic venous leg ulceration have demonstrated that these patients experience a reduced quality of life compared with their 'healthy' peers. The dominant themes to emerge from these studies are: pain, reduced mobility, depression, increased anxiety, feeling helpless, loss of control over their lives and despair that their ulcers will never heal (Hamer *et al*, 1994; Hyland *et al*, 1994; Walshe, 1995; Charles, 1995; Chase *et al*, 1997). In addition, many studies suggest that these patients suffer from social isolation due to the presence of ulcers (Phillips *et al*, 1994; Walshe, 1995; Krasner, 1998; Rich and McLachlan, 2003). In these qualitative studies, patients understandably have isolated themselves from others because of their wet, malodorous bandages and fear of further trauma to their legs. Many of these studies were conducted prior to the universal introduction of compression bandaging which reduces oedema, and wound dressings designed to absorb exudate and reduce odour. Despite improved clinical management of leg ulceration, the theme of 'social isolation' still continues to emerge from more recent studies into the lives of leg ulcer patients, however, few attempts have been made to explore this concept any further (Mudge *et al*, 2006).

To investigate the concept of social isolation in more depth, I conducted a small, phenomenological study with eight venous leg ulcer patients. As part of the literature review, a literature search was conducted to find a definition of 'social isolation'. It became apparent that, while loneliness and social isolation have been linked to many physical illnesses, the concept of social isolation has been explored by psychologists and sociologists rather than healthcare professionals or healthcare academics (Schwarz and Olds, 1997) and only one study relevant to the subject was retrieved.

To find out more about social isolation, the psychology and sociology databases, such as PsychINFO were searched and revealed several definitions of 'social isolation'. Victor *et al* (2002) defined social isolation as 'an objective measure of low social interaction and relates to the integration of individuals into the wider social environment'. As a measure used in quantitative studies, Bowling (1991) quantifies 'social isolation' as a social network of between five and seven contacts per month. Victor *et al* (2002) described a person's dissatisfaction with the number, but more importantly, the quality of his/her interactions as loneliness, rather than social isolation. The terms social isolation, loneliness and living alone are often used interchangeably, however, Victor *et al* (2002) believe it is important to distinguish between them since, while they are closely linked, they are actually quite different concepts. The term, 'social isolation', therefore, is ill-defined and is very subjective, unique to each individual. It also appears that some people who are often alone, do not feel lonely since their solitude may be a personal choice (Brown, 2003).

It became apparent that some of the authors of the studies who claimed that patients with venous leg ulceration suffered from social isolation may have made assumptions based on the number of contacts each patient claimed to have received, rather than how satisfied the patients were with their social network. This concurred with the findings of Flett *et al* (2003) who conducted a study of 14 leg ulcer patients and compared them with a control group of 14 people with similar demographic data but without leg ulcers. They investigated levels of psychological well-being, self-esteem, life satisfaction and social support and found no significant differences between the two groups.

The results of my study indicated that none of the eight participants felt socially isolated by their leg ulcers and these findings supported those of Flett *et al* (2003). Most of the patients interviewed in my study were very elderly, with poor mobility and suffering from concurrent chronic conditions, such as arthritis, heart disease or diabetes. They did not appear to suffer significantly greater feelings of loneliness or dissatisfaction with their social relationships because of their leg ulceration, since they experienced problems in their everyday lives as a result of their other disorders. Indeed, they appeared to feel resigned to the fact that their leg ulcer was part of the normal ageing process and they had to 'put up with it'. The majority of patients, however, expressed a feeling of being the 'only person in the world with a leg ulcer, a fact which they felt set them apart from their peers.

These feelings are common to many leg ulcer patients, particularly the housebound, as many community healthcare professionals will verify. As a former district nurse, I was frequently asked by patients with venous leg ulceration whether I had anybody else on my caseload suffering from the same condition and my affirmative reply was often met with disbelief and surprise. This may well be due to the stigma that often surrounds chronic venous leg ulceration, the negative stereotyping of leg ulcer patients and the low profile afforded this distressing condition by the Government and even some healthcare providers (Brown, 2005).

More recently, research has been undertaken into the role social support may play in improving the quality of life of leg ulcer patients (Franks and Moffatt, 2006). Levels of social support have been linked to improved health outcomes and psychological well-being across a range of acute and chronic illnesses, such as myocardial infarction, stroke, hypertension, multiple sclerosis, chronic back pain and arthritis (Franks and Moffatt, 2006; Morgan *et al*, 2004), although the mechanism by which social support protects against morbidity is unclear (Morgan *et al*, 2004).

Several authors have investigated whether the social support offered at leg ulcer clinics improves patients' quality of life (Liew *et al*, 2000; Charles, 2004; Morgan *et al*, 2004) and report positive outcomes. Results indicate that a patient's quality of life improves as his/her leg ulcer heals and equally improves in cases even where ulcer healing does not occur (Charles, 2004). Although these are encouraging results, patients in these studies are only monitored for a limited period of time, and, what about the patients for whom healing is never likely to occur? These patients have a long-term condition defined by the Department of Health as 'an illness or condition which is currently not curable and can only be managed' (DoH, 2005).

Anecdotally, there is a commonly held belief by some healthcare professionals that some patients do not want their ulcer to heal in order to maintain contact with their nurses (Brown, 2005). This widely held belief has been discussed elsewhere in the literature (Bland, 1999; Charles, 1995; Walshe, 1995; Wise, 1986); however, it is the result of one study (Wise, 1986) and is based on anecdotal evidence only. Wise (1986) conducted a case study with one patient and used the findings to suggest that there was a relationship between social isolation and poor ulcer healing and/or recurrence of a leg ulcer. She used Townsend's (1963) scale of isolation to measure the number of contacts her patient received. The score defined social contact as 'meeting with another person, other than a casual exchange of greetings' and Townsend (1963) defined a score of less than 21 contacts per week as being very isolated. The patient in Wise's study (1986) had many other physical and psychological problems in addition to a leg ulcer, and also suffered recurrent ulceration. Coincidentally, she had a low number of social contacts and based on these findings, Wise described the existence of the 'social ulcer'. This inferred that the patient did not wish her ulcer to heal as she relied on the frequent visits by the nurses to increase her social contacts and a healed ulcer, therefore, would result in reduced social contacts again. The 'social ulcer' continues to be cited as a common phenomenon by healthcare professionals, particularly community nurses, despite lack of robust evidence.

As is now known, social isolation cannot be measured by counting contacts alone, and it is the patient's satisfaction or dissatisfaction with the quality of those contacts, rather than the number, that defines social isolation. In view of this, it would be difficult to conclude that there is any robust evidence to support the belief of the healthcare professionals that patients deliberately interfere with their bandages to delay healing to maintain the nurses' visits. Rather, it may be that the healthcare professionals caring for these patients are experiencing stress at their perceived failure to heal these wounds and use this phenomenon as a coping mechanism by shifting blame from themselves onto the patient. In addition, there appears to be a dichotomy of treatment expectations between patients and healthcare professionals. For the latter, healing may be the main objective of treatment, whereas the patient may just seek relief of unpleasant symptoms, such as pain or malodour rather than complete closure of their ulcer. This may cause frustration on the part of the healthcare professionals when the patient refuses compression therapy and is then viewed as non-concordant. It is well documented in the health psychology literature that people weigh up the benefits and disadvantages of adhering to particular treatments which they feel are unpleasant, and will only change their behaviour if they feel the outcome justifies the change (Dines, 1994; Preston, 1997). Finally, it is unlikely that healthcare professionals would be able to satisfy all aspects of social support for their patient, which the literature defines as encompassing many elements such as emotional, instrumental, and financial. Despite this, Palmer (1995) concedes that the 'psychosocial aspect of community nursing is often the most vital part of dealing with wounds that will not heal'.

The current government policy of encouraging patients with long-term conditions to self-manage their illness has resulted in the development of support groups and self-management programmes (*The Expert Patient*, DoH, 2002) for conditions such as multiple sclerosis, rheumatoid arthritis and diabetes. The emphasis of these initiatives is on enabling patients to learn to cope and adapt to living with their chronic condition, rather than focusing on total cure. They have been shown to lead to increased information and education for the patient, exposure to new coping strategies, positive health behaviours, increased motivation and enhanced social networks (Subramaniam *et al*, 1999). Members have also demonstrated enhanced self-esteem and improved morale through the peer support they received by attending these groups. Other aspects of social support, such as a sense of belonging, the opportunity to help others, the development of new friendships and taking pleasure in the achievements of others were also seen as significant benefits (Subramaniam *et al*, 1999). Many of these initiatives are patient-led and it has been suggested that they fill a gap in current services, providing empathy and peer support in a way that healthcare professionals cannot possibly deliver. Currently, there are support groups for many chronic conditions, however, to date, there are few support groups available for patients with chronic or recurrent venous leg ulceration.

In light of the findings of my study, this gap in local service provision was identified and a Lindsay Leg Club was opened locally. The Lindsay Leg Club model is an innovative model of delivering leg ulcer care in the community, combining evidence-based, clinical management of venous leg ulceration with psychosocial support for patients or members (*Chapter 5*). Held in a non-medical environment, the aims of the Leg Club are:

- to empower patients to become stakeholders in their own treatment, promoting a sense of ownership and involvement
- to meet the needs of isolated patients by providing a mechanism for social interaction, empathy and peer support
- to rebuild patients' self-esteem and self-respect by destigmatising their condition
- to facilitate an informal support network
- to achieve compliance with treatment through informed beliefs and modified behaviour
- to provide an informal forum for health promotion and education (Lindsay, 1999).

This unique model of care has become increasingly popular, with 25

Lindsay Leg Clubs now in existence throughout the United Kingdom and Australia. The growing number of Leg Clubs indicates that this model meets the needs of many leg ulcer patients because of its supportive role. Why has this model of care become so successful? To suggest a possible explanation, the sociological literature was reviewed, in particular in relation to group behaviour theory.

Social capital theory

During the last 25 years, a new term 'social capital' has emerged as a popular concept with both sociology theorists and government policy makers in relation to group theory (Hean *et al*, 2003). Coleman (1990) defines 'social capital' as 'the quality and quantity of the social relations embedded within a community that share similar norms'. The theory proposes that, in society, people form groups or associations based on common themes, such as ancestry, residence or beliefs. These groups or associations help shape individual identity, norms, beliefs and priorities (Collins, 1994) and through these networks people share information, provide and receive support and work together to achieve collective goals that could not be accomplished by an individual working in isolation (Macinko and Starfield, 2001). Putnam (2000), a leading theorist, defined social capital as having the following characteristics:

- the existence of community networks —— this involves human interaction within a community through clubs, societies, the church and other organisations/networks
- civic engagement — the participation of people in communal processes and the use of the above networks
- civic identity — the feeling of equal participation within a community
- reciprocity — mutual help among members in a community
- trust as opposed to fear.

Many researchers propose that social capital may lead to potentially useful health interventions which, in turn, may lead to significant improvements in health status (Pesut, 2002; Ervin *et al*, 1999). Veenstra (2002), researching 30 health districts in Canada, found that areas where people did not settle for long periods and had no sense of belonging, tended to have low social capital scores and poorer health.

These are usually places with proportionately high levels of minority groups, for example, single parents, women and elderly people, and he suggests that community nursing should target these places/groups and make effective interventions to improve their health.

Coleman (1988) agrees and believes that social capital is most effective in communities or groups which are characterised by social and environmental isolation from others. It may be that people in these minority groups know each other better, participate in the same organisations/clubs and strengthen their relationships on the basis of cultural, social and moral elements. In other words, they have a sense of belonging and an 'internal identity'. Conversely, these communities may demonstrate high rates of intolerance to anything that is foreign to them or clashes with their established ideas, which are characteristics of communities with low levels of social capital (Putnam, 2000). Bourdieu (1991) even suggests that, in social capital, there is the potential for the concept to be used by those in power to maintain their power, for example, the Mafia organisation, and refers to this as the 'darker side' or disadvantage of social capital.

As interest in social capital has increased, the concept itself has become increasingly dense and regarded by some sociologists as contentious (Coleman, 1988). In addition, the rapidly expanding body of literature on social capital has begun to obscure a clear understanding of the concept itself, making it difficult to translate into policy or practice (Hean *et al*, 2003). As a result, some critics claim that the concept is 'falsely inflated' (Labonte, 1999) or 'a new term for an old product' (Portes *et al*, 1996). Kritsotakis and Gamarnikow (2004) even suggest that the positive findings of the many research studies into social capital may be due to the high levels of social support received, rather than social capital itself, and discuss how the terms social support and social capital are often used interchangeably in the literature, resulting in a concept that is poorly defined or understood.

The purpose of this review was to explore whether the concept of social capital could be offered as a possible sociological framework underpinning the success of the Lindsay Leg Club model of leg ulcer service provision. Clearly, the five major building blocks of social capital — the existence of community networks, civic engagement, civic identity, reciprocity and trust are demonstrated consistently through anecdotal evidence gleaned from informal discussions with Leg Club members and observation of how the members interact with each other. As a group, people with leg ulceration may feel isolated by their condition (Brown, 2003) and attendance at a Leg Club allows them to meet other people with similar problems, reducing the feeling that they are alone in suffering from this chronic condition. Reciprocity is also clearly demonstrated by the willingness of the members to 'give something back' to Leg Clubs in return for the help and support they have received and is also evident from the fundraising activities and volunteer help offered at the Leg Clubs and to individual members who require help with transport, etc. The numerous subgroups that have been formed by members as a result of attending Leg Clubs, examples of which include a Fish and Chip Night group, and a Steak and Pub Night group have enabled members to benefit from an improved and active social life, thus improving their quality of life.

Anecdotally, the Lindsay Leg Club does not appear to meet the needs of all leg ulcer patients, with some preferring the more traditional leg ulcer clinic model of service delivery. The literature on support groups and patients' health beliefs was reviewed to explore why this may be.

Galinsky and Schopler (1994) investigated the negative experiences of people attending support groups. The findings of their study revealed that for some people, the pressure to conform to the group, stress related to reciprocal obligations, feelings of inadequacy, embarrassment and feeling overwhelmed by the group led to negative experiences. Some people felt depressed to hear other members talk openly about their deteriorating condition and sensed the despair of others who were in a similar situation (Galinsky and Schopler, 1994). It must be noted, however, that the study took place within a cancer support group and the findings may not be generalisable within a Leg Club due to differences in symptoms and prognosis between the two conditions. Nevertheless, Galinsky and Schopler (1994) point out that support groups are not beneficial to everybody and healthcare interventions should be developed to suit the varying social support needs of all patients.

For some patients, their health beliefs influence their choice of treatment location. A venous leg ulcer may represent a medical condition, which, in the patient's view, requires treatment within a 'medical environment', and so the Leg Club may not sit comfortably with their expectations, with its non-medical venue and collective treatment policy. This has also been expressed by some healthcare professionals and may be the result of practising within the 'medical model' of healthcare delivery, where the primary focus is on delivering medical interventions and providing objective outcome measures in terms of complete healing.

The majority of patients who attend Leg Clubs will achieve complete healing of their leg ulcer, as excellent healing rates have been reported (Edwards *et al*, 2004; Edwards *et al*, 2005; Gordon *et al*, 2006). For a small minority of patients, despite appropriate clinical interventions, a healed ulcer may never be an achievable outcome. For such patients, nursing interventions may need to focus on improving their quality of life and, thus, attendance at a Leg Club would appear to achieve that aim.

The question remains: is social capital the theoretical framework that underpins its success or is it due to the health beliefs of those who attend Leg Clubs? We do not currently have the answers to these questions, and further research is required to investigate why some patients benefit from the Leg Club environment while others do not. If we as healthcare professionals wish to deliver truly individualised patient care, should we not be able to offer our patients a choice of where they attend for their leg ulcer management?

References

Bland M (1999) On living with chronic leg ulcers. In: Madjar M, Walton JA, eds. *Nursing and the Experience of Illness: phenomenology in practice*. Routledge Press, London

Bowling A (1991) Social support and social networks — their relationship and the successful and unsuccessful survival of elderly people in the community: an anlysis of concepts and a review of the evidence. *Family Practice* 8(1): 68–83

Bourdieu P (1991) The Forms of Capital. In: Richardson JG, ed. *Handbook of Theory and Research for the Sociology of Education*. Greenwood, New York

Brown A (2003) Social isolation and the management of venous leg ulceration. *J Community Nurs* 17(2): 32–8

Brown A (2005) Chronic venous leg ulcers, part 1: do they affect a patient's social life? *Br J Nurs* 14(17): 894–8

Charles H (1995) The impact of leg ulceration on patients' quality of life. *Professional Nurse* 10(9): 571–4

Charles H (2004) Does leg ulcer treatment improve patients' quality of life? *J Wound Care* 13(6): 209–13

Chase S, Mellori M, Savage A (1997) A forever healing: the lived experience of venous ulcer disease. *J Vasc Nurs* 15(2): 73–7

Coleman JS (1988) Social capital in the creation of human capital. *Am J Sociol* 94: S95–S120

Coleman JS (1990) *Foundations of Social Theory*. Harvard University Press, Cambridge, Massachussetts

Collins R (1994) *Four Sociological Traditions*. Oxford University Press, Oxford

Department of Health (2005) *Supporting people with long-term conditions. An NHS and Social Care model to support local innovation and integration.* DoH, London

Department of Health (2002) *The Expert Patient: a new approach to chronic disease management for the 21st century.* DoH, London

Dines A (1994) A review of lay health beliefs research: insights for nursing practice in health promotion. *J Clin Nurs* **3**: 329–38

Ervin NE, Nelson LL (1999) Preventing adverse outcomes: a population focus. *J Nurs Care Qual* **13**: 25–31; 92–3

Edwards H, Courtney M, Finlayson K, Lewis C, Lindsay E, Dumble J (2004) Improved healing rates for chronic venous leg ulceration: pilot study from a randomised, controlled trial of a community nursing intervention. *Int J Nurs Practice* **11**: 169–276

Edwards H, Courtney M, Finlayson K, Lindsay E, Lewis C, *et al* (2005) Chronic venous leg ulcers: effect of a community nursing intervention on pain and healing. *Nurs Standard* **19**(52): 47–54

Flett R, Harcourt B, Alpass F (2003) Psychosocial aspects of chronic lower leg ulceration in the elderly. *West J Nurs Res* **16**(2): 183–92

Franks PJ, Moffatt C (2006) Do clinical and social factors predict quality of life in leg ulceration? *Lower Extremity Wounds* **5**(4): 236–43

Gordon L, Edwards H, Courtney M, *et al* (2006) A cost-effectiveness analysis of 2 community models of care for patients with venous leg ulcers. *J Wound Care* **15**(8): 348–53

Galinsky MJ, Schopler JH (1994) Negative experiences in support groups. *Soc Work Health Care* **20**(1): 77–95

Hamer C, Cullum NA, Roe BH (1994) Patients' perceptions of chronic leg ulcers. *J Wound Care* **3**(2): 99–101

Hean S, Cowley S, Forbes A, Griffiths P, Maben J (2003) The 'M-C-M' cycle and social capital. *Soc Sci Med* **56**: 1061–72

Hyland ME, Ley AM, Thompson B (1994) Quality of life of leg ulcer patients: questionnaire and preliminary findings. *J Wound Care* **3**(6): 294–8

Krasner D (1998) Painful venous ulcers: themes and stories about the impact on quality of life. *Ostomy/Wound Management* **44**(9): 38–49

Kritsotakis G, Gamarnikow E (2004) What is social capital and how does it relate to health? *Int J Nurs Stud* **41**: 43–50

Labonte R (1999) Social capital and community development: Practitioner emptor. *Aust J Public Health* **23**(4): 430–3

Liew IH, Law KA, Sinha S (200) Do leg ulcer clinics improve patients' quality of life? _J Wound Care_ **9**(9): 423–6

Lindsay E (1999) Show a leg. _Nurs Times_ **95**(11): 67–73

Macinko J, Starfield B (2001) The utility of social capital in research on health determinants. _Milbank Q_ **79**(3): 387–427

Morgan P, Franks PJ, Moffatt C, Doherty DC, _et al_ (2004) Illness behaviour and social support in patients with chronic venous ulcers._Ostomy/ Wound Management_ **50**(1): 25–32

Mudge F, Holloway S, Simmonds W, Price P (2006) Living with venous leg ulceration: issues concerning adherence. _Br J Nurs_ **13**(15): 1166–71

Palmer I (1995) Healing the mind as well as the body. _Community Nurse_ **1**: 18–20

Pesut JD (2002) Awakening social capital. _Nurs Outlook_ **50**: 3

Philips T, Stanton B, Provan A, Lew R (1994) A study of the impact of leg ulcers on quality of life. Financial, social and psychological implications. _J Am Acad Dermatol_ **31**(1): 49–53

Portes A, Landolt P (1996) The downside of social capital. _The American Prospect_ 26 May–June. Available online at: www.prospect.org/ archives/26/26-cnt2/html

Preston RM (1997) Ethnography: studying the fate of health promotion in coronary families. _J Adv Nurs_ **25**: 554–61

Putnam R (2000) _Bowling alone. The Collapse and Revival of American Community_. Simon and Schuster, New York

Rich A, McLachlan L (2002) How living with a leg ulcer affects peoples' daily lives — a nurse-led study. _J Wound Care_ **12**(2): 51–4

Schwarz RS, Olds J (1997) Loneliness in psychosocial issues. _Harvard Rev Psychiatry_ **5**: 94–8

Subramaniam V, Stewart MW, Smith J (1999) The development and impact of a chronic pain support group: a qualitative and quantitative study. _J Pain Symptom Management_ **17**(5): 376–83

Townsend P (1963) _The Family Life of Old People_. Penguin Books, London

Veenstra G (2000) Social capital, SES and health: an individual-level analysis. _Soc Sci Med_ **50**: 619–29

Victor C, Scambler S, Bond J, Bowling A (2002) Loneliness in later life: preliminary findings from the Growing Older project. _Ageing Policy Practice Res_ **3**(1): 34–41

Walshe C (1995) Living with a venous leg ulcer: a descriptive study of patients' experiences. _J Adv Nurs_ **22**: 1092–1100

Wise G (1986) The social ulcer. _Nurs Times_ May 21: 47–9

Section III: Practical issues

CHAPTER 12

UNDERSTANDING COMPRESSION THERAPY

Joan Enric Torra i Bou and Christine Moffatt

This chapter focuses on the use of compression therapy in patients with venous or mixed ulcers. Compression therapy is a basic step in the holistic approach to patients with leg ulcers, and has been used for a long time. Hippocrates was already referring to the use of dressings around the year 450 BC; Guy de Chauliac described the use of compression therapy for the treatment of venous ulcers in his work *Chirurgica magna*, published in 1363 (Hohlbaum, 1999).

To analyse in depth the effect of compression therapy in the treatment of leg ulcer patients, the following aspects will be examined in this chapter:

- anatomy of the venous system
- physiopathology of venous ulcers
- treatment of venous ulcers
- venous ulcers and compression therapy
- skin care in patients who use compression
- what to do after the ulcer has gone.

Anatomy of the venous system

The venous system is a fundamental part of the circulatory system. Its function is to return blood to the heart. Anatomically, the venous system is divided into the deep vein system, which is protected by muscle and bone structures, and the superficial venous system, which is situated above the muscular fasciae. Communication between both systems is achieved by anastomosis.

The veins, the basic element of the venous system, are highly flexible and on the interior have valves that prevent the backflow of blood.

The venous system in the lower limbs has a series of characteristics that are of great importance in understanding how venous ulcers arise, namely:

- the presence of one-way valves, ie. valves which, under normal circumstances, allow circulation in one direction only
- the return of venous blood in the lower limbs is assisted by the action of the muscles that make up the so-called calf and foot pumps
- the increase in pressure in the superficial venous system due to valve insufficiency is responsible for the dilation of the superficial veins (varicose veins), resulting in a risk of ulceration and haemorrhage.

Blood circulating through the venous system is continuously subjected to an external pressure corresponding to the column of blood between the foot and the right atrium as a result of the effect of gravity. When standing, blood pressure in the ankles is thus approximately 80–100 mmHg (Partsch, 2003; Moffatt, 2007). When walking, these levels can decrease to 10–20 mmHg (*Figure 12.1*; Moffatt, 2007).

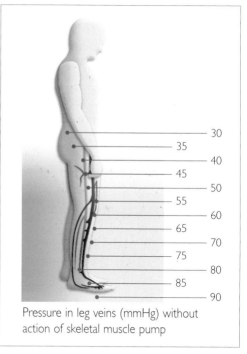

Pressure in leg veins (mmHg) without action of skeletal muscle pump

Figure 12.1: Weight of the column of blood

Physiopathology of venous ulcers

Venous ulcers are a result of chronic venous insufficiency (CVI). This can arise because of primary varicosis, when the lumina of the superficial and perforating veins dilate and the valves are insufficient. It can also result from post-thrombotic syndrome with decompensated subfascial veins, this being the most common cause of venous ulcers (VU).

Circulatory disease of the veins in the lower limbs manifests as one or more of the following symptoms: heaviness, pain, pruritus, fatigue, muscle cramp and swelling in the lower limbs, which worsen with orthostatism or heat and improve with decubitus or cold.

If the venous system fails, this manifests as severe skin abnormalities that can range from oedema to trophic disorder, such as atrophie blanche, ochre dermatitis and venous ulcers.

A deficiency in returning blood to the heart caused by venous insufficiency translates to an increase in venous pressure in the lower limbs. This overload secondarily affects the lymphatic system because of an increase in exudate in the interstitial spaces, which this system is not capable of counteracting. This causes a considerable disruption to the metabolism, which can trigger fibrotic, degenerative and inflammatory processes.

The inflammatory processes affect the venules and arterioles and promote the development of venous ulcers, as a visible sign of the existence of decompensated venous hypertension.

A lower limb with venous insufficiency has various characteristics and processes which can interact to cause a skin lesion and, in this case, is called a venous ulcer (_Figure 12.2_).

The mechanism by which venous ulcers are produced can have various origins. In a large number of cases, the trigger is an external trauma combined with primary varicosis.

There are various theories about the formation of venous ulcers in relation to the organism's metabolic processes. The first, described by Coleridge _et al_ (1988), is known as the platelet aggregation theory (_Figure 12.3_); the second, described by Browse and Burnard in 1982, is the fibrin cuff theory (_Figure 12.4_) (Browse and Burnand, 1982) and, finally, Herrick _et al_ (1992) described a combination of the above theories whereby, following prolonged hypertension in the lower limbs, messengers such as cytokines are released for other cells, stimulating the haemostatic process and causing the synthesis of a fibrin cuff. This inhibits angiogenesis, limiting the oxygen and nutrient supply to the affected region, resulting in tissue damage and the onset of a venous ulcer.

In a discussion of the physiopathology of venous ulcers, the important role played by the lymphatic system in the lower limbs must not be forgotten. This was described by Mortimer (1995) when he showed that leg oedema is caused by a defect in capillary filtration and the drainage capacity of the lymphatic system.

Therefore, lymphoedema can be described as oedema resulting from a lymphatic system failure. Prolonged oedema causes an accumulation of protein molecules in the tissues, which causes skin abnormalities. This problem may be due to two main situations:

- *Primary failure:* no extrinsic causes (eg. a congenital absence of lymph vessels)
- *Secondary failure:* due to extrinsic factors such as infection, bacterial lymphangitis, cellulitis, surgery, tumours and radiotherapy.

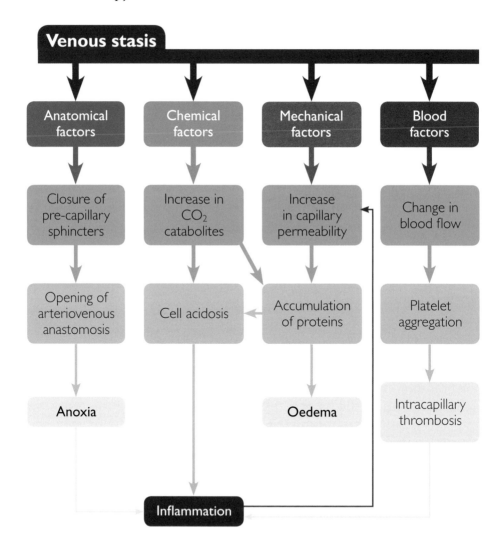

Figure 12.2: The physiopathology of venous ulcers (Soldevilla *et al*, 2004; Rueda *et al*, 2004)

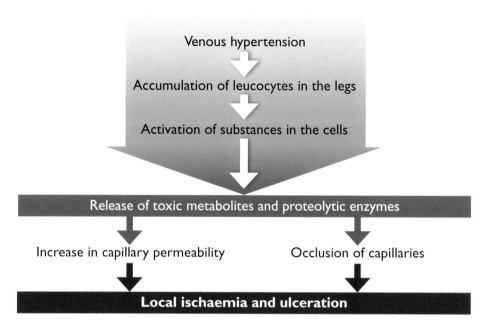

Figure 12.3: Leucocyte aggregation theory (Coleridge *et al*, 1988)

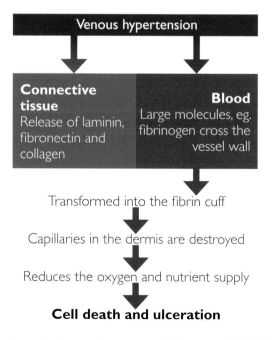

Figure 12.4: Fibrin cuff theory (Browse and Burnand, 1982)

Lymphoedema is common in patients with chronic venous ulcers. In this process there are two predisposing factors: an increase in capillary filtration as a result of venous hypertension on the one hand, and a lack of drainage from the lymphatic system on the other.

The severity and persistence of the venous return defect, as well as the grade and duration of the overload to the venous system in the legs, determine the various clinical pictures of venous disease (Gericke, 1997; Abenhaim *et al*, 1994; Widmer, 1978). These are grouped under the term chronic venous insufficiency and are usually classed in three levels of severity according to Widmer (1978) (*Table 12.1*).

Table 12.1: Levels of chronic venous insufficiency (Widmer, 1978)	
Grade I	Branched veins around the ankle and arch of the foot. With or without malleolar oedema
Grade II	Hyperpigmentation of the skin, oedema in the leg, and dermatolipodystrophy (white atrophy or atrophy blanche)
Grade III	Open venous ulcer at the perimalleolar region or gaiter region

A venous ulcer is the highest grade of venous insufficiency, regardless of its classification.

Venous ulcers usually appear in the internal supramalleolar region, although they may also appear in the external region or slightly above the mid-calf. They vary in size and are typically not very painful, but this symptom must in no way be used in a differential diagnosis.

Venous ulcers are the result of a series of disorders that affect the returning blood flow, such as:

- prolonged venous hypertension in the lower limbs, of which oedema is the most obvious symptom
- functional deficiency of the venous valves, which, together with the effect of the hypertension, cause dilation of the veins, giving rise to varicose veins
- thrombophlebitis, which causes an increase in blood flow through the deep vein system, which in the perilesional region translates to trophic changes with eczematous dermatitis, ochre pigmentation and dermatolipodystrophy
- deep vein thrombosis (DVT) or thrombophlebitis (Morrison and Moffatt, 1994; Rodrigo and Villa, 2002; Botella *et al*, 2000) is responsible for 50% of lesions of venous origin. It is usually

located on the internal malleolar region (in the area of Cockett's perforating veins). This disease generates changes in the skin and causes oedema, giving the limb the appearance of an inverted 'champagne bottle'. This is known as Cornwall's ulcer (Cornwall *et al*, 1986).

Ulcers of venous aetiology can be classified as varicose ulcers, postphlebitic ulcers or stasis ulcers. The diagnosis of venous ulcers is based on various elements (*Chapter 15*).

Treatment of venous ulcers

The treatment of venous and mixed (arteriovenous) ulcers of the lower limbs is based on both local and systemic measures to treat the underlying disease.

Local treatment includes measures such as cleansing and debridement of the devitalised tissue, as well as the use of dressings that promote optimum healing of the wounds and, if appropriate, healing of the wound in a moist environment. The TIME method is an extremely useful tool in the local

> T – tissue non-viable or deficient
> I – infection or inflammation
> M – moisture imbalance
> E – edge of wound non-advancing or undermined

Figure 12.5: The acronym TIME to describe some common clinical observations in chronic wounds

treatment of leg ulcers (*Figure 12.5*), allowing the wound bed to be prepared adequately (Schultz *et al*, 2004; Fletcher, 2005; Dowsett and Ayello, 2004).

Among local treatments, and considering the aetio-pathogenesis of venous ulcers, compression is a basic strategy for the treatment of these wounds since it reverses the effects of the cause and optimises the care of the wounds.

Venous ulcers and compression therapy

According to the available evidence, the treatment of venous ulcers is based on two mainstays: management of the ulcer as a chronic wound and management of venous hypertension, its main cause, using sustained and decreasing high-pressure systems (Torra *et al*, 2003).

With regard to the cause of venous ulcers, ie. the cascade of events that are triggered by venous hypertension in the distal third of the leg, which greatly limits the venous circulation, external compression is a fundamental approach to treatment, as it allows a great improvement in the venous return, effectively acting on the aetiology of the venous ulcer (Morrison and Moffatt, 1994; Gardon-Mollard, 1999).

Compression therapy, used for over 300 years in the treatment of venous ulcers (Alexander House Group, 1992; Alos *et al*, 2003), pursues two major objectives: to control the oedema and to reverse the effect of venous hypertension (Ruckley, 1992). In practice, suitable compression allows the following (Chaveau, 1999; Williams *et al*, 1999; Partsch, 2000; Kunimoto, 2001; Partsch, 2002; Partsch, 2003; Clark, 2003):

- reduction of the calibre of the superficial and deep veins and promotion of venous flow, reducing the local volume of blood, and redistribution of the blood to central compartments of the body (*Figure 12.6*)
- acceleration of the venous flow by reducing the diameter of the vessels and increasing velocity
- reduction in the distension in the superficial veins to counteract the effect of the increase in pressure
- reduction of the oedema by mechanically returning fluids to the lymph vessels and veins
- improvement in the effect of the calf muscle pump to increase venous return (*Figure 12.7*)

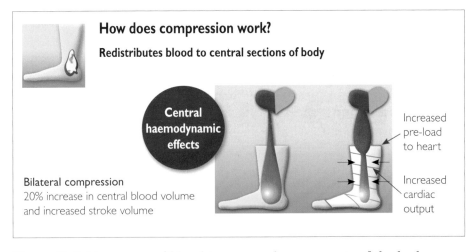

Figure 12.6: Movement of blood into central components of the body

- reduction in orthostatic reflux, the residual volume and venous pressure by facilitating the performance of the venous valves (*Figure 12.8*)
- reduction in the symptomatology of venous dysfunction, such as heaviness, pain, etc.

Compression therapy is based on the use of a number of devices, bandages and stockings or socks, made with textile products with the appropriate elastic properties. The arrangement of fibres in each of these systems allows differing levels of pressure to be achieved (Gardon-Mollard, 1999; Giménez *et al*, 2003).

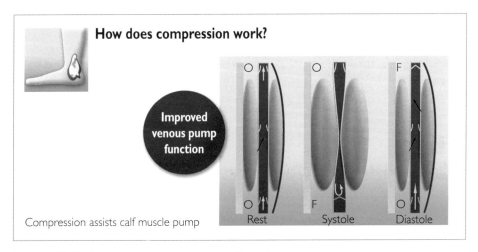

Figure 12.7: Improved venous pump function

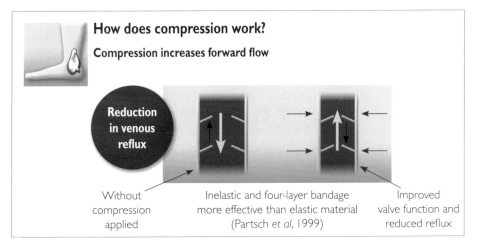

Figure 12.8: Reduction in venous reflex

There is no single European standard that classifies the various compression systems. *Table* 12.2 gives a summary of the various classifications of elastic compression.

Table 12.2: Classification systems for elastic compression stockings				
Name of grade of compression in Spain (Ferrer *et al*, 2003)	Pressure at ankle according to Hohenstein's method (Aznar, 2002)	Pressure at ankle according to Hatra's method (Aznar, 2002)	Federal Association of Panel doctors of the German Federal Republic (Partsch, 2000)	Indications (Partsch, 2000; Aznar, 2002)
Normal compression (I) 22–29 mmHg	Slight compression 18–21 mmHg	Slight compression 11–16 mmHg	Slight compression (I) about 20 mmHg	Varicose veins measuring 0.1–1 mm Prevention of varicose veins in persons at risk Sensation of heaviness and fatigue in the limbs
Tight compression (II) 30–40 mmHg	Normal compression 20–29 mmHg	Normal compression 13–23 mmHg	Moderate compression (II) about 30 mmHg	Varicose veins measuring 0.5–1 cm with or without mild oedema Predisposition to or presence of varicose veins during pregnancy Following healing of venous ulcers, superficial thrombophlebitis, sclerotherapy and venous surgery
Very tight compression (III) >40 mmHg	Tight compression 30–40 mmHg	Tight compression 23–33 mmHg	Tight compression (III) about 40 mmHg	Following varicose vein surgery Postphlebitic syndrome Venous insufficiency with resistant oedema, secondary varicosis, white atrophy and dermatosclerosis. Following healing of considerable venous ulcers
			Extremely tight compression (IV)	Lymphoedema and elephantiasis

As far as compression bandages are concerned, the level of compression produced by a given system for a given period of time is due to complex interactions between four factors (Clark, 2003; Marinel lo *et al*, 2003; Cahuveau, 1999):

- the physical structure and elastomeric properties of the bandage
- the dimensions of the leg to which it will be applied
- the skill and competence in the bandaging technique of the person who applies the bandage
- the level of physical activity of the patient in terms of walking.

Laplace's law explains how compression bandaging functions: **P: T/R** (where **P** is the pressure, **T** is the tension and **R** is the radius) and we can summarise this by saying more simply: The pressure applied (to the limb) is directly proportional to the tension of the bandage (force applied), but inversely proportional to the radius of the curvature of the limb to which it is applied (**P** increases as **T** increases but **P** decreases as **R** increases) (Partsch, 2002). *Figure 12.9* shows the extended version of Laplace's law.

The pressure exerted by a bandage can be calculated by using the following equation:

$$P = \frac{N \; T \; K}{C \; W}$$

Where:
P = pressure exerted by the bandage in mmHg
T = tension of the bandage
N = number of layers
C = circumference of the limbs
W = thickness of the bandage
K = constant (4630)

Figure 12.9: Laplace's law

As with compression stockings, there is no European consensus on the levels of pressure that various types of bandage can achieve. *Table 12.3* summarises these.

As far as the elasticity of compression bandages is concerned, we can divide these into inelastic and elastic systems.

Inelastic compression (short stretch) is based on the application of a rigid bandage around the leg. This compression system is effective when the patient walks since muscle contraction improves vein emptying, but it is not effective when the patient is at rest. The efficacy of the inelastic compression system is related to the tension used during application. It is made up of a bandage impregnated with zinc paste or adhesive, known as 'Unna's boot'. The Viscopaste® PB7 (Smith and Nephew) bandage is also marketed, as are the magistral formulae of the Unna paste (Fronek, 2007; Stacey *et al*, 2002).

Table 12.3: Classification systems for elastic compression bandages		
English standard (British Standards Institute, 1995)	German standard (Detusches Institut für Gütesicherung und Kennzeichnung Medizinische Kompressionsstrümpfe RAL-GZ 387)	Indications (Dale, 1995)
Slight compression I (3A) up to 20 mmHg	Slight compression (1) 18.4–21.2 mmHg	Treatment of superficial or early varicose veins and varicosis that developed during pregnancy
Moderate compression (3B) 21–30 mmHg	Moderate compression (2) 25.1–32.1 mmHg	Treatment of varicose veins during pregnancy, moderate varicose veins, as well as the prevention and treatment of venous ulcers and treatment of moderate oedema
High compression (3C) 31–40 mmHg	High compression (3) 36.4–46.5 mmHg	Treatment of large varicose veins, post-thrombotic venous insufficiency, and considerable oedema
Very high compression (3D) 41–60 mmHg	Very high compression (4) >59 mmHg	Treatment of lymphoedema and considerable oedema

This type of compression can be applied by:

- *Bandages*: their efficacy depends on the skill in application, they are usually made up of one or two layers.
- *'Unna's boot', Viscopaste® PB87*: application of a bandage with paste. This system is effective, even on mixed lesions, but a problem arises in the bandage fitting to the limb when the oedema subsides. Removing the bandage may cause lesions and there is a risk of allergy. When a short-stretch bandage is applied it behaves like a rigid compression system. It must be applied by specialised professionals.
- *'Circ-Aid'*: a series of nylon strips that surround the leg and are adjusted with Velcro®.

Elastic compression (long stretch) is based on the application of a compression system that is active when the patient is at rest and when active. There is a large variety of bandages on the market, eg. Setopress[TM] and Suropress[TM] (ConvaTec) and Tensopress[TM] (Smith and Nephew) which, being single-layer systems, require application by specialised personnel. Not all achieve a therapeutic level of pressure for the treatment of venous ulcers. The recommended pressure for the treatment of this type of ulcer is 35–40 mmHg at the ankle to reverse the effect of venous hypertension.

Pneumatic compression pumps are indicated in addition to other compression methods; they were initially developed to prevent deep vein thrombosis, but their indications have extended to lymphoedema, severe oedema and venous ulcers.

It is a device made up of a compressor and a pneumatic boot that applies a cyclical pressure, which can reach a maximum level of 90 mmHg. It is indicated in patients who cannot tolerate other types of compression and is completely contraindicated in patients with arterial disease and acute deep vein thrombosis.

The Royal College of Nursing (RCN) of the United Kingdom (RCN, 1998) has established the following recommendations on the treatment of venous leg ulcers and compression:

> *Multilayer high compression systems (including short-stretch regimens) with adequate padding, capable of sustaining compression for at least a week (heavily exuding ulcers may require more frequent changes) should be the first line of treatment for uncomplicated venous ulcers (APBI must be ≥ 0.8).*

The Scottish Intercollegiate Guidelines Network (SIGN) guide on the care of patients with chronic leg ulcers (SIGN, 1998) includes various recommendations relating to venous ulcers:

- gradual compression should be used (more compression at the ankle that decreases towards the knee) in order to improve venous insufficiency (level B, evidence levels IIa and IIb)[1]
- gradual compression should be used to heal uncomplicated venous ulcers (level A, evidence level Ia)
- elastic compression is the first choice for uncomplicated venous ulcers (level A, evidence level Ib)
- multilayer bandage systems are recommended (level A, evidence level Ia).

A systematic review by the NHS Centre for Reviews and Dissemination of the University of York (1997), supports the use of high compression systems (40 mmHg at the ankle) for the treatment of venous ulcers and reported the results of a clinical trial with a large sample, and two trials with small samples which showed there to be a higher percentage of fully healed venous ulcers after 24 weeks of treatment with a four-layer system versus low compression or single-layer bandages.

A systematic review published recently with the collaboration of Cochrane was able to establish that ulcers treated with compression had better results than those treated without compression, and that multilayer compression systems, which allowed high levels of pressure to be achieved, were more effective than low pressure or single-layer systems (Cullum *et al*, 2001; Franks and Posnett, 2003).

The origin of the multilayer compression system lies in the increasing attention being paid to venous ulcers in the United Kingdom in the mid-1980s, which brought about care structures that allowed two major objectives to be achieved: to treat patients in the community and to enable patients to be treated by non-specialist personnel using systems with a good cost/benefit/efficacy ratio.

The outcome of this new approach has been put into practice in community venous ulcer clinics (Moffatt *et al*, 1992; Bosanquet *et al*, 1993; Franks *et al*, 1994; Moffatt and Oldroyd, 1994; Freak *et al*, 1995; Taylor *et al*, 1998). Continuing this sequence of events and in response to the need for an effective compression system easily applicable in non-specialist settings, in 1987 Charing Cross hospital in London developed a multilayer bandaging system that allowed the compressive properties of various bandages existing on the market to be combined (King's Fund, 1988; Moffatt and Stubbings, 1990; Bosanquet *et al*, 1993; Franks *et al*, 1994) and acceptable levels of pressure to be achieved. The Charing Cross multilayer system proved to be very effective in the treatment of venous ulcers

1. Evidence levels of the Scottish Intercollegiate Guidelines Network

Level A:

Ia: Evidence obtained from meta-analysis of randomised clinical trials
Ib: Evidence obtained from at least one randomised clinical trial

Level B:

IIa: Evidence obtained from at least one good controlled study without randomisation
IIb: Evidence obtained from at least one other type of well-designed quasi-experimental study
III: Evidence obtained from non-experimental descriptive studies, such as comparative studies, correlation studies and case studies

Level C:

IV: Evidence obtained from the expert committee report or opinions and/or clinical experiences of persons of recognised authority and subsequently, based on this system, specific kits started to be developed for multilayer compression.

The first of these specific systems was the Profore™ multilayer compression bandage developed by Smith and Nephew that enables effective, gradual, sustained pressure to be applied. This bandaging regimen applies a pressure of 40 mmHg at the ankle, which decreases to 17 mmHg under the knee, leaving the bed of the ulcer in optimum conditions for healing (Blair *et al*, 1988; Becker and Molland, 1995). The system is usually applied and maintained stable for seven days, keeping the pressure constant (Moffatt *et al*, 1992), and allowing the patients to carry out their activities of daily living (ADL) as much as possible. The levels of pressure achieved by this system make it incompatible with arterial insufficiency. For this reason, its use is conditional upon the diagnosis of venous ulceration and verification by Doppler ultrasound that the patient does not have severe arterial insufficiency.

It functions based on the use of four layers of bandage that allow the necessary levels of pressure under the bandage to be reached for effective treatment of the venous ulcer (Nelson, 1996; Moffatt and O'Hare, 1995). The arrangement of the multilayer system prevents problems relating to excessive pressure and its positioning is easier and more comfortable than any other compression system for healthcare professionals who are not used to compression therapy. The different presentations of the system, suited to various ankle diameters, can be used on all patients with venous problems.

For patients with moderate arterial insufficiency, specific multilayer presentation systems exist that exert a reduced pressure of 23 mmHg. Greater supervision of the patient is advised because of the arterial insufficiency. Patients with diabetes should be examined by a vascular surgeon or specialist before any type of compression is applied, as neither arterial insufficiency nor calcification can be detected by examinations carried out by non-specialist professionals (Becker and Molland, 1995).

According to the literature, the Profore™ multilayer system has been clinically shown to have an 80% healing rate at 12 weeks of treatment (Moffatt and O'Hare, 1995), making it the most effective existing treatment so far for the management of venous ulcers, with sufficient clinical evidence to prove its efficacy both clinically and in terms of improvement in the quality of life of patients who suffer this type of lesion (Torra *et al*, 2003).

Multilayer systems with two layers have subsequently appeared on the market such as Proguide™ (Smith and Nephew), a system based on the use of advanced elastomers in the elastic bandage that allow effective, safe, and sustained levels of pressure to be reached, and the 3M Coban™ system.

In summary, the ideal requirements of a compression system are those that (Moffatt, 1997; Moffatt, 2002):

- provide clinical efficacy
- allow effective levels of compression to be achieved for periods of at least one week
- promote the action of the calf muscle pump
- are made from non-allergenic products
- are easy to apply and remove
- are flexible and comfortable (does not slip)
- are durable.

Skin care in patients who use compression

However an effective compression system reduces the oedema and therefore the volume of the limb, the skin of patients wearing compression requires specific care involving adequate hydration. For this purpose, lanolin-free moisturisers or hyperoxygenated fatty acids in lotion form (Mepentol milk) can be used. They improve the fatty layer of the skin and reduce the effect of anoxia and free radicals. There is a large amount of experience on their use both in pressure ulcers (Declair, 1997; Torra i Bou *et al*, 2005; Segovia *et al*, 2001; Torra i Bou *et al*, 2003) and, more recently, in vascular and diabetic foot ulcers (Puentes *et al*, 2006).

In the case of heavily exudating ulcers, it can be very useful to protect the skin around the wound with barrier creams containing zinc oxide (Triple Care Cream or Triple Care EPC).

What to do after the ulcer has gone

Once the venous ulcer has healed, the care team must evaluate the possibility of correcting its cause and consider if surgical measures would be possible that would re-establish full vein function.

If this is not possible, it is important that the patient follows the following recommendations:

- maximising local care of vulnerable areas with lanolin-free moisturisers or hyperoxygenated fatty acid products
- using special stockings or socks that allow high levels of compression to be achieved (to reverse the venous insufficiency)
- avoiding involuntary trauma to the vulnerable areas.

The perseverance of the patient and the care team in telling people about these preventative measures and in following them are fundamental to preventing relapse.

References

Abenhaim M, Clément D, Norgren L, *et al* (1994) The management of chronic disorders of the leg: an evidence-based report an international task force. *Phlebology* **14**(suppl 2): 1–26

Alexander House Group (1992) Consensus paper on venous leg ulcers. *Phlebology* **7**: 48–55

Alós J, Moga JL, Rubio P (2003) Referentes históricos de la terapéutica de compresión. En: Marinel lo Roura J, ed. *Terapéutica de compresión en patología venosa y linfática*. Editorial Glosa, Barcelona

Aznar GMA (2002) *La úlcera venosa. Pautas para su tratamiento.* Universidad Católica San Antonio, Murcia

Becker F, Molland JM, *et al* (1995) Contention elástique et arteriopathie des members inférieurs. *Phebologie* **48**(1): 83–5

Blair SD, Wright DI, Backhouse CM, Riddle E, McCollum N (1988) Sustained compression and healing of chronic venous ulcers. *Br Med J* **297**: 1159–61

Bosanquet N, Franks P, Moffatt C, *et al* (1993) Community leg ulcer clinics: Cost effectiveness. *Health Trends* **25**: 146–8

Botella FG, Labiós Gómez M, Brasó Aznar JV (2000) Trombosis venosa profunda: presente y futuro. *Med Clin (Barcelona)* **114**: 584–96

British Standards Institute (1995) Specification of the elastic properties of flat, non-adhesive, extensible fabric bandages. BS 7505. British Standards Institute, London

Browse NL, Burnand KG (1982) The cause of venous ulceration. *Lancet* **II**: 243–45

Cahuveau M (1999) Effects of compression on venous haemodynamics. In: Gardon-Mollard C, Ramelet AA, eds. *Compression therapy*. Masson, Paris

Chaveau M (1999) Effects of compression on venous haemodynamics. In: Gardon-Mollard C, Ramelet AA, eds. *Compression Therapy*. Masson, Paris

Clark M (2003) Compression bandages: principles and definitions. In: *Understanding compression therapy*. EWMA Position document. London: MEP Ltd, 2003

Coleridge SPD, Thomas P, Scurr J H, Dormandy JA (1988) Causes of venous ulceration: a new hypothesis. *Br Med J* **296**: 1726–7

Cornwall J, Dore C J, Lewis JD (1986) Leg ulcers: epidemiology and aetiology. *Br J Surgery* **73**: 693–6

Cullum N, Nelson EA, Fletcher AW, *et al* (2001) *Compression bandages and stockings for venous leg ulcers*. Cochrane Database of Systematic Reviews 2001, Issue 2. Art No: CD000265

Dale J (1995) The anatomy and physiology of the circulation of the legs. In: Cullum N, Roe B, eds. *Leg Ulcers: nursing management — a research-based guide*. Scutari, London

Declair V. The usefulness of topical application of essential-fatty acids (EFA) to prevent pressure ulcers. *Ostomy/Wound Management* **43**(5): 48–54

Deutsches Institut für Gütesicherung und Kennzeichnung Medizinische (1987) Kompressionsstrümpfe RAL-GZ 387. Beuth-Verlag, Berlin

Dowsett C, Ayello E (2004) TIME principles of chronic wound bed preparation and treatment. *Br J Nurs* **13**(15): S16–23

Ferrer C, Gomón P, González R, *et al* (2003) Metodología y criterios de homologación de la terapeútica de compresión. En: Marinel lo Roura J, ed. *Terapeútica de compresión en patología venosa y linfática*. Barcelona: Editorial Glosa, Barcelona

Fletcher J (2005) Wound bed preparation and the TIME principles. *Nurs Standard* **20**(12): 57–65

Franks P, Moffatt CH, Conolly M, *et al* (1994) Community leg ulcers: cost-effectiveness. Health Trends. *Phlebology* **9**: 83–6

Franks PJ, Posnett J (2003) Cost-effectiveness of compression therapy. In: *Understanding compression therapy*. EWMA Position document. London: MEP Ltd, 2003

Freak L, Simon D, Kinsella A, McColum C, Walsh J, Lane C (1995) Leg ulcer care: an audit of cost effectiveness. *Health Trends* **27**: 133–6

Fronek HS (2007) *Conservative therapy for venous disease*. American College of Phlebology, Oakland, CA. Available online: www.phlebology.org/syllabus4.htm (last accessed 1 June 2007)

Gardon-Mollard, Ramelet AA (1999) *Compresión Therapy*. Masson, Paris

Gardon-Mollard C (1999) Textiles used for medical stockings. In: Gardon-Mollard C, Ramelet AA, eds. *Compression therapy*. Masson, Paris

Gericke A (1997) *Diagnóstico y tratamiento de las úlceras venosa*. Wound Forum 2

Giménez A, González R, Halcón M, *et al* (2003) Bases fisiológicas de la terapeútica de compresión. En: Marinel lo Roura J, ed. *Terapeútica de compresión en patología venosa y linfática.* Editorial Glosa, Barcelona

Herrick SE, Sloan P, McGurk M, Freak L, McCullum CN, Ferguson MWJ (1992) Sequential changes in histological pattern and extracellular matrix deposition during the healing of CVI. *Am J Pathol* **141**(5): 1085–95

Hohlbaum GG (1999) History of compression therapy. In: Gardon-Mollard C, Ramelet AA, eds. *Compression Therapy.* Masson, Paris

King's Fund (1988) Grant to help treat leg ulcers (editorial). *Br Med J* **297**: 1412

Kunimoto BT (2001)Management and prevention of venous leg ulcers: A literature guided approach. *Ostomy/Wound Management* **47**(6): 36–49

Marinel lo J, Alós J, Rosendo A (2003) Fundamentos fisiológicos en los que se basa la terapeútica de compresión. En: Marinel lo Roura J, ed. *Terapeútica de compresión en patología venosa y linfática.* Barcelona: Editorial Glosa, Barcelona

Morrison MJ, Moffatt CJ (1994) *A Colour Guide to the Assessment and Management of Leg Ulcers.* 2nd edn. Mosby, London

Mortimer PS (1995) Managing lymphoedema. *Clin Exp Dermatol* **20**: 98–106

Moffatt CHJ (1997) Know how. Four-layer bandaging. *Nurs Times* **93**(16): 82–3

Moffatt CH (2002) Four layer bandaging: From concept to practice. *Low Extrem Wounds* **1**(1): 13–26

Marston W, Vowden K (2003) Compression therapy: a guide to safe practice. In: *Understanding compression therapy.* EWMA Position document. London: MEP Ltd, 2003

Moffatt CH (2007) *Compression Therapy in Practice.* Wounds UK, Aberdeen

Moffatt CH, Franks PJ, Oldroyd M, *et al* (1992) Community clinics for leg ulcers and impact on healing. *Br Med J* **305**: 1389–9

Moffatt CH, Oldroyd M (1994) A pioneering service to the community. The Riverside Community leg ulcer project. *Prof Nurse* **9**(7): 486–90

Moffatt CH, Stubbings N (1990) The Charing Cross approach to venous ulcers. *Nurs Standard* **5**(12): 6–9

Moffatt CHJ. O'Hare L (1995) Venous leg ulceration: Treatment by high compression bandaging. *Ostomy/Wound Management* **41**(4): 16–25

NHS Centre for Reviews and Dissemination, University of York (1997) Compression therapy for venous leg ulcers. *Effective Health Care* **3**(4): 1–12

Nelson EA (1996) Compression bandging in the treatment of venous leg ulcers. *J Wound Care* **5**(9): 415–8

Partsch H (2000) *Contributions towards compression therapy.* Lohmann Rauscher, Neuwied

Partsch H (2002) Compression therapy in venous leg ulcers. How does it work? *J Phlebol* 2(2): 129–36

Partsch H (2003) Understanding the pathophysiological effects of compression. In: *Understanding compression therapy.* EWMA Position document. London: MEP Ltd, 2003

Puentes J, Pardo CM, Pardo MB, Navarro F, Puentes R, Méndez JM, González J (2006) Prevención de úlceras vasculares y pie diabético. Evaluación clínica abierta no aleatorizada sobre la efectividad de Mepentol leche. *Rev Rol Enf* 29(10): 663–8

Rodrígo JA, Villa R (2002) Trombosis venosa. *Guías Clínicas* 2(26):

Royal College of Nursing Institute, Center for Evidence-based Nursing University of York, School of Nursing, Midwifery and Health Visiting, University of Manchester (1998) *Clinical practice guidelines. The management of patients with venous leg ulcers.* RCN, London

Rueda López J, Torra i Bou JE, Arboix i Perejamo M, *et al* (2004) Úlceras venosas. Atención al paciente con úlceras venosas. In: Soldevilla Agreda JJ, Torra i Bou JE, eds. *Atención integral a las heridas crónicas.* SPA, Madrid

Ruckley CV (1992) Treatment of venous ulceration. Compression therapy. *Phlebology* (suppl 1): 22–6

Schultz GS, Barillo DJ, Mozingo DW, Chin GA (2004) Wound bed preparation and a brief history of TIME. *Int Wound J* 1(1): 19–32

Scottish Intercollegiate Guidelines Network (1998) *The care of patients with leg ulcers.* SIGN, Edinburgh

Segovia T, Bermejo M, Rueda J, Torra JE (2001) Cuidados de la piel y úlcera por presión. Los ácidos grasos hiperoxigenados en la prevención de Upp y el tratamiento de lesiones de estadio I. *Rev Rol Enf* 24(9): 578–82

Soldevilla Agreda JJ, Torra i Bou JE, Rueda López J, Arboix i Perejamo M (2004) Etiopatogenia de las úlceras vasculares. In: Soldevilla Agreda JJ, Torra i Bou JE, eds. *Atención integral a las heridas crónicas.* SPA, Madrid

Stacey M, Falange V, Marston W, *et al* (2002) The use of compression therapy in the treatment of venous leg ulcers: a recommended management pathway. *EWMA J* 2(1): 9–13

Taylor AD, Taylor RJ, Marcuson RW (1998) Prospective comparison of healing rates and therapy costs for conventional and four-layer high compression bandaging treatments of venous leg ulcers. *Phlebology* 13: 20–4

Torra JE, Rueda J, Blanco J, Ballester T, Toda L (2003) Úlceras venosas. Sistema de compresión multicapa o venda de crepe? Estudio comparativo sobre la efectividad, coste e impacto en la calidad de vida. *Rev Rol Enf* **26**(6): 59–66

Torra i Bou JE, Segovia Gómez T, Verdú Soriano J, *et al* (2005) The effectiveness of a hyper-oxygenated fatty acid compound in preventing pressure ulcers. *J Wound Care* **14**(3): 117–21

Torra i Bou JE, Rueda López J, Segovia Gómez T, Bermejo Martínez M (2003) Aplicación tópica de un compuesto de ácidos grasos hiperoxigenados. *Rev Rol Enf* **26**(1): 54–61

Widmer LK (1978) *Peripheral venous disorders. Prevalence and sociomedical importance. Basel Study III*. Hans Huber, Bern: 43–50

Williams RJ, Wertheim D, Melhuish J (1999) How compression therapy works. *J Wound Care* **8**(6): 297–8

CHAPTER 13

TRENDS IN COMPRESSION THERAPIES

Michael Clark

Compression, particularly of the legs, is considered to be 'the most important component in the conservative treatment of venous leg ulcers and lymphoedema' (Moffatt *et al*, 2007). There have been many reviews and reports on why compression can benefit oedema management along with leg ulcer healing and help in the prevention of ulcer recurrence (Moffatt, 2007), and it is not the purpose of this chapter to consider the potential modes of action through which compression can help. Accepting that compression can provide marked benefits to patients (Cullum *et al*, 2001), this chapter considers different approaches through which compression can be provided to explore current trends in the utilisation, comparison and classification of different methods of applying compression, namely; compression bandages, compression hosiery and intermittent compression therapy.

Compression bandages and hosiery

Compression bandages probably represent the main intervention for the treatment of venous leg ulcers and have been described in a number of ways depending upon their construction, elasticity and level of compression they apply (*Table 13.1*). None of these systems are ideal and none are in universal use. For example, the use of elasticity to separate different groups of compression bandages typically results in general definitions such as 'elastic' and 'inelastic' bandages, or terms such as 'long' or 'short' stretch are used (Clark, 2003). However, how is elasticity defined, measured and used to classify bandage products? Technically, elasticity can be reported as the maximum stretch achieved by a bandage when a specified force is applied to a known bandage width. This gives a separation of long- and short-stretch bandages, where the maximum stretch of an elastic bandage will be over 100%, while the maximum stretch of an inelastic bandage will be lower than 100%. Such classifications may assist the manufacturer and technical staff but are likely to be of limited, or no value to clinicians, given that the maximum stretch of a bandage is unlikely to be achieved when applying it to the leg with an intended sub-bandage pressure of around 40mmHg (Partsch *et al*, 2006). If a force is applied to a bandage to achieve a sub-bandage pressure of 40mmHg at the ankle, the bandage may stretch by 20–50% for a 'so-called' short-stretch bandage, and by 40–120% for a 'so-called' long-stretch bandage, with the overlap between the two systems negating this approach to classifying bandages into discrete categories (Partsch *et al*, 2006).

Table 13.1: Examples of the terms used to describe compression bandages
● Elastic
● Inelastic
● Rigid
● Stiff
● Long-stretch
● Short-stretch
● Mild compression
● Moderate compression
● High compression
● Single component
● Multi-component
● Single layer
● Multilayer

If there remain challenges regarding the classification of compression bandages, this weakens the ability of the clinician to select appropriate products for use in individual cases. As discussed above, at present there are challenges separating elastic from inelastic systems and this is further compounded by the observation that bandages may perform differently when applied as single layers or as a multilayer bandage system, for example, consider the well-known 'four-layer' system in which each layer may behave as an elastic bandage, but the overall bandage system may be inelastic (Partsch *et al*, 2006).

The preceding discussion regarding the classification of compression bandages highlights the challenges faced by clinicians seeking to select the most appropriate forms of compression bandage. This can be further complicated by the observation that reported sub-bandage pressures are typically higher for a given bandage product applied at different tensions than would be expected from the British Standard 7505: 1985 sub-bandage pressure ranges marking mild, moderate and strong compression (Partsch *et al*, 2006), leaving experts to propose a new classification of mild to very strong compression (*Table 13.2*) based upon sub-bandage pressure measurements.

If the field cannot be confident of the levels of compression applied by different classes of compression bandage and can offer limited classification of bandage and bandage systems based upon their ability to stretch under load, there remains considerable work to be done to derive an internationally agreed format for compression bandage specification and classification. Until such systems are in place, there will remain uncertainty regarding the selection of appropriate compression bandage systems and this can, perhaps, be seen within the limited literature that has compared the effectiveness of different compression bandages and bandage systems.

Cullum *et al* (2001) reported a systematic review of the effect of compression bandages upon venous leg ulcer healing. This review was restricted to randomised controlled trials (n = 20) and controlled clinical trials (n = 2), with the majority of the studies described being at least 12 years old (published in 1995 or before). The review provided three key conclusions:

- compression was more effective than where no compression was applied
- elastic bandages appeared to be more effective than inelastic compression

Table 13.2: Proposed revision of sub-bandage pressures used to mark different levels of compression

Level of compression	Current sub-bandage pressure thresholds (from BS 7505; 1985)	Recommended amendments to bring thresholds in line with *in vivo* pressure measurements
Mild	<20	<20
Moderate	21–30	20–40
Strong	31–40	40–60
Very strong	41–60	>60

Adapted from from Partsch *et al*, 2006

- no apparent differences between the effectiveness of multilayer compression systems.

These conclusions have been frequently reported in discussion of compression bandages (for example, Moffatt *et al*, 2007), and form an apparent foundation for our clinical understanding of the likely effects of different compression bandage systems. There are, of course, weaknesses given the challenges of classifying elastic and inelastic bandage systems and it appears that the comparisons between elastic and inelastic systems reported by Cullum *et al* (n = 3, latest publication date 1992) actually were comparisons between high and low compression systems, rather than strictly elastic or inelastic compression bandages. Where multilayer high compression systems were compared with inelastic bandages (n = 4 studies), there appeared to be no difference in the effectiveness of these approaches to providing adequate compression. It would appear that Cullum *et al's* (2001) second conclusion that elastic bandage systems are more effective than inelastic ones may be too strong, with the difference being negligible between multilayer (elasticity unreported) and inelastic systems, and unproven between elastic and inelastic bandages. These confusions highlight the challenges faced by clinicians when attempting to identify effective bandage systems in the absence of clear, clinically relevant classifications of the available bandage systems. Of course, the Cullum *et al* review could only consider publications to the end of the last century and further work has emerged since then. Of these, perhaps one of the most relevant was the VenUS I trial (Nelson *et al*, 2004), which reported a randomised controlled trial that compared the effects of the four-layer bandage system with an inelastic bandage system. In this study, the venous leg ulcers treated with the inelastic system had a lower probability of healing, with more adverse events and withdrawals within the inelastic group. However, other studies have reported contradictory findings, for example, Partsch *et al* (2001) noted that the leg ulcer healing rate or median time to healing did not differ among people treated with four-layer and inelastic bandages. Some of these apparent differences may mark the statistical handling of the data, for Nelson *et al* (2004) also found no apparent difference between the median time to healing between the four-layer and inelastic bandage groups when unadjusted data was used to undertake the analysis, with the difference between the four-layer and inelastic groups appearing only upon inclusion of prognostic factors within their regression model. This again highlights the challenge for clinicians attempting to identify the most effective compression bandage systems, given the growing complexity and subtlety of the statistical analyses performed upon the growing body of controlled and randomised clinical trials that compare different bandage systems.

From the above, it is evident that there remains confusion regarding the most effective form of compression bandage system. There is a need for the existing systematic reviews to be updated to include the growing body of literature comparing different compression bandages. Clinical comparisons will be clarified if there is an underlying agreed system for describing and classifying compression bandages, thus allowing valid comparison groups to be established when planning future trials.

One possible approach to clarifying the performance (and hence classification) of compression bandages may be to include a new measure of their physical effect to supplement reported sub-bandage pressures. This new measure, stiffness, records the change in sub-bandage pressure, as the bandaged leg changes in volume either while walking or through changes in static posture (Partsch *et al*, 2006; Partsch, 2007). A high stiffness value means that increases in limb circumference produce greater sub-bandage pressures potentially beneficial to the management of venous leg ulcers. While the measurement of stiffness could be technically challenging given that it may (in research terms) require dynamic measurement of changes in limb volume, a simple test has been proposed in which static stiffness can be measured as the change in sub-bandage pressure that occurs when the person with the bandaged leg stands having been in a seated position (Partsch, 2005). Such stiffness indices could be used to classify bandage systems (Partsch *et al*, 2006) where inelastic bandage systems produce a change in sub-bandage pressure of less than 10mmHg on standing, while elastic systems give rise to greater than 10mmHg difference between the seated and standing sub-bandage pressures. One future trend may be that the terminology for compression bandages will shift from descriptions based on elasticity, to systems founded on stiffness (Partsch, 2007).

All of the above discussion regarding the challenges of defining and evaluating compression bandages becomes truly academic if bandages are not used to manage venous leg ulcers. In 2001, the UK Royal College of Nursing reported an audit of leg ulcer management across fourteen sites with data collected in early 1999, and then repeated after local support for implementation of appropriate clinical practice guidelines in early 2000 (Royal College of Nursing [RCN],

2001). Within the first audit, 80.1% of all venous leg ulcers reported upon received compression, with this percentage rising to 91.5% in the second audit. While this rise in the use of compression is encouraging, there remained 6.5% of patients who did not receive any compression, even during the second audit phase. Of equivalent concern was the observation that 25/28 (first audit) and 30/31 (second audit) of patients with evidence of arterial disease also received lower leg compression. It is interesting to note that the sites audited by the RCN formed a random stratified sample of volunteer institutions — it might have been expected that these centres considered themselves proficient in leg ulcer management prior to volunteering to participate. Regardless, almost 20% of patients in the first audit and 6.5% in the second did not receive compression and, in many cases, compression was perhaps applied inappropriately (presence of arterial disease). These results indicate that prior to over-emphasis upon classification and evaluation, there remains a need for further education regarding the importance of compression bandaging.

Many of the challenges posed by the use, evaluation and classification of compression bandages also apply to compression hosiery. For example, within the RCN audit, questions were posed on whether compression hosiery was provided to patients with healed ulcers (to help prevent recurrence) and, where provided, was education given regarding the correct use of the hosiery? For both questions, almost half of all audit forms contained missing data, for example, in the first audit, 49.8% of all returned forms did not indicate whether compression hosiery had or had not been provided. By the time of the second audit a year later, this proportion of missing information fell to 42.2%. It is unclear what the widespread failure to answer questions related to the use of compression hosiery indicated. Where responses were given, compression hosiery was often provided to patients with healed ulcers — 84.3% in the first audit and 89.7 in the second. This meant that almost 16% of patients with healed ulcers were not provided with compression hosiery at the time of the first audit, potentially giving rise to recurrence of the leg ulcers at a future date. Interestingly, education regarding the use of compression hosiery was provided to 86% (first audit) and 96.9% (second audit), indicating that some patients with healed leg ulcers were educated about the use of compression hosiery, but then not provided with the hosiery. While the use of compression hosiery is widely considered to help prevent the recurrence of leg ulcers, the evidence underpinning this is relatively weak (Nelson *et al*, 2000; Moffatt *et al*, 2007), based upon two randomised controlled trials. Neither study compared recurrence rates with and without compression and, given the strong belief that compression does prevent recurrence, such studies would probably not be feasible (Nelson *et al*, 2000). After five years use of high or moderate compression stockings, no significant differences were seen in leg ulcer recurrence rates (Harper *et al*, 1999), with 48/149 patients developing new leg ulcers where high compression hosiery was used and 59/151 where the level of compression was moderate. In this study, changes in the level of compression occurred frequently: in the high compression hosiery arm 64/149 patients could not tolerate the level of compression and their hosiery was changed to provide less strong compression. There may be benefits in using high compression hosiery to prevent recurrence (although this needs to be clarified in future studies), however, high compression may not be tolerated by those wearing the hosiery.

Intermittent pneumatic compression (IPC)

The use of intermittent pneumatic compression (IPC) to manage leg ulcers and lymphoedema deserves mention, for this physical modality often appears overlooked when considering the application of compression. In 2001 there was a systematic review of four randomised controlled trials that compared IPC (with or without additional compression applied by bandages) and compression bandaging alone (Mani *et al*, 2001). These studies tended to be small (numbers recruited ranged from 16 to 53), often limiting the interpretation of the data available. While IPC remains poorly evaluated, it may offer clinical benefits in the healing of leg ulcers resistant to improvement through the use of compression bandages alone (Moffatt *et al*, 2007). One impediment to the consideration of IPC as a valid alternative or supplement to compression bandaging lies in the dissimilar ways in which these modalities are evaluated and classified. Perhaps, if there were to be a common classification pathway based on the compression applied and the change in compression that results upon movement, it may become easier to consider directly the place and use of compression stockings, bandages and intermittent pneumatic compression?

This chapter has attempted to highlight current challenges in the use, evaluation and classification of the different modalities through which compression of the lower leg can be achieved. In reviewing these issues, it has hopefully become clearer why a robust, generally agreed classification of these modalities, ideally with little or no distinctions made between static and dynamic (IPC) modes of compression, will offer great potential benefits to clinicians, manufacturers and patients. Without such a common language being available to describe the likely effects of these interventions, there will continue to be confusion regarding the most effective forms of compression, leading to confused clinical comparisons of products, for example, the laboratory data indicates the four-layer system behaves as an inelastic bandage system, but it is often viewed as an elastic system within clinical studies. Before we can achieve progress and more effective leg compression, the current 'Tower of Babel' that is the classification of compression therapies must be resolved.

References

Clark M (2003) Compression bandages: principles and definitions. In: EWMA, Position Document: *Understanding compression therapy.* Medical Education Partnership Ltd, London: 5–7

Cullum N, Nelson EA, Fletcher AW, Sheldon TA (2001) *Compression for venous leg ulcers.* Cochrane Database of Systematic Reviews 2001, Issue 2. Art No: CD000265. DOI: 10.1002/14651858.CD000265

Harper DR, Ruckley CV, Gibson B, Brown D, Prescott RJ (1999) Randomised trial of two grades of compression stockings in the prevention of venous ulcer recurrence — 5-year outcomes. *Phlebology* **14**: 91

Mani R, Vowden K, Nelson EA (2001) *Intermittent pneumatic compression for treating venous leg ulcers.* Cochrane Database of Systematic Reviews 2001, Issue 4. Art No: CD001899. DOI: 10.1002/14651858.CD001899

Moffatt CJ, Partsch H, Clark M (2007) Compression therapy in leg ulcer management. In Morison MJ, Moffatt CJ, Franks PJ, eds. *Leg Ulcers: A problem-based learning approach.* Mosby-Elsevier, Edinburgh: 169–98

Moffatt C (2007) *Compression Therapy in Practice.* Wounds UK, Aberdeen

Nelson EA, Bell-Syer SEM, Cullum NA (2000) *Compression for preventing recurrence of venous ulcers.* Cochrane Database of Systematic Reviews 2000, Issue 4. Art No: CD002303. DOI: 10.1002/14651858.CD002303

Nelson EA, Iglesias CP, Cullum N, Torgerson DJ (2004) VenUS collaborators. Randomised clinical trial of four-layer and short-stretch compression bandages for venous leg ulcers (VenUS I). *Br J Surg* **91**(10): 1292–9

Partsch H (2005) The use of pressure change on standing as a surrogate measure of the stiffness of a compression bandage. *Eur J Vasc Endovasc Surg* **30**(4): 415–21

Partsch H, Damstra RJ, Tazelaar, *et al* (2001)Multicentre, randomised controlled trial of four-layer bandaging versus short-stretch bandaging in the treatment of venous leg ulcers. *Vasa* **30**(2): 108–13

Partsch H, Clark M, Bassez S, *et al* (2006) Measurement of lower leg compression in vivo: recommendations for the performance of measurements of interface pressure and stiffness: consensus statement. *Dermatol Surg* **32**(2): 224–32

Partsch H, Clark M, Bassez S, Benigni JP, Becker F, Blazek V, *et al* (2006) Measurement of lower leg compression in vivo: recommendations for the performance of measurements of interface pressure and stiffness: consensus statement. *Dermatol Surg* **32**(2): 224–32; discussion 233

Partsch H (2007) Assessing the effectiveness of multilayer inelastic bandaging. *J Lymphoedema* **2**(2): 55–61

Royal College of Nursing (2001) *The management of patients with venous leg ulcers*. Report of the National Sentinel Audit Pilot Project. RCN, London

Chapter 14

Effective skin care

Ellie Lindsay and Fiona Stephens

The condition of the skin can give an indication as to the state of general health. Raising the profile of skin care is important in all age groups, especially the elderly. As part of the ageing process, natural changes occur in the skin (Davies, 1988) placing older people at risk of poor or compromised skin health (Penzer and Finch, 2001).

It is vital that practitioners have an understanding of the skin and its functions, the anatomical and physiological changes of ageing skin, and the use of appropriate washing products, creams, ointments and lotions.

Anatomy and physiology

The skin is known as the largest organ in the human body; it has an area of approximately two square metres and makes up 10% of a person's total body weight (Butcher and White, 2006). It is highly vascular and varies in thickness from 0.5 mm over the tympanic membrane, to 4 mm on the palms of the hands and soles of the feet. It forms an outer cover for the body and acts as a protective barrier against micro-organisms, heat loss, radiation, chemicals and water loss. The skin is a sensory organ, some areas being more sensitive than others, and it is involved in the formation of vitamin D. It assists in the regulation and maintenance of body temperature and, in so doing, plays a significant role in homeostasis (Elias, 2007).

The skin is composed of two distinct layers, the outer epidermis and the dermis (*Figure 14.1* and *14.2*). The dermis contains accessory structures such as glands, nails, and hair follicles. The topmost layer of the epidermis is called the stratum corneum, and is about 0.04 mm thick except on palmar and plantar surfaces. This layer contains keratin protein and lipids which act as a barrier to water loss. The cells are continuously worn away and normally shed at a rate of 0.5–1 g per day.

The dermis is approximately 2 mm thick and contains touch receptors, sebaceous glands, hair follicles and their erector muscles and sweat glands. This layer helps the body to maintain its temperature, and the nerve endings send impulses when stimulated by pressure, heat or irritation, causing a sensation of pain.

The subcutaneous layer, or superficial fascia, is made up of adipose tissue, with elastic fibres running through connecting the dermis to the deeper tissues, such as the muscles. This layer helps maintain the shape of the skin after stretching or distortion and contains fat molecules that form part of an important insulating layer, which is also an extra source of nutrition (Hodgkinson and Nay, 2005). The skin requires the provision of a good supply of nutrients, water and oxygen from the blood stream and the removal of waste products through sweat gland elimination and lymphatic mechanisms.

With age, the epidermis becomes thinner as skin cells decrease, the subcutaneous fat layer thins and the production of protective lipids is reduced. These changes affect the normal functions of the skin, making it less able to endure normal wear and tear because its ability to act as a barrier to irritants and microorganisms and its thermo-regulatory and water retention functions are all compromised.

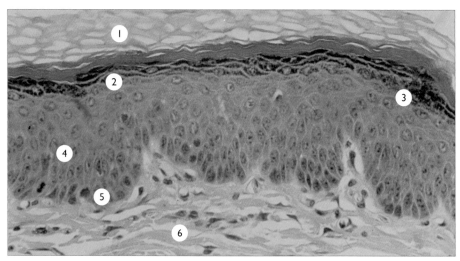

Figure 14.1: Histology of typical epidermis and superficial dermis
1. Stratum dysjunctum; 2. Stratum compactum (these two together form the stratum corneum); 3. Stratum granulosum (granular layer); 4. Stratum spinosum; 5. Stratum basale (basal layer); 6. Stratum (papillary) dermis

Generally, Caucasians will show earlier signs of wrinkling and sagging, and increased pigmentation and discolouration is more common (Rawlings, 2006).

Flexures

Flexures are any area of the body where two skin surfaces rub closely together, such as groins, under breasts, axillae and between toes. These areas are frequently neglected and skin health is compromised. The warm, relatively damp conditions that are found are ideal conditions for fungal growth and infection risk. To promote skin health, these areas must be given particular attention when washing and drying. Intertrigo often occurs as a result of obesity and poor hygiene (Yosipovitch *et al*, 2007). It is an erythematous maceration caused by friction and sweat retention, and can largely be avoided by

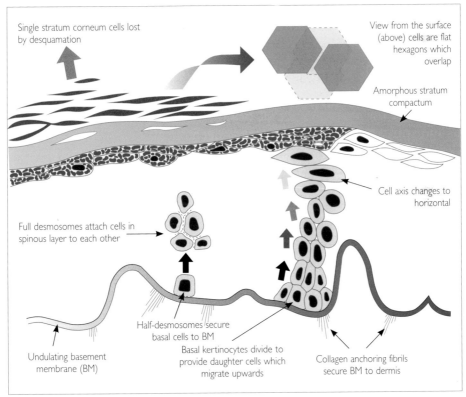

Figure 14.2: A diagrammatic view of the skin section, shown in *Figure 14.1* illustrating key features of epidermal biology

drying well and sparing use of unperfumed talcum powder. Talcum powder should not be used on other areas of the skin because of its drying effect (Rawlings, 2006). Care should be taken when using talc as it can cause caking which can exacerbate the skin trauma in intertrigo.

Skin assessment

Assessment of the general condition of the skin is important in all patients, but especially in the older person (Barr, 2006). Assessment can reveal the patient's fluid and nutritional status, their standard of personal hygiene and, to an extent, their medical history. It will also indicate any potential healing problems (Crooks, 2005; Rawlings, 2006) and the need for a pressure ulcer risk assessment. Darkly-pigmented skin can be difficult to assess, due to the pigmentation potentially concealing areas where skin integrity may be at risk of, or have signs of, damage.

There are a number of physical changes that affect ageing skin (*Table 14.1*), and ensuring adequate hydration and a well-balanced diet should be a priority. It is important to encourage the regular inspection of vulnerable areas, mobility and repositioning, thus reducing pressure on at-risk areas and improving circulation. Campbell *et al* (2006), stated that the maintenance of healthy skin depends on factors such as moisture, nutritional status and mechanical forces. Although skin disorders vary in severity, they all adversely affect an older person's health status and/or quality of life.

There are multiple factors that increase the risk of skin tissue breakdown, eg. restrictive mobility, excessive wound exudate, or other bodily fluids such as urine or sweat. Underlying disease processes should also be considered, for example, myxoedema, hypertension or congestive heart failure, where the use of diuretics may cause drier skin and can lead to skin-related problems (Monk and Graham-Brown, 1988).

Continence should be promoted and incontinence well managed. Individuals who are not able to care for their own personal hygiene are usually washed and dressed by a carer or a nurse. This is an ideal time to examine skin and to assess for potential future problems such as eczema, leg ulceration or diabetic foot ulceration. Thorough assessment and care that may highlight potential problems, may well prevent years of misery in the future (Bale, 2005).

Table 14.1: Normal physiological changes that affect ageing skin

- The stratum corneum becomes less moist and flexible. The epidermis becomes thinner, so reducing its effectiveness as a barrier. Melanin production is also reduced, offering less protection from the harmful rays of the sun

- The dermis can thin by up to 20% due to a reduction in collagen and elastin. The blood supply deteriorates providing poorer regulation of the skin's surface temperature. The skin also appears paler

- Wound healing is affected by a reduced blood supply and the resulting decrease in macrophages, fibroblasts and mast cells results in a reduced immune response

- The epidermis — dermal junction is less stable and easily slides across the dermis, increasing the likelihood of skin tears due to damage, friction or rough handling

- There is a decrease in sebum secretion. In the older person sebum contains less fatty acids, increasing the vulnerability and dryness of the skin

- Dehydration can be caused by thinning of the epidermis, reduced ability of the kidneys to produce concentrated urine and a decreased ability to sense thirst (Tong, 1999). The decrease in the skin's elasticity due to dehydration increases the risk of damage

- Poor hygiene, or the ability to maintain hygiene levels, emotional stress, poor mobility and reduced nutritional uptake all compromise skin integrity

- A general loss of subcutaneous fat increases the risk of tissue damage, especially to over-exposed and bony areas

Skin cleansing

Cleaning products used on the skin should maintain the skin's natural pH, between 5 and 6. When washing older skin, harsh soaps and shampoos, which can increase pH levels and remove natural oils from the skin, should be avoided (Graham-Brown, 1996; Kirsner and Frolich, 1998). Over-enthusiastic washing can cause dehydration and rupturing of the skin's surface, leaving it vulnerable to bacterial infection (Penzer and Finch, 2001). After cleansing, the skin should be patted dry using a soft towel. The use of cotton underclothing should be encouraged as protection, and to help with moisture absorption. A high factor sun screen should be used and lengthy periods of exposure to sunlight avoided.

Barrier creams

Barrier creams and talcum powder should be avoided as they can interfere with the skin's function, and may affect the absorptive qualities of continence products. Barrier creams provide no relief from the risk of pressure damage to the skin. They are intended for use as a barrier against body fluids which may alter the pH levels of the skin, causing irritation and leading to breakdown.

There is no research evidence that any barrier cream is more effective than traditional compound zinc ointments. If barrier creams are used, vulnerable areas should not be massaged or rubbed. It is important to consider known sensitivities, such as perfumes, wool fats and preservatives.

Creams and lotions are more easily absorbed than ointments, although they require more frequent application. All topical products should be applied in the direction of the hair growth to prevent damage to underlying tissues. If the skin is itchy, it may be dry and require a moisturiser; if it is scaly, it is too dry and requires an emollient.

Emollients

Emollients are used as a first-line treatment for a wide range of dermatological conditions, as well as being a proactive therapy for those people with dry, itchy skin. They can make the skin much more comfortable, allow other treatments to work more effectively and reduce scaling. *Figure 14.3* provides a guide to the severity of skin dryness. They are available in a variety of presentations, namely:

Lotions: These are water-based liquids, which have a cooling effect. They are useful after psoriasis settles to maintain good skin.

Creams: These are thicker and slightly greasier. They are easy to use and are suitable for daily use.

Ointments: Being oil-based these are very greasy and thick. They are excellent moisturisers, but are less acceptable to patients. They are best used at night.

Oils: Oils can be messy, but are comforting. Bath oils can be hydrating.

0 None	Naturally soft supple skin	
1 Mild	Soft skin maintained by 1–2 daily applications of emollients, powdery with occasional irritation	Cream or lotion
2 Moderate	Dry skin in patches, environmental conditions causing drying easily, skin is mildly flaky with irritation	
3 Severe	Very dry skin feels rough and flaky, distressingly irritant	Ointment or gel
4 Very severe	Extremely dry skin with possible fissuring or peeling, or acanthosis (epidermal thickening) or dry desquamation without trauma, distressingly irritant	

Figure 14.3: Plymouth hydration flow chart

To a certain extent, patient choice should guide prescribing, rather than being solely research-based, as this will assist with compliance to treatment. Emollients need to be used at least twice a day for best effect, although the frequency of application is as individual as the patient's skin condition. Application should be smooth, gentle and in the direction of the growing hairs to avoid blocking pores, causing irritation, and thickening of the skin and folliculitis. It has been found that not prescribing enough emollient is the biggest barrier to effective patient use (Oor-van-der-Molen, 1999). Some products can be used both as a soap substitute and as an emollient, see *Table 14.2*.

Table 14.2: Emollients that can be used as soap substitutes (East Kent Primary Care Trust, 2006)			
Presentation	First line	Second line	Third line
Cream	Aqueous cream	Cetraben® (Sankyo)	Zerobase® (Zeroderm)
Ointment	Emulsifying ointment	Hydrous ointment	50:50

Topical steroids

Topical steroids are extremely useful in inflammatory disorders but are not the panacea for everything. They are contraindicated in acne, rosacea, infections (bacterial, viral and fungal) and infestations. As the condition improves, potency should be gradually reduced rather than stopped abruptly. *Figure 14.4* shows the four steps of potency of topical steroids.

The mode of action of topical steroids is not completely understood, however, it is thought to work on three stages: receptor binding, synthesis of specific mRNA and/or synthesis of protein. Anti-inflammatory effects are still being studied. Absorption through the skin can rarely suppress a patient's adrenal glands.

Topical steroids can have the following side-effects:

- skin atrophy, striae and tearing of the skin through loss of dermal collagen
- bruising due to loss of collagen and support for blood vessels in the dermis
- telangiectasia (small thread veins)
- rebound phenomenon and tachyphylaxis
- sensitisation resulting in eczema
- susceptibility to infection.

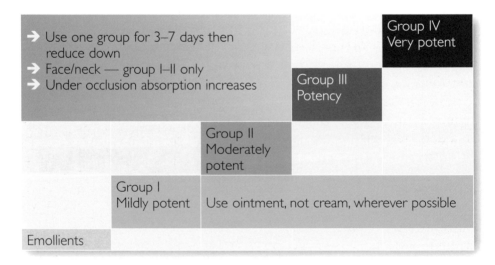

Figure 14.4: Four steps of potency of topical steroids

Skin conditions

Pruritus

Pruritus (*Figure 14.5*) is unpleasant and a considerable threat to skin integrity through scratching, which can lead to inflammation and skin damage. It is necessary to understand the possible causes of itching to prevent and treat the problem. The cause of an itch is not always easy to ascertain, as it might not be accompanied by a visible rash or other symptom that will assist diagnosis. Pruritus is common in older people, and can be a result of many factors, such as renal failure, metabolic diseases (thyroid disease, diabetes), iron-deficiency anaemia, leukaemia, lymphomas, Hodgkin's disease, scabies, *dermatitis herpetiformis* and early bullous pemphigoid and other conditions (Graham-Brown and Monk, 1988).

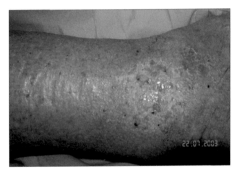

Figure 14.5: Pruritic skin in area of lymphoedematous changes in lower limb. Weeping is adding to the irritation

Itching can be aggravated by heat, sudden changes in temperature, sweating, clothing, fatigue and emotional stress. Adverse drug reactions, including contact dermatitis, might also lead to itching skin. Management should include prevention, identification and treatment of the problem, management of the environment and skin care strategies. In all cases of pruritus, a thorough holistic assessment is required and if necessary referral to a dermatologist.

Maceration

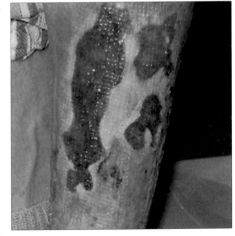

Figure 14.6: Example of maceration

Maceration of the skin and wound bed is caused by prolonged exposure to excess and inappropriately managed exudate

167

(*Figure 14.6*). The specific wound types below may increase the propensity to macerate because of the pathology or the anatomic location (White and Cutting, 2004):

Leg ulcers: Ulcerated legs have raised intra-capillary pressure resulting from damage to the venous system. This can lead to uncontrolled oedema, which may cause maceration. Exudate management involves a combination of dressings, compression, and limb elevation. The skin directly below the wound is at greatest risk of maceration from leakage.

Pressure ulcers: Pressure ulcers over the sacrum are particularly at risk of maceration due to urinary incontinence (Collins *et al*, 2002). Skin protection is vital.

Diabetic foot ulcers: Diabetic foot ulcers may develop into chronic, non-healing wounds. The predominantly neuropathic nature of plantar ulcers, where exudate is in contact with thick callus, makes maceration a real risk.

Incontinence: Faecal or urinary incontinence can cause maceration of the skin, and a continence assessment should be undertaken to determine the cause, treating where possible. Where treatment is unavailable or ineffective, disposable pads or absorbent disposable pants are recommended.

Incontinence can lead to skin breakdown and the development of pressure ulcers. Regular inspection of the skin, the use of repositioning, transfer techniques and the reduction of shear and friction can, along with a barrier cream (such as Cavilon™ Durable Barrier Cream, 3M), assist in protecting the skin.

Lymphoedema: Lymph is high in protein, which, in combination with fluid, provides a warm, moist environment that can lead to bacterial infections. Skin changes, such as hyperkeratosis, often accompany lymphoedema, and may lead to cracks, fissures or fungal infection.

Dry cracked skin

Soap should be avoided with dry, cracked skin (*Figure 14.7*), as it removes the protective lipid barrier, increasing the tendency of the skin to be dry, itchy, and more permeable to allergens (Nix, 2000). Emollient soap substitutes are recommended when washing, bathing and showering, followed by intensive emollient therapy. Bath emollients and oils are a useful additional treatment to a lotion, cream, or ointment, as they clean and hydrate the whole body.

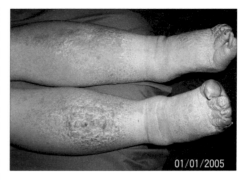

Figure 14.7: Dry, cracked skin

Ensure that the individual or caregiver is warned about the risk of slipping or falling in the bath, as emollients tends to form a greasy film on the skin.

Folliculitis

Folliculitis is an infection of the superficial part of the hair follicle with staphylococci. One predisposing factor is the use of occlusive ointment-based topical preparations. It appears as an erythematous area centred on the hair follicle with occasionally localised pustules.

Candidiasis

Candidiasis or 'thrush' is a yeast infection caused by _Candida albicans_ that may develop on the skin. Warm, moist folds of skin such as in the groins, fold of the abdomen, axillae or under the breasts are the areas most likely to become infected with candida. Skin infected with candida looks red and feels itchy and sore, and tiny yellow pustules may be present. Affected areas can often be effectively treated with a topical anti-fungal/steroid combination cream (Hunter _et al_, 1989).

Sensitisation and irritation

The skin can react to allergens and/or irritant chemicals by either an allergic reaction (allergic contact dermatitis, ACD) or an irritant reaction. ACD can be a complication of leg ulcer management and polysensitisation in patients with chronic wounds is frequent (Machet _et al_, 2004; Tavadia _et al_, 2003). The source is often discovered by noting the demarcation line of the product that has been the causal factor (*Figure 14.8*). A bland product should be used until the inflammation has resolved, and then reintroduce a cream, lotion or new dressing and evaluate the outcome to ensure the patient is not allergic to that product.

Steroid creams or ointments will help to reduce inflammation, redness and sore areas. However, they can also delay wound healing so should only be used in the short term. Steroid therapy should be discontinued as soon as the soreness and redness is completely clear. Bathing with emollients and the application of film barriers or barrier creams will further protect the skin against damage (Atherton, 1995).

Skin care relating to leg ulcer management

Figure 14.8: Sensitisation

Cleansing should be kept simple. It can prevent the build up of exudate, slough and toxic components, but should not damage granulation or epithelialising tissue.

Removal of loose flakes of skin allows new epithelium to grow and aims to prevent hard areas of accumulated scale (appearing like scabs) acting as pressure points beneath bandaging.

Washing technique

1. If practical, soak the leg in a clean (plastic-lined) bucket of warm water at each treatment.
2. Dry scale and wound edge encrustations should be removed if this can be done easily. This will allow emollients to moisturise the surrounding skin and aid the process of wound epithelialisation.

Cleansing should never involve scrubbing the wound with gauze or cotton wool balls, as this will damage granulating and epithelialising tissue.

To help remove dead skin cells, emollients may be added to water or applied to dry skin as creams/ointment surrounding the ulcer. Where possible, avoid using products containing agents commonly known to produce skin sensitisation in patients with leg ulcers, such as lanolin and fragrances.

Eczema

Eczema tends to present as small cracks and fissures on any part of the skin surface, due to scratching or tissue breakdown. This damage can provide an entry point for bacteria to cause infection. *Staphylococcus aureus* is the most common bacterial source of skin infection, causing eczema to deteriorate and making treatment more difficult. Infected eczema presents as inflamed (red) and is usually 'weepy' with a yellowish crust. Yellow, pus-filled spots may also be present (pustules), and small red spots around the base of hairs (folliculitis). Bacterial infection of eczema should be treated with specific antiseptics or antibiotics in cases where pustules are present under the skin, or when the skin is cracked, broken or weeping. Some specific points to remember when treating eczema include:

- the prescription of combination creams containing both a topical steroid and antibiotic to help combat inflammation and infection
- treatment to control eczema that breaks out over the body secondary to uncontrolled eczema on the ulcerated leg, or the leg at risk of ulceration. This should occur alongside the treatment for the leg irritations
- potassium permanganate at the start of a course treatment for weeping eczema should only be applied long enough to dry up the eczema to facilitate topical steroids, as it can be an irritant.
- powder-free gloves should be used when applying steroid creams/ointments
- clinicians and carers treating individuals with eczema and dry skin conditions should understand the basic principles of emollient usage. They should be aware of the relative benefits of steroid creams (to reduce inflammation) and emollients (to combat dry skin).

Eczema management

Intensive emollient therapy and topical steroids are indicated. It is important to remember that there may be sensitivity to constituents such as the preservatives, fragrances, and biologically-derived ingredients such as lanolin. There are products currently available that do not usually contain a preservative (eg. Epaderm, arachis oil, 50/50 liquid/white soft paraffin).

Infected eczema
A topical steroid/antibiotic combination is indicated, adding in an oral antibiotic if the condition does not start to resolve in seven days.

Severely infected eczema
This should be treated with intensive emollient therapy with topical steroid antibiotic preparation plus oral antibiotics.

Venous eczema

Incompetence of the deep and perforating veins causes backflow of blood into the superficial veins. The superficial vein pressure rises to 90 mmHg and above (normal pressure, 30 mmHg), causing venous hypertension. The capillaries become engorged and dilated, eventually failing and leaking fluid into the interstitial spaces, which results in oedema.

Oedema causes a 'waterlogging' effect and contains proteolytic enzymes which act as irritants, and, together with the presence of bacteria, cause irritable venous eczema.

Management of venous eczema

The term venous eczema is now more common than older terms such as varicose, gravitational and stasis eczema, eg. venous (stasis) eczema occurs on those who have severe varicose veins, often following a deep vein thrombosis many years previously. The lower leg above the ankle is often swollen with tense, shiny skin which can develop greasy scaling and pigmentation. After minor trauma the area may break down and form a venous ulcer which is often hard to heal.

Treatment includes:

- rest
- elevation
- soaking and de-scaling
- the use of emollients to normalise the skin
- the use of topical steroids to reduce inflammation
- compression bandaging to aid venous hypertension
- avoiding allergens (lanolin, parabens, antiseptics).

Cellulitis

Cellulitis is an acute spreading infection of the subcutaneous tissues usually caused by _Staphylococcus aureus,_ but group A streptococci are also frequently involved (_Figure 14.9_). The clinical manifestations include spreading erythema with oedema, warmth and tenderness. It should be distinguished from erypsipelas. Cellulitis often accompanies skin trauma where bacteria gain access through fissures and damage to the skin surface (Gabillot-Carre and Roujeau, 2007). The criteria for wound infection are numerous (Cutting and Harding, 1994). All practitioners who regularly manage wounds should be familiar with these criteria and with the fact that they have been validated.

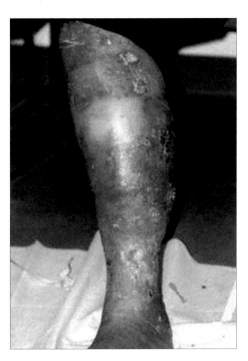

Figure 14.9: Cellulitis

Assessment and management of cellulitis

The main symptom of infection is pain. Other symptoms include:

- redness around ulcer (more than recently or a brighter intensity which is painful to light pressure)
- localised heat

- swelling around wound margins
- yellow pus
- offensive odour
- green slough.

Investigations may include: bloods — full blood count (FBC), erythrocyte sedimentation rate (ESR), liver function tests (LFTs), urea and electrolytes (U&Es) to identify any contributory underlying pathology; and wound swab, if clinically indicated, for culture and sensitivity. The empirical choice and dose of antibiotics is in the first instance governed by local antibiotic formulary and then modified, if necessary, on swab or blood culture results. Investigations will be a swab from the ulcer or areas of newly broken skin for culture and sensitivity and, if the cellulitis is spreading or there are signs of systemic illness, a blood culture to identify the invading pathogen and guide antibiotic treatment and c-reactive protein test (CRP) to monitor response to antibiotic treatment and determine timing of switching from intravenous to oral therapy.

Treatment includes:

- gentle cleansing with a soap substitute, such as aqueous cream. Particular attention needs to be paid to foot hygiene
- topical therapy, limited to bland emollients that soothe the lesions. Erosions or blisters require simple non-adherent dressings
- treating leg ulceration as appropriate
- discontinuing compression bandages until the acute phase is resolved
- applying mild compression bandages during the healing phase, especially when mobilising. In uncomplicated cases of cellulitis, consider class 2 below-knee compression hosiery for four to six months following the acute phase
- elevating and resting the limb, and keeping the skin clean, free of scale and hydrated with emollients.

Conclusion

As well as treating specific conditions, there are many strategies that can be used to prevent skin breakdown in older people and promote skin health. These strategies are neither costly nor time-consuming, particularly when compared to the cost and resources required to treat conditions resulting from poor skin health, such as pressure ulcers, wounds and leg ulcers (Rawlings, 2006). Guidance is available for nurses, patients and carers for the use of skin care products and maintaining a healthy, nutritious diet (*Best Practice Statement: Care of the Older Person's Skin*). The older person's skin can provide us with information about their physical condition. A good knowledge and understanding of normal ageing, skin physiology and structure is essential to the provision of evidence-based nursing care and the prevention or reduction of related problems. Regular assessment of any vulnerable areas, appropriate use of skin cleansing and moisturising products can help to maintain and promote skin integrity. Finally, on a psychological level, patients will benefit, whatever their age, as the appearance of their skin improves.

Figures 14.1 and 14.2 are reproduced by kind permission of Richard White.

Advice

- Patients should be advised to protect vulnerable areas to prevent damage, notice any signs of damage by inspecting their skin regularly, especially if they suffer with neuropathy.

- Ensure the skin is kept dry, as if allowed to remain moist it will become macerated and heavily colonised.

- Contrary to popular belief, rubbing or massaging the skin will not improve circulation, but may cause damage due to friction and potentially reduce blood flow.

- Maintaining an adequate fluid intake can improve skin hydration, and a diet high in protein and vitamin-rich foods can assist in maintaining healthy tissue integrity while, if necessary, promoting an ideal healing environment.

- Mobility must be encouraged, as should maintenance or management of continence.

- Lastly, patients should consult the nurse if they have any concerns or identify damage related to their skin.

References

Atherton DJ (1995) How should eczema be treated? In: *Eczema in Childhood.* Oxford Medical Publications: chap 8, 91–203

Bale S (2005) Incontinence care. In: White R, ed. *Skin Care in Wound Management.* Wounds UK, Aberdeen: 115–7

Barr JE (2006) Impaired skin integrity in the elderly. *Ostomy/Wound Management* **52**(5): 22–8

Best Practice Statement: Care of the Older Person's Skin. Wounds UK, a subsidiary of HealthComm UK Ltd, Aberdeen, 2006

Cameron J (2005) Allergic reactions to treatment. In: White R, Harding K, eds. *Trauma and Pain in Wound Care.* Wounds UK, Aberdeen: chap 6, 100–18

Campbell DK, Woodbury MG, Whittle H, Labate T, Hoskin A (2006) A clinical evaluation of 3M No Sting Barrier Film. *Ostomy/Wound Management* **46**(1): 24–30

Collins F, Hampton S, White RJ (2002) *A–Z Dictionary of Wound Care.* Quay Books division, MA Healthcare Ltd, London

Crooks A(2005) How does ageing affect the wound healing process? *J Wound Care* **14**(5): 222–3

Davies (1988) The mechanisms of aging. In: Monk BE, Graham-Brown RA, Sarkeny I, eds. *Skin Disorders in the Elderly.* Blackwell Scientific, Oxford: chap 1, 2–29

East Kent PCT (2006) *Clinical Guideline for the Assessment and Management of Wounds.* Unpublished

Elias PM (2007) The skin barrier as an innate immune element. *Semin Immunopathol* **29**(1): 3–14

European Pressure Ulcer Advisory Panel (1998) *Pressure ulcer prevention guidelines.* EPUAP, London. Available online at: www.epuap.org/glprevention.html

Gabillot-Carre M, Roujeau JC (2007) Acute bacterial skin infections and cellulitis. *Curr Opin Infect Dis* **20**(2): 118–23

Gfatter R, Hackl P, Braun F (1997) Effects of soaps and detergents on skin surface pH. *Dermatology* **195**(3): 258–62

Graham-Brown RA, Monk BE (1988) Pruritus and xerosis. In: Monk BE, Graham-Brown RA, Sarkany I, eds. *Skin Disorders in the Elderly.* Blackwell Scientific, Oxford: chap 7, 1133–46

Graham-Brown RA (1996) Soaps and detergents in the elderly. *Clin Dermatol* **14**(1): 85–7

Hodgkinson B, Nay R (2005) Effectiveness of topical skin care provided in aged care facilities [Review]. *Int J Evidence-based Healthcare* **3**(4): 65–101

Hunter JAA, Savin, JA, Dahl MV (1989) Infections. In: *Clinical Dermatology*. Blackwell Scientific, Oxford: chap 15, 136–65

Kirsner RS, Frolich CW (1998) Soaps and detergents: understanding their composition and effects. *Ostomy/Wound Management* 44(3 suppl): S62–S70

Machet L, Couhe C, Perrinaud A (2004) A high prevalence of sensitisation still persists in leg ulcer patients. *Br J Dermatol* 150(5): 929–35

Monk BE, Graham-Brown RA (1988) Eczema. In: Monk BE, Graham-Brown RA, Sarkany I, eds. *Skin Disorders in the Elderly*. Blackwell Scientific, Oxford: chap 8, 147–58

Nix DH (2000) Factors to consider when selecting skin cleansing products. *J Wound Ostomy Continence Nurs* 27(5): 260–8

Oor-van-der-Molen M (1999) The basics of quality care. *Elderly Care* 11(1): 14–6

Penzer R, Finch M (2001) Promoting healthy skin in older people. *Nurs Standard* 15(34): 46–52, 54–5

Peters G (2005) Exploring the use of emollients. *Br J Nurs* 14: 9

Rawlings A (2006) Ethnic skin types: are there differences in skin structure and function? *Int J Cosmetic Sci* 28(2): 79–93

Stephens F (2001) Raising the profile of effective skin care in the older person. *Community Nurse* March: 23–4

Tavadia S, Bianchi J, Dawe RS, *et al* (2003) Allergic contact dermatitis in venous leg ulcer patients. *Contact Dermatitis* 48(5): 261–5

Tong A (1999) More than skin deep. *Nurs Times* 95(3): 65–8

White RJ, Cutting K (2003) Interventions to avoid maceration of the skin and wound bed. *Br J Nurs* 12(20): 1186–1203

Yosipovitch G, Devore A, Dawn A (2007) Obesity and the skin, skin physiology and skin manifestations of obesity. *J Am Acad Dermatol* 55(6): 901–20

Chapter 15

Differential diagnoses in ulceration of the lower limb

John Buchan

The correct diagnosis of the cause of leg ulceration is of paramount importance when selecting the most appropriate treatment. The application of compression, for example, to an arterial ulcer can have disastrous consequences leading to gangrene, and even amputation. This chapter gives practical guidance on diagnosing the common, and some of the not so common causes of ulceration of the lower limb, along with their complications, and covers the following topics:

- venous ulcers
- mixed venous and arterial ulcers
- vasculitic ulcers

- *necrobiosis lipoidica*
- pressure ulcers
- infection (as a cause of ulceration)

- contact dermatitis
- trauma and dermatitis artefacta.

- arterial ulcers
- hypertensive ulcers
- ulcers associated with diabetes mellitus
- thrombotic ulcers
- malignant ulcers
- infection (as a complication)
- varicose eczema

History-taking

It is all too tempting when presented with a patient with a leg ulcer (or, indeed, any other skin complaint) to examine them without first taking a history. This is a serious mistake, and, if you are lucky, the diagnosis may be apparent. However, often you are left looking foolish, usually on your knees, staring at an oozing leg ulcer and asking questions that you now regret not asking when both you and the patient were far more comfortable. History-taking should include:

- *Noting the age of the patient.* This may seem obvious, but young or very old people developing leg ulcers should sound a warning that there may be an unusual cause, eg. infection or malignancy.
- *Asking the patient's occupation.* It will be far harder to treat a patient with a venous ulcer whose job involves their standing all day. A patient who has lived or worked in the tropics may have a rare type of infection that requires further investigation.
- *Asking about any personal or family history of skin disease.* In particular, one would want to know about atopic or contact eczema (dermatitis) and any previous leg ulceration.
- *Taking a past medical history.* It is relevant to discover if there is a history of diabetes mellitus, hypertension, ischaemic heart disease, stroke, transient ischaemic attack, peripheral vascular disease, intermittent claudication, rheumatoid or other autoimmune conditions. One should specifically ask about varicose veins, deep or superficial thromboses or phlebitis, previous leg fractures, trauma or surgery.
- *Enquiring about present general health.* Is the patient well or unwell? Could there be undiagnosed underlying disease, such as diabetes or heart failure? Ask if their weight is stable and if they smoke. Any indication that the patient is unwell needs further elaboration, investigation or referral.
- *Making a note of any medication that the patient is taking.*
- *Finding out if the patient has symptoms suggestive of venous insufficiency,* such as aching, heavy or swollen legs? Are the legs discoloured, itchy or weeping?
- *Learning about the ulcer itself.* This should include; site, duration, progress (better, worse or static), level of pain, whether the ulcer is itching, bleeding or has any discharge. It is also important to know what treatment has been tried and with what effect and noting anything that has made things worse, as contact reactions are not uncommon.

Examination

From the history one should already have a 'mental' list of differential diagnoses. The examination should confirm or refute the diagnosis, or indicate the need for further investigation.

Generally, it is worth noting if the patient looks well or ill. This may be obvious, but it is worth reiterating that one is dealing with a patient with a leg ulcer, not a leg ulcer with a person attached. Is the patient mobile or immobile, fat or thin, pale or plethoric, breathless, confused or alert, happy or sad? Remember, chronic illness and chronic leg ulceration can be extremely depressing.

When examining the leg, it is important to look specifically for and assess:

- oedema
- varicose veins
- varicose eczema
- contact reactions
- brown staining — from haemosiderin or iron pigments in the skin
- lipodermatosclerosis — ' champagne bottle legs' caused by dermatitis, induration and dermal fibrosis
- atrophie blanche — ivory white scarring dotted with red, dilated capillary loops surrounded by increased pigmentation
- poor circulation — is the foot cold or warm? (pedal pulses are difficult to palpate and measuring an ankle brachial pressure index (ABPI) is much more reliable. An ABPI less than 0.8 suggests significant arterial disease)
- capillary refill.

The ulcer should be examined and, if possible, photographed. The following should be assessed:

- site
- size
- depth
- discharge
- slough
- ulcer bed for signs of healing
- odour
- surrounding skin for signs of infection (redness, swelling, heat and tenderness)
- surrounding skin for signs of eczema.

Further investigation should also be considered, namely:

- urinalysis for sugar, protein and blood
- blood tests for random and/or fasting blood sugar
- urea, electrolytes, creatinine and epidermal growth factor receptor (EGFR) for renal function
- protein and albumin for nutritional sate
- C-reactive protein, erythrocyte sedimentation rate and auto-antibodies for inflammatory disease such as rheumatoid arthritis
- swab for bacteriology to see if there are clinical signs of infection (pain, fever, increase in size, cellulitis, smell, friable ulcer bed)
- venography, duplex scanning to assess surgically treatable causes of venous incompetence
- cardiac evaluation for heart failure.

Differential diagnoses

Venous ulcers

Venous (stasis or varicose) ulcers account for 80–85% of leg ulceration. The typical patient is middle-aged and overweight. There is usually a history of varicose veins and/or thrombosis. Ulceration is commonest around the medial malleolus. Although ulcers can be large, they tend to be shallow with granulation tissue in the ulcer bed. There may be small islands of grey epithelial cells within the ulcer and at the margins. The leg is often swollen with red or purple discolouration. There may be hair loss, brown pigmentation, atrophie blanche, lipodermatosclerosis and signs of eczema. With the patient standing, incompetent perforating branches between the superficial and deep veins of the leg may be seen or felt. Despite appearances, the ulcers are relatively pain free.

Arterial ulcers

Arterial ulcers are far less common. Typically, there is little evidence of varicose veins. The leg is often thin, cold with poor peripheral circulation and capillary return. There may be associated nail dystrophy. Severe pain is not uncommon, particularly when the legs are elevated. Nocturnal pain is a common feature and patients may find they are more comfortable sleeping in a chair. There may be a history of intermittent claudication. The ulcers are most often found on the toes, dorsum of the foot, heel, calf and shin. They may be multiple with sharply-defined punched-out edges and are tender. They may be deep, even gangrenous and there may be a dry adherent slough in the ulcer base, possibly covering exposed tendons.

Arterial leg ulceration is often associated with generalised arterial disease, in particular, atherosclerosis. They are also found in Buerger's disease, a peripheral arteriopathy affecting young men who smoke heavily, giant cell arteritis, *polyarteritis nodosa* and systemic sclerosis. Diseases that affect smaller blood vessels such as diabetes mellitus, systemic lupus erythematosis, rheumatoid arthritis and allergic vasculitis may produce ulcers with similar clinical features (see below).

Mixed venous and arterial ulcers

Between 10 and 20% of leg ulcers will be caused by a combination of arterial and venous insufficiency. It is important to reassess these ulcers frequently and tailor treatment accordingly, especially if any form of compression is used or there is a sudden worsening of the ulcer.

Hypertensive ulcers

This is an unusual type of leg ulcer, more commonly found in women. It is usually extremely painful. It occurs on the anterior external aspect of the lower leg and is often bilateral. The ulcer is superficial with a bright red or yellowish edge surrounded by ruddy mottling of the skin. Peripheral pulses are present and there is no lipodermatosclerosis. Untreated high blood pressure causes small vessel wall hypertrophy, and/or vasospasm in areas of the skin with sparse arterioles.

Vasculitic ulcers

Any pathological process which affects small or medium-sized blood vessels may result in leg ulceration. These ulcers start as painful, palpable, purplish lesions which later become small, well-demarcated ulcers. The involvement of larger vessels leads to painful nodules that may break down. The ulceration is usually deep, necrotic and multiple with an atypical distribution. There may be evidence of vasculitis elsewhere, eg. subcutaneous nodules or subungual splinter haemorrhages. The patient may be generally ill and have a low grade fever.

These ulcer are often found in the mid-calf area in rheumatoid disease. They have a sloughy, poorly granulating base and are slow to heal. There is usually evidence of rheumatoid disease in the hands and other joints. Associated venous disease is not uncommon. Poor mobility, dependent oedema, neuropathy and systemic corticosteroids may also delay healing. *Pyoderma gangrenosum*-like inflammation may cause exacerbation of the ulceration process.

Pyoderma gangrenosum initially presents as boils which rapidly break down to leave large, painful ulcers due to a combination of vasculitis and thrombosis.

The ulcers may have an undermined, indurated or pustular margin. Patients are systemically unwell. The disease is not only associated with rheumatoid arthritis, but also with ulcerative colitis, Crohn's disease, monoclonal gammopathies and myeloma.

Vasculitic ulcers may also be seen in systemic lupus erythematosis, systemic sclerosis, *polyarteritis nodosa*, Wegner's granulomatosis and allergic vasculitis.

Ulcers associated with diabetes mellitus

Ulceration in the patient with diabetes requires special mention. These patients are prone to both small and large vessel disease. In addition, there may be a mixed sensory and motor neuropathy. The older patient with an insidious onset is at particular risk with loss of temperature, pain and fine touch sensation. Cutaneous infections, due to *Staphylococcus aureus* and *candida albicans* are more common.

Sensory loss in the lower limbs clinically similar to that found in diabetes is also a feature of syphilis, leprosy, syringomyelia and peripheral neuropathy.

Necrobiosis lipoidica

Although less than 1% of patients with diabetes will have *necrobiosis lipoidica*, most patients with the condition will be, or may well develop, diabetes. Patients range from being young adults to those in early middle life. Lesions appear as discoloured areas on the front of the shins. As the disease progresses, the areas become waxy, atrophic with a dirty, yellow brown discolouration. The underlying small blood vessels are easily seen. If looked at side-on, the lesions are indented. Minor trauma may lead to very slow healing ulcers.

Thrombotic ulcers

Arterial embolism or increased coaguability of the blood, as seen in polycythaemia or cryoglobulinaemia, can cause leg ulceration. The appearance is similar to that of arterial ulcers, however, there may be no other evidence of arterial disease.

Pressure ulcers

Pressure ulcers of the lower limb usually occur at the back of the heels. Initially there is a patch of skin discolouration or a blister which may subsequently become necrotic and break down. Pressure ulcers occur in the debilitated or immobile patient, for example, in the postoperative period. Most, but not all, can be predicted and hence avoided.

Malignant ulcers

Malignancy as a primary cause of leg ulceration is rare. Malignant change occurring in a chronic leg ulcer is uncommon but important to recognise or at least to consider in any non-healing ulcer.

Malignant change should be suspected if the edge of an ulcer becomes progressively heaped up, proliferative and does not flatten with compression therapy. There may be increased pain and smell. Ulcers may appear to heal superficially, then break down again.

Squamous cell carcinoma is the most frequent form of malignant change. Several biopsies may need to be taken, including the edge and the ulcer bed. Most squamous cell carcinomas develop as a result of sun exposure but they can also be caused by exposure to X-rays and infrared rays. Chronic exposure to heat causes a condition known as erythema abigne and presents as a reticulated pigmented erythema most commonly on the lower legs ('granny's tartan'). Any ulcer occurring in association with erythema abigne should be viewed with suspicion. Squamous cell carcinomas have the potential to metastasise. The local lymph glands should be examined

Basal cell carcinomas do occur in venous ulcers and may remain quite flat and undetected for some time. More commonly, basal cell carcinomas arise as a primary malignancy and are a result of prolonged exposure to ultraviolet (UV) rays from the sun. Typically, the cancer has a pearly, rolled edge with fine telangectasiae. Biopsy will confirm the diagnosis. Basal cell carcinomas rarely spread but, locally, they can be destructive.

Occasionally, Bowen's disease will present on the lower limb as an isolated erythematous plaque, which may look very similar to psoriasis. However, unlike psoriasis, the lesions will not respond to topical steroids. The underlying pathology is of a slow-growing intra-epidermal squamous cell carcinoma. A small proportion (about 3%) progress into invasive squamous cell carcinoma. Multiple patches of Bowen's disease are seen in association with excessive sun exposure and the ingestion of arsenical tonics as a child.

Over 50% of melanomas in women occur on the lower leg, presumably due to sun exposure. Superficial spreading melanoma is the most common type. It presents as an irregularly-shaped and irregularly-pigmented lesion, often with some inflammation. Ulceration within the lesion suggests vertical invasion of tumour cells into the dermis, with potential secondary spread and is a bad prognostic sign.

Secondary tumours, for example from breast cancer, may present as an ulcerated nodule on the leg. It would be rare for this to be an isolated lesion and the underlying diagnosis is usually already known.

Infection (as a cause of ulceration)

Primary infection is a rare cause of leg ulcers in the western world. In the tropics, tuberculosis, atypical mycobacteria, leprosy, diphtheria and deep fungal infections such as *sporotrichosis* are still seen. A good history, along with the presentation of eroding, malodorous ulcers should alert one to the possibility of unusual infection. Liaison with the microbiologist is recommended.

Infection (as a complication)

All broken areas of skin will rapidly become colonised with bacteria in any normal environment. Most of these will cause no harm and, in fact, some may be beneficial to the healing process. Most chronic leg ulcers will become colonised with *Staphylococcus aureus* and *Pseudomonas aeruginosa*. This does not mean that there is clinical infection. Signs of infection include localised inflammation, increased pain and tenderness, friability of the ulcer bed, pyrexia or the patient becoming systemically unwell. This may require treatment with systemic antibiotics, as will the isolation of beta-haemolytic streptococci from an ulcer swab.

Contact dermatitis

Contact dermatitis takes two forms. The first is contact irritant dermatitis in which repeated exposure to an irritant substance such as a detergent causes a mechanically-induced inflammatory response in the skin.

On the other hand, allergic contact dermatitis is an immunologically-induced hypersensitivity (type IV). Allergies can also occur from repeated exposure to a particular substance. There are a wide variety of substances that can cause allergies, ranging from metals, such as nickel, through to complex proteins (*Chapter 19*).

It is not always easy on clinical grounds alone to separate contact irritant from allergic dermatitis. The conditions may even overlap. Patients with chronic leg ulcers appear vulnerable to developing contact allergies, often to several different topical treatments. This is not surprising considering that one is repeatedly exposing broken skin to a range of medicaments under moisture-retaining bandages.

Common sensitisers include parabens and chlorocresol, antibacterial agents, colophony and additives which prevent rubber and elastic from perishing. Sensitivity reactions tend to follow the shape of application of the ointment, dressing or bandage. Patch testing may help differentiate allergic from irritant reactions, but requires skilled interpretation. Many patients with allergic dermatitis will have positive reactions to several agents.

Varicose eczema and stasis changes

It is too easy to overlook and hence not treat varicose eczema in the presence of a large venous ulcer. In contrast to contact reactions, the eczema is less acute, more chronic and diffuse, being largely confined to the skin over the distended varicose veins. Scaling, thickening and ultimately lichenification of the skin, particularly around the ankle may occur. Occasionally the eczema may flare and become exudative or even generalised. As contact dermatitis is not uncommon and difficult to distinguish from varicose eczema, some authorities argue that patch testing should be carried out on all patients with venous stasis associated eczema.

Trauma and dermatitis artefacta

Not surprisingly, acute abrasive trauma may lead to ulceration of the lower limb. The diagnosis should be obvious. Chronic trauma may be more subtle, eg. due to ill-fitting foot wear. A patient's apparent lack of awareness should make one suspect sensory neuropathy.

Iatrogenic trauma, usually in the form of dressings that are too tight, should not be overlooked, and nor should patients' complaints of too tight a dressing be dismissed.

Self-induced harm does occur. Sometimes this is in direct response to contact irritant or allergic reactions (the 'knitting needle down the plaster syndrome'). Sadly, there are cases of patients self-perpetuating their ulcer for fear of losing what may be, for them, their only social contact.

Conclusion

To diagnose the cause of ulceration of the lower limb requires taking a good history, followed by a methodical examination that involves not just looking at the ulcer but at the whole patient. The healthcare professional should be aware of any underlying disease that may exacerbate or delay the healing process. It is, after all, far easier to heal an ulcer in a healthy patient.

Around 80% of leg ulcers are of venous origin, however, that also means that around 20% have another cause. It is vital to exclude significant arterial disease before applying compression.

If an ulcer is not healing, you should consider what else could be going on, eg. malignant change or vasculitis. It is important to reassess both the ulcer and the surrounding skin. Redness does not necessarily indicate infection and contact reactions are common.

Further reading

Nicolaides AN (2000) Investigation of chronic venous insufficiency : a consensus statement. *Circulation* **102**(20): e126–e163

Smith PC (2006) The causes of skin damage and leg ulceration in chronic venous disease. *Int J Lower Extremity Wounds* **5**(3): 160–8

Simon DA, Dix FP, McCollum CN (2004) Management of venous leg ulcers. *Br Med J* **328**: 1358–62

Grey JE, Harding KG, Enoch S (2006) Venous and arterial leg ulcers. *Br Med J* **332**: 347–50

London NJM, Donnelly R (2000) ABC of arterial and venous disease: Ulcerated lower limb. *Br Med J* **320**: 1589–91

Graves JW, Morris JC, Sheps SG (2001) Martorell's hypertensive leg ulcer: case report and concise review of the literature. *J Hum Hypertension* **15**(4):279–83

Burch J, Jones M (2006) *Pyoderma gangrenosum* and leg ulcers associated with vasculitis: importance of addressing the underlying disease process when treating inflammatory wounds. *J Wound Ostomy Continence Nurs* **33**(1):77-81; discussion 81–2

Nelzen O, Bergqvist D, Lindhagen A (1993) High prevalence of diabetes in chronic leg ulcer patients: a cross-sectional population study. *Diabetic Med* **10**(4): 345–50

Okuwa M, Sanada H, Sugama J, Inagaki M, Konya C, Kitagawa A, Tabata K (2006) A prospective cohort study of lower-extremity pressure ulcer risk among bedfast older adults. *Adv Skin Wound Care* **19**(7):391–7

Cruickshank AH, McConnell EM, Miller DG (1963) Malignancy in scars, chronic ulcers, and sinuses. *J Clin Pathol* **16**: 573–80

Mekkes JR, Loots MA, Van Der Wal AC, Bos JD (2003) Causes, investigation and treatment of leg ulceration. *Br J Dermatol* **148**(3):388–401

Oluwasanmi JO, Alao MO, Ofodile FA (1979) Tropical ulcers. *Plast Reconstruct Surg* **64**(1): 41–6

Cameron J, Wilson C, Powell S, Cherry G, Ryan T (1992) Contact dermatitis in leg ulcer patients. *Ostomy/Wound Management* **38**(9):8, 10–1

Hofman D, Moore K, Cooper R, Eagle M, Cooper S (2007) Use of topical corticosteroids on chronic leg ulcers. *J Wound Care* **16**(5): 227–30

Millard LG (1984) Dermatological pathomimicry: a form of patient maladjustment. *Lancet* **2**(8409): 969–71

CHAPTER 16

THE DIABETIC FOOT

Alistair McInnes and Richard White

The diabetic foot or diabetic foot syndrome includes the diabetes-related complications of peripheral neuropathy, peripheral arterial disease, foot ulcer, Charcot arthropathy and infection. It is often a combination of these factors that leads to lower limb amputation. The International Diabetes Federation has reported that a diabetes-related amputation occurs every 30 seconds on a worldwide basis (Bakker, 2005). Clearly, the burden of diabetic foot disease poses a significant health challenge both nationally and globally. This chapter will focus on the diabetic complications and the evidence-based practice for the healthcare practitioner.

Epidemiology

Diabetes mellitus is a chronic metabolic disorder which affects between 2–5% of the population in Europe (Williams *et al*, 1999) and is increasing at epidemic rates worldwide. The prevalence in the UK is estimated to be around 2.5 million adults today and expected to increase to approximately 3 million by the year 2010 (Diabetes UK, 2004).

Foot ulcers are one of the main complications of diabetes mellitus and it has been estimated that people with diabetes have a 12–25% lifetime risk of developing foot ulceration (Abbott *et al*, 2005). There is a wide variation in reported prevalence and incidence as a result of different populations studied (community-based and clinic-based). However, in a large population study of over 10000 patients, there was a 5% history of past or current ulceration (Abbott *et al*, 2005). Furthermore, it has been estimated that 20% of diabetic patients are admitted to hospital because of foot problems (Levin, 1996), and that 50% of the hospital bed occupancy of diabetic patients in the UK is due to diabetic foot disease (Levin, 2001). Foot ulcers precede 85% of lower extremity amputations in diabetes (Pecoraro *et al*, 1990) and considering that diabetes is the most common reason for lower extremity amputation, it is imperative that all possible preventable measures are taken to avoid this complication. When foot ulcers do occur, early aggressive management should be undertaken to prevent further morbidity and possible mortality.

Economics

In the UK, the economic burden of diabetes has been estimated at 5% of the total national health budget (currently approaching £100 billion). The cost of diabetes-related foot complications has been estimated at £252 million pounds on an annual basis (Dang and Boulton, 2003). In addition to these costs, there is a further estimate of seven-fold more in the community (Dang and Boulton, 2003). There is evidence to suggest that the more severe the foot condition in terms of infection, the more costly the episode of care (Dang and Boulton, 2003). These estimates do not include the cost of amputations.

In a cost-utility analysis based on the Markov model, there is a suggestion that the implementation of a preventative strategy could be cost-effective. The most cost-effective programme is one that targets those people with diabetes with recognised risk factors for foot ulceration (Ortegon *et al*, 2004). This may aid in the development of screening and assessment programmes to identify those at-risk for tailored intervention strategies.

Pathogenesis

The route to the development of a foot ulcer involves both intrinsic and extrinsic factors. The majority of diabetic foot ulcers involve peripheral neuropathy and peripheral arterial disease, which are direct results from prolonged periods of chronic hyperglycaemia (Marston, 2006). These complications alone are unlikely to lead to foot ulceration. However, in combination with the presence of plantar callus and foot deformity, the likelihood of developing an ulcer is significantly increased (Ledoux *et al*, 2005; Leese *et al*, 2006). There are a number of factors that contribute to abnormal high pressures on the diabetic foot and with the lack of sensory feedback, due to neuropathy, soft tissue damage and the resultant responses of the tissues leads to ulceration and infection (Dinh and Veves, 2005; Ledoux *et al*, 2005; Leese *et al*, 2006).

Table 16.1: Intrinsic and extrinsic factors to consider when assessing the patient

Intrinsic factors	Observations
• Foot deformity	For example, pes cavus, excessive pronation, hallux abducto valgus, hallux rigidus, claw toes
• Limited joint mobility syndrome	Positive prayer sign: inability to approximate both palmar surfaces of the hands together
• Peripheral neuropathy	Claw toes, high arch, muscle atrophy, dry skin and Ward's sign (distended dorsal veins)
• History of past ulceration	Callus present and/or scar tissue
• Peripheral arterial disease	Nutritional loss, dystrophic toenails, shiny skin, dry skin, loss of hair on digits, skin and muscle atrophy. Colour change, ie. pale, cyanotic, dependent rubor
• Plantar callus	Thickened epidermis, appears yellowish/brown and presents as circular plaques over pressure sites
• Poor glycaemic control • Smoking • Retinopathy and nephropathy • Poor visual acuity • Age and being male • Social background • Psychosocial factors	
Extrinsic factors	
• Walking barefoot • Treading on a nail • Dropping something on foot • Trips and falls • Inappropriate footwear • Self-treatment, eg. use of over-the-counter remedies • Too hot footbath • Walking on hot sand • Prolonged bedrest • Lack of foot and shoe inspection	

Table 16.1 provides an aide memoire for the healthcare practitioner when taking a history of the patient presenting with a foot ulcer. In the section on assessment and screening for risk factors (*pp 196–198*), more information is available on the simple tests that can determine the risk factor status of the patient.

Peripheral neuropathy

This complication of diabetes is the most common finding in patients with foot disease. Kumar *et al* found that over 40% of type 2 diabetic patients had significant neuropathy and overall about 30% of all people with diabetes have neuropathy (Kumar *et al*, 1994). Peripheral neuropathy results from glucose toxicity which causes significant metabolic abnormalities and damage to the *vasa nevorum* (Ilnytska *et al*, 2006). The pathological mechanisms are complex and, unsurprisingly, can manifest in different types of neuropathic syndromes including peripheral sensory neuropathy, painful mono-neuropathies and autonomic neuropathy (*Table 16.2*; Tesfaye, 2006). With sensory neuropathy, loss of protective sensation is arguably the most significant clinical finding and several studies have now shown that peripheral neuropathy is the strongest initiating factor for the development of a foot ulcer. Motor neuropathy affects the foot in quite subtle ways which can lead to foot deformity, altered gait and abnormal pressure loading on the foot. This can contribute to the formation of callus, which, in turn contributes to the risk of developing a foot ulcer (Pitei, 1999; Abouaesha, 2001; Baker, 2002).

Painful diabetic neuropathy may include several forms of neuropathy and the diagnosis is made by exclusion. The differential diagnosis is made by a physician or specialist neurologist, as there are many reasons for patients to experience pain. Diabetic painful neuropathy may present as acute painful neuropathy, asymmetrical (focal) neuropathy, proximal amyotrophy and chronic painful diabetic neuropathy. The acute

Table 16.2: Proposed hypothesis of diabetic peripheral nerve damage

- Chronic hyperglycaemia
- Nerve microvascular dysfunction
- Protein kinase C hyperactivity
- Increased free-radical formation
- Polyol pathway hyperactivity
- Non-enzymatic glycation
- Abnormalities of nerve growth

neuropathy is associated with glycaemic control and may be experienced by the patient who experiences rapid metabolic control. This form of neuropathy often resolves within 12 months or so (Burden and Burden, 2002). Proximal amyotrophy is characterised by profound proximal leg weakness and the patient may complain of burning pain which can extend below the knee (Taylor and Dunne, 2004). The patients suffering from this type of neuropathy have profound wasting of the quadriceps and may experience difficulty in raising from a chair and climbing stairs.

Chronic painful neuropathy poses a major challenge to the multidisciplinary team, as the patients may be unable to cope with all the difficulties of living with diabetes and suffering constant pain. Many of these patients also suffer from depression which exacerbates the situation. It is important that the team members adopt an empathic approach and consider psychological support and counselling.

The management of painful neuropathy has improved over the years and there are various treatments recommended (see section on management).

The Charcot foot

Aetiopathology

This is a complication of peripheral neuropathy which is characterised by joint dislocation, subluxation and pathologic fractures of the foot. This condition may also be termed Charcot neuroarthropathy. Charcot believed that intrinsic bone weakness was the underlying condition, caused by neurogenic deficiencies in bone nutrition. It was subsequently felt that such dystrophy was mediated by sympathetic denervation of the bone vasculature (neurotrophic, or neurovascular theory). Now, Charcot foot is mostly seen in diabetic neuropathy, which has replaced syphilis as a frequent cause of peripheral nerve dysfunction. Recent studies in the diabetic Charcot foot and bone turnover indicate that the neurotrophic theory is a myth (Chanteleau and Onvlee, 2006). The assumption that bone resorption is due to sympathetic denervation proved to be false; sympathetic activity increases osteoclastic activity and thereby bone loss (sympathomimetic bone resorption). Except for the transient, inflammatory stage of the diabetic Charcot foot, there is no evidence of relevant osteoporosis or demineralisation of the foot skeleton. Another theory for the aetiopathology is the neurotraumatic and neurovascular explanation (Jude and Boulton, 2001; Salgami *et al*, 2006). The neurotraumatic theory proposed that continued weight bearing on an insensitive foot with loss of proprioception could lead to bone fracture and joint destruction (Trepman *et al*, 2005; Chanteleau *et al*, 2006). The neurovascular theory was based on the assumption that an autonomically stimulated vascular reflex led to a hyperaemia and periarticular osteopenia. The continued weight bearing on the weakened demineralised bones leads to microfractures, compounded by further episodes of inflammation (Schoonbeek *et al*, 2002). These theories have been recently challenged, notably by Jeffcoate *et al* (2005). The pronounced inflammatory reaction characteristic of the acute Charcot foot has not yet been fully elucidated. Jeffcoate has suggested a role for the increased expression of pro-inflammatory cytokines in the altered state of inflammation. This triggers a cascade of reactions that results in osteoclastogenesis, leaving the bones vulnerable to fracture and dislocation (Jeffcoate, 2005a, b). The possibility of a systemic inflammatory response in the acute Charcot foot has been postulated (Petrova *et al*, 2007).

Clinical features

Typically, the patient presents with a hot, painless, swollen foot. A history of minor trauma has been recorded in about 50% of cases (Caputo *et al*, 1998). It is important to discriminate this condition from cellulitis and osteomyelitis or an inflammatory arthropathy. There is a temperature difference of $>2°C$ when compared to the contralateral foot. At this stage (acute), there may not be any visual deformity or evidence of fracture from X-ray.

It is also important to note that most investigations at this early stage may be normal. If a Charcot foot is suspected, prompt referral to the multidisciplinary diabetic foot team is essential (Sinacore, 1998).

Peripheral arterial disease

Approximately 30% of all people with diabetes have peripheral arterial disease. This is a major cause of morbidity and mortality in the diabetic population (Heikkinen *et al*, 2007; Coccheri, 2007). Atherosclerosis is more widespread and accelerated among patients with diabetes. It is the cause of stroke, heart disease and gangrene. It accounts for

>70% of deaths in type 2 diabetes. Peripheral vascular disease is 20 times more common in diabetes. The prothrombotic status as a result of diabetes is complex; suffice to say that oxidative stress is more profound with diabetes and contributes to the disease. The risk factors include: smoking, hypertension, dyslipidemia, abnormal fibrinolysis and altered platelet function (Grant, 2007; Heikkinen *et al*, 2007). Peripheral arterial disease is a major contributing factor in the development of foot ulceration in around 35% of cases and may cause delayed healing, gangrene and subsequent amputation (Pataky and Vischer, 2007).

Clinical features

The ischaemic foot may be red, dry and atrophic. The skin may be shiny, hairless with dystrophic toenails. The foot may be cadaverous in appearance. Peripheral neuropathy may accompany the ischaemia which can lead to difficulty with assessment (see section on assessment).

Infection

Infection is a consequence of ulceration and is the greatest threat to the limb in diabetes (Lipsky *et al*, 2007). The immune response is defective in diabetes, which permits pathogenic bacteria to multiply and destroy viable tissue. It is vital to inspect the foot for all signs and symptoms of infection, as outlined by various authors (Edmonds, 2006; Lipsky *et al*, 2006; Lipsky, 2007). The infected neuroischaemic foot may not show all of these signs and symptoms (Edmonds, 2006).

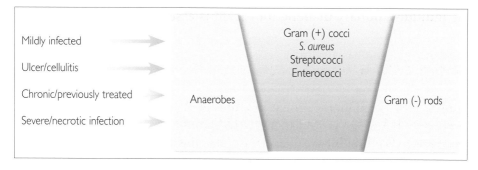

Figure 16.1: Multiple pathogens. Modified from Van der Meer *et al*, 1996

Clinical features

The foot may be swollen, red and warm. There may be purulent discharge from the ulcer which may be malodourous. Depending upon the severity of the infection, there may be ascending cellulitis and the patient may have an increase in blood glucose levels. Pain may not be present as a result of any neuropathy. In addition, the cellulitis may be masked by the rubor of ischaemia. It is vitally important to assess the severity and type of infection to enable appropriate early antibiotic therapy (see section on assessment). There have been several studies that have identified the pathogens responsible for the infected diabetic foot. The more severe the infection, the greater likelihood for multiple pathogens (Jude and Unsworth, 2004; *Table 16.3*)

Table 16.3: Diabetic foot risk classification system		
Risk status	**Risk definition**	**Plan of care**
Low risk	Diabetes, but no evidence of established risk factors	Basic education and open access if problems
High risk, not yet ulcerated	Diabetes and established risk factors	Structured care with regular review by appropriately skilled healthcare professionals
Active ulceration	Diabetes and active foot problem, eg. ulcer or Charcot foot	Review and treatment by specialist diabetic footcare services
Aftercare of the person with a healed ulcer or amputation	Diabetes with healed ulcer or amputation	Review and tailored education, renew shoes and orthoses as required

Management

Screening and assessment

Part of the annual review process for all those persons with both type 1 and type 2 diabetes must include inspection and assessment of both feet. There is an evidence base that has informed national and international guidelines for screening. For those healthcare practitioners in primary care, a simple screening must include assessment of risk. This enables appropriate referral to podiatry services and/or the specialist multidisciplinary team. This has been described as the 'pyramid of foot care' (*Figure 16.2*; Young, 2006).

Risk factor assessment can be carried out fairly simply. It is important to keep the system in a standardised format to allow collection of data for audit purposes and prevent misinterpretation. Any attempt to introduce a screening programme should be accompanied by an education programme for all those involved. It is vital that all stakeholders are involved from the beginning.

Key risk factors to look for: ischaemia, neuropathy and foot deformity

1. Ascertain if there is a history of ulceration.
2. Vascular status: check foot pulses in both feet. If one or more pulses are absent, then consider further evaluation, eg. pain history, intermittent claudication or night/rest pain.
3. Check for peripheral neuropathy. For assessing any loss of protective sensation, select a 10 g nylon monofilament and test

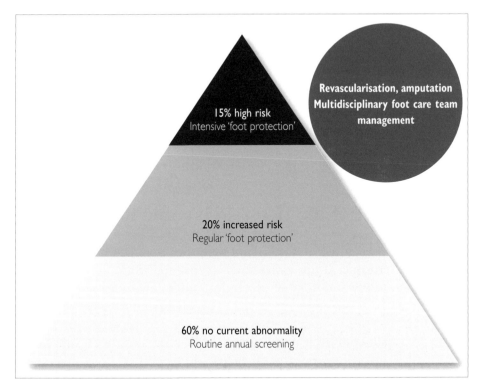

Figure 16.2: Pyramid of foot care

pressure sites. Sites to check for sensation: plantar aspect of hallux, and first and fifth metatarsal heads. Avoid areas of callus and test normal skin closest to the recommended sites.

4. Select a 128 Hz tuning fork and test for loss of vibration perception sense at the apex of the hallux, medial eminence of the first metatarsal head and the malleoli.

5. Look for callus and for significant deformity, eg. Charcot foot, hallux valgus, claw toes, pes cavus and hallux rigidus.

6. Record findings and allocate risk factor status. Refer to national guidelines (Foster, 2004; National Diabetes Support Team, 2006, or Scottish Intercollegiate Guidelines Network [SIGN], 2001, or the Foot in Diabetes UK, 2006).

This is a simple primary screening process to allocate the patient to an appropriate level of care. It is important that any primary care trust has agreed protocols of care and that all of the stakeholders have signed up in agreement. This will allow effective and efficient use of limited resources.

Table 16.3 is a simplified version of risk category classification which considers the aftercare of the person with a healed ulcer or amputation (Diabetic Foot Journal, 2007). Having a history of a foot ulcer is the most significant risk factor for development of another ulcer. This group of patients require periodic review and a tailored education programme in an attempt to prevent further episodes of ulceration. Sadly, the recurrence rates for ulcers are very high. In a prospective study following up patients after foot ulcer healing, re-ulceration rates at one, three and five years were 34%, 61% and 70%, respectively (Boulton *et al*, 2005). This risk category group require close monitoring and regular review.

Assessment of the neuroischaemic foot

The acutely presenting diabetic foot may be associated with varying degrees of chronic limb ischaemia. Ischaemia may be critical or insignificant in the aetiology of ulceration, infection and tissue necrosis. In some diabetic patients, a history of claudication and rest pain (ischaemic neuritis) and eventual tissue loss, accompanied by absent pulses in a pale cool limb may suggest ischaemia. However, significant neuropathy, infection and the presence of ulceration may mask the symptoms and make assessment difficult. Ischaemia and infection are the most significant clinical findings and warrant prompt action.

Practice tip: gently elevate the limb while listening to Doppler sounds over a foot pulse. If the sounds disappear quickly on elevation, the severity of ischaemia warrants further investigation, refer to the vascular services.

Practice tip: if on elevation of the limb, the redness on the dorsal aspect of the foot remains, the chances are the redness is a result of cellulitis and not of ischaemia.

Practice tip: if any new pain is reported in a neuropathic foot, consider the presence of infection.

Pain history

The presence of foot pulses is the most reliable clinical test for lower limb ischaemia, although foot pulses can be absent in the normal population. In addition, the foot pulses may be masked by oedema. It is important to record any pain history, either intermittent claudication or rest pain. Rest pain is often preceded by night pain and is a burning pain felt in the dorsal aspect of the toes and foot. This is a sign of critical ischaemia and urgent referral is required (same day) to the vascular services.

Ankle/brachial pressure index (ABPI)

The ankle/brachial pressure index (ABPI) can be performed by recording the systolic pressures of the brachial artery (arm) and posterior tibial artery/dorsalis pedis (Marshall, 2004).

Ankle
Arm   eg. brachial systolic pressure = 120 mmHg
       Ankle systolic pressure = 70 mmHg

ABPI = 120/70 = 0.58

Values: ABPI for ischaemia

ABPI		
	<0.5	severe or critical ischaemia
	0.5–0.8	significant arterial disease
	0.8–1.3	normal arterial flow
	>1.3	arterial calcification, unreliable

Note: If foot pulses are not palpable and the ABPI pressure index >1, reduced Doppler arterial waveform indicates ischaemia (Korzon-Burakowska and Edmonds, 2006).

Practice tip: 'Red herrings' — thickened toenails, discolouration, loss of hair and cold feet are not reliable indicators of arterial insufficiency. Capillary refill test is an unreliable test.

Assessment of infection

Early detection of infection in a diabetic foot ulcer is of paramount importance to minimise tissue destruction and prevent delayed healing and possible amputation. Signs of infection can be masked in the neuroischaemic foot and clinicians should thoroughly inspect the foot:

- observing the skin for trauma, erythema, dryness, callus and oedema
- checking between web spaces for macerated or fissured skin
- remembering that erythema may indicate cellulitis, or, irritation from a shoe
- recording redness, streaking, fullness, fluctuation and the extent of inflammatory process.

The use of an ulcer classification system should be considered for clinical management, research and audit and for medico-legal reasons. There are several classifications described in the literature, including the Wagner (Wagner, 1983), Texas (Armstrong *et al*, 1998), SAD (size, sepsis, area/depth, arteriopathy, denervation: Jeffcoate *et al*, 2006) systems and the PEDIS system (Schaper, 2004). This latter system has been developed by the International Working Group on the Diabetic Foot (IWGDF) for research purposes. Part of the classification system includes a section on severity of infection, which is useful for clinical management (*Table 16.4*).

Management of infection

It is vital to remember that the management of infection is part of the therapeutic regimen in the management of foot ulceration. All other aspects need to be considered, namely:

- infection control
- metabolic control
- vascular control
- education control
- mechanical control (Foster and Edmonds, 2001).

Infection control

An example of standard antibiotic regimens is as follows:

Micro-organism   **Antibiotics**

Staphylococcus aureus   Flucloxacillin 500 mg qds
                            Clindamycin 300 mg qds

Table 16.4: Clinical classification of a diabetic foot infection		
Clinical manifestations of infection	Infection severity	PEDIS grade
Wound lacking purulence or any manifestations of inflammation	Uninfected	1
Presence of >2 manifestations of inflammation (purulence, or erythema, pain, tenderness, warmth, or induration), but any cellulitis/erythema extends <2 cm around the ulcer, and infection is limited to the skin or superficial subcutaneous tissues; no other local complications or systemic illness	Mild	2
Infection (as above) in a patient who is systemically well and metabolically stable but which has >1 of the following characteristics: cellulitis extending >2 cm, lymphangetic streaking, spread beneath the superficial fascia, deep tissue abscess, gangrene, and involvement of muscle, tendon, joint or bone	Moderate	3
Infection in a patient with systemic toxicity or metabolic instability (eg. fever, chills, tachycardia, hypotension, confusion, vomiting, leukocytosis, acidosis, severe hyperglycaemia, or azotemia)	Severe	4

	Co-amoxiclav 625 mg tds
Streptococcus	Amoxycillin 500 mg tds
(B, C and G)	Erythromycin 500 mg qds
	Clindamycin 300 mg qds
	Co-amoxiclav 625 mg tds
Anaerobes	Metronidazole 400 mg tds
	Clindamycin 300 mg qds
Gram negatives	Ciprofloxacin 500 mg bd

It is important to consider the particular challenges with the infected diabetic foot, namely methicillin-resistant *Staphylococcus aureus* (MRSA) and osteomyelitis. If infection is suspected, the patient must be referred to the specialist multidisciplinary diabetic foot care team where added input from the microbiologist is necessary (Lipsky *et al*, 2006).

Metabolic and vascular control

Medical management of diabetes is required, particularly with more severe infections. Vascular intervention may be required in the form of endovascular procedures, ie. angioplasty and the use of stents to improve arterial blood flow.

Education control

The patient with a diabetic foot ulcer requires education and support. Basic education must include preventative strategies to prevent further trauma to the foot and to recognise any deterioration of the condition. The ability to recognise any problem and contact a member of the healthcare team is the absolute minimum. Patient concordance and other psychosocial factors should be considered. Many patients suffering from diabetes and foot ulceration experience a poor health-related quality of life and may also suffer from depression (Egede, 2007; Simson *et al*, 2007), even during their first episode of ulceration (Ismail *et al*, 2007).

Mechanical control

Off-loading pressure from the ulcer site is a key aspect of management. Diabetic neuropathic ulcers will not heal unless off-loading is achieved.

While the literature is weak on this topic, the most compelling evidence is for the use of a total contact cast (Armstrong and Stacpoole-Shea, 1999). Other means of off-loading include commercially available aircasts (Lavery *et al*, 1996), half shoes, splints, modified shoes and sandals. Custom-moulded insoles are also useful to off-load from the ulcer site (Branthwaite *et al*, 2004).

Careful and prompt attention to these key areas of diabetic foot ulcer management, can help to reduce morbidity, costs, and ultimately mortality.

References

Abouaesha F, van Schie CH, Griffiths GD, *et al* (2001) Plantar tissue thickness is related to peak plantar pressure in the high-risk diabetic foot. *Diabetes Care* 24(7): 1270–4

Abbott CA, Garrow AP, Carrington AL, *et al* (2005) Foot ulcer risk is lower in South-Asian and African-Caribbean compared with European diabetic patients in the UK: the north-west diabetes foot care study. *Diabetes Care* 28: 382–7

Armstrong DG, Lavery LA, Harkless LB (1998) Validation of a diabetic wound classification system. The contribution of depth, infection, and ischaemia to risk of amputation. *Diabetes Care* 21(5): 855–9

Armstrong DG, Stacpoole-Shea S (1999) Total contact casts and removable cast walkers. *J Am Podiatr Med Assoc* 89(1): 50–3

Baker N (2002) Debridement of the diabetic foot: a podiatric perspective. *Int J Lower Extrem Wounds* 1(2): 87–92

Bakker K, van Houtum WH, Riley PC (2005) 2005: The International Diabetes Federation focuses on the diabetic foot. *Curr Diab Rep* 5(6): 436–40

Boulton AJ, Vileikyte L, Ragnarson-Tennvall G, Apelqvist J (2005) The global burden of diabetic foot disease. *Lancet* 366(9498): 1719–24

Branthwaite HR, Payton CJ, Chockalingam N (2004) The effect of simple insoles on the three-dimensional foot motion during walking. *Clin Biomech* (Bristol) 19(9): 972–7

Burden ML, Burden AC (2002) Resolution of diabetic autonomic neuropathy. *Postgrad Med J* 78(920): 360–1

Caputo GM, Ulbrecht J, Cavanagh PR, Juliano P (1998) The Charcot foot in diabetes: six key points. *Am J Family Physician* 57(11): 2705–10

Chanteleau E, Richter A, Schmidt-Grigoriadis P, Schwerbaum WA (2006) The diabetic charcot foot. *Exp Clin Endochrinol Diabetes* 114(3): 118–23

Chanteleau E, Onvlee GJ (2006) Charcot foot in diabetes: farewell to the neurotrophic theory. *Horm Metab Res* **38**(6): 361–7

Coccheri S (2007) Approaches to prevention of cardiovascular complications and events in diabetes mellitus. *Drugs* **67**(7): 997–1026

Dang CN, Boulton AJM (2003) Changing perspectives in diabetic foot ulcer management. *Int J Low Extrem Wounds* **2**(4): 4–12

Diabetes UK (2004) *Diabetes in the UK 2004. A report from Diabetes UK October 2004.* Diabetes UK, London

Dinh TL, Veves A (2005) A review of the mechanisms implicated in the pathogenesis of the diabetic foot. *Int J Low Extrem Wounds* **4**(3): 154–9

Edmonds M (2006) Diabetic foot ulcers: practical treatment andrecommendations. *Drugs* **66**(7): 913–29

Egede LE (2007) Major depression in individuals with chronic medical disorders: prevalence, correlates and association with health resource utilisation, lost productivity and functional disability. *Gen Hosp Psychiatry* **29**(5): 409–16

Foot in Diabetes UK, Diabetes UK, The Association of British Clinical Diabetologists, The Primary Care Diabetes Society and The Society of Chiropodists and Podiatrists (2006) *The National Minimum Skills Framework for Commissioning of Foot Care Services for People with Diabetes* (online) Available online at: www.feetforlife.org/download/4033/NatMinSkillFramewkFootNov06.pdf (last accessed 28 September, 2007)

Foster A (2004) An evaluation of NICE guidelines in foot care for patients with diabetes. *Nurs Times* **100**(22): 52–3

Foster A, Edmonds M (2001) An overview of foot disease in patients with diabetes. *Nurs Standard* **16**(12): 45–52

Grant PJ (2007) Diabetes mellitus as a prothombotic condition. *J Intern Med* **262**(2): 157–72

Heikkinen M, Salmenpera M, Lepantalo A (2007) Diabetes care for patient with peripheral arterial disease. *Eur J Vasc Endovasc Surg* **33**(5): 583–91

Ilnytska O, Lyzogubov VV, Stevens MJ, *et al* (2006) Poly(ADP-Ribose) polymerase inhibition alleviates experimental diabetic sensory neuropathy. *Diabetes* **55**(6): 1686–94

Ismail K, Winkley K, Stahl D (2007) A cohort study of people with diabetes and their first foot ulcer: the role of depression on mortality. *Diabetes Care* **30**(6): 1473–9

Jeffcoate WJ (2005a) Theories concerning the pathogenesis of the acute charcot foot suggest future therapy. *Curr Diab Rep* **5**(6): 430–5

Jeffcoate WJ (2005b) Abnormalities of vasomotor regulation in the pathogenesis of the acute charcot foot of diabetes mellitus. *Int J Low Extrem Wounds* **4**(3): 133–7

Jeffcoate WJ, Game F, Cavanagh PR (2005) The role of pro-inflammatory cytokines in the cause of neuropathic osteoarthropathy (acute Charcot foot) in diabetes. *Lancet* **366**(9502): 2058–61

Jeffcoate WJ, Chipchase SY, Ince P (2006) Assessing the outcome of the management of the diabetic foot using ulcer-related and person-related measures. *Diabetes Care* **29**(8): 1784–87

Jude EB, Boulton AJ (2001) Update on Charcot arthropathy. *Curr Diab Rep* **1**(3): 228–32

Jude EB, Unsworth PF (2004) Optimal treatment of infected diabetic foot ulcers. *Drugs Aging* **21**(13): 833–50

Korzon-Burakowska A, Edmonds M (2006) Role of the microcirculation in diabetic foot ulceration. *Int J Low Extrem Wounds* **5**(3): 144–8

Kumar S, Ashe HA, Parnell LN, *et al* (1994) The prevalence of foot ulceration and its correlates in diabetic patients: a population-based study. *Diabet Med* **11**(5): 4804

Lavery LA, Vela FA, Lavery DC (1996) Reducing dynamic foot pressures in high risk diabetic subjects with foot ulcerations. *Diabetes Care* **19**(8): 818–21

Ledoux WR, Shofer JB, Smith DG, *et al* (2005) Relationship between foot type, foot deformity, and ulcer occurrence in the high-risk diabetic foot. *J Rehabil Res Dev* **42**(5): 665–72

Leese GP, Reid F, Green V, *et al* (2006) Stratification of foot ulcer risk in patients with diabetes: a population-based study. *Int J Clin Pract* **60**(5): 541–5

Levin ME (1996) Foot lesions in patients with diabetes mellitus. *Endocrinol Metab Clin N Am* **25**(2): 447–62

Levin ME (2001) Pathogenesis and general management of foot lesions in the diabetic patient. In: Bowker JH, Pfeifer MA, eds. *Levin and O'Neal's The Diabetic Foot*, 6th edn. Mosby, St Louis: 219–60

Lipsky BA (2007) Empirical therapy for diabetic foot infections: are there clinical clues to antibiotic selection? *Clin Microbiol Infect* **13**(4): 3513

Lipsky BA, Berendt AR, Deery HG, *et al* (2006) Diagnosis and treatment of diabetic foot infections. *Plast Reconstr Surg* **117**(7) Suppl: 212–38

Marshall C (2004)The ankle brachial pressure index: a critical appraisal. *Br J Podiatry* **7**(4): 93–5

Marston WA (2006) Risk factors associated with healing chronic diabetic foot ulcers: the importance of hyperglycaemia. *Ostomy/Wound Management* **52**(3): 26–32

National Diabetes Support Team (2006) *Diabetic Foot Guide*. NHS Clinical Governance Support Team, London

Ortegon MM, Redekop WK, Niessen LW (2004) Cost-effectiveness of prevention and treatment of the diabetic foot: a Markov analysis. *Diabetes Care* **27**(4): 901–07

Pataky Z, Vischer U (2007) Diabetic foot disease in the elderly. *Diabet Metab* 33(Suppl 1): S56–S65

Pitei DL, Foster A, Edmonds M (1999) The effect of regular callus removal on foot pressures. *J Foot Ankle Surg* 38(4): 251–5

Pecoraro RE, Reiber GE, Burgess EM (1990) Pathways to diabetic limb amputation. *Diabetes Care* 13(5): 513–21

Petrova NL, Moniz C, Elias DA, *et al* (2007) Is there a systemic inflammatory response in the acute charcot foot? *Diabetes Care* 30(4): 997–8

Salgami EV, Bowling FL, Whitehouse RW, Boulton AJ (2006) Charcot neuroarthropathy. *Int J Low Extrem Wounds* 5(3): 207–12

Schaper NC (2004) Diabetic foot ulcer classification system for research purposes: a progress report and criteria for including patients in research studies. *Diabetes Metab Res Rev* May–June, 20(Suppl 1): S90–95

Schoonbeek A, Ottens RL, Lutterman JA (2002) Charcot-arthropathy in diabetes mellitus. *Ned Tijdschr Geneeskd* 146(2): 60–3

Scottish Intercollegiate Guidelines Network (2001) *Management of diabetic foot disease.* Guideline 55, section 7. SIGN, Edinburgh

Simson U, Nawarotzky U, Porck W, *et al* (2007) Depression, anxiety, quality of life among in-patients suffering from diabetic foot syndrome. *Psychother Psychosom Med Psychol* Sept 10 (epub ahead of print)

Sinacore DR (1998) Acute Charcot arthropathy in patients with diabetes mellitus: healing times by foot location. *J Diabet Complic* 12(5): 287–93

Taylor BV, Dunne JW (2004) Diabetic amyotrophy progressing to severe quadriparesis. *Muscle Nerv* 30(4): 505–9

Tesfaye S (2006) CNS involvement in diabetes mellitus. *Curr Diab Rep* 6(6): 431–8

Trepman E, Nihal A, Pinzur MS (2005) Current topics review: Charcot neuroarthropathy of the foot and ankle. *Foot Ankle Int* 26(1): 46–63

Van der Meer JW, Koopmans PP, Lutterman JA (1996) Antibiotic therapy in diabetic foor infection. *Diabetic Med* 13(Suppl 1): S48–51

Wagner FW (1983) Supplement: algorithms of foot care. In: Levin ME, O'Neal LW, eds. *The Diabetic Foot.* 3rd edn. Mosby, St Louis: 291–302

Walters DP, Gatling W, Mullee MA, *et al* (1992) The distribution and severity of diabetic foot disease: a community study with comparison to non-diabetic group. *Diabetic Med* 9: 354–8

Williams G, Pickup JC (1999) Introduction to diabetes. In: *Handbook of Diabetes*, 2nd edn. Blackwell, Oxford: 2–4

Young RJ (2006) The organisation of diabetic foot care: evidence-based recommendations. In: Boulton AJM, Cavanagh PR, Rayman G, eds. *The Foot in Diabetes.* 4th edn. John Wiley and Sons, Ltd, Chichester: chap 36

CHAPTER 17

WOUND INFECTION OF THE LOWER LIMB

Keith Cutting

It has been stated that between 0.6% and 3.6% of people have a leg ulcer. These figures are dependent on the populations studied and the methodology employed (Graham *et al*, 2003). Nonetheless, it can be seen that leg ulceration is an important cause of patient morbidity.

Factors that influence healing of chronic wounds regardless of aetiology present a challenge to the clinician (*Table 17.1*).

Table 17.1: Factors that influence healing of chronic wounds	
Patient factors	Wound bed factors
Age	Tissue type
Underlying disease	Infection
Mobility	Size and site of the wound
Nutrition	Exudate levels
Medication	Oedema/lymphoedema
Psychosocial issues	Biochemical imbalance
	Inappropriate wound management

Table 17.1 indicates that infection is one of the identified factors that may adversely influence healing. Wound infection remains a major cause of morbidity and mortality and warrants particular attention as a cause of delayed healing.

Prompt and accurate diagnosis of infection is essential. Currently, two options may be considered when attempting to determine if a wound is infected; placing reliance on a microbiological assay obtained from sampling the wound or making a clinical decision based on the appearance of the wound. Many clinicians, though not all, opt for making a decision based on the clinical findings. This clinical decision may be followed, if thought necessary, by obtaining a microbiological report derived from swabbing the wound surface, which can be used to guide antimicrobial choice. A wound swab should only be taken when the wound is clinically infected, there are no signs of infection but the wound is deteriorating, or when there is a long history of failure (chronic wounds). Clinical signs of wound infection are closely aligned with the classic signs of inflammation; redness, swelling, heat and pain. These have served us well over two millennia. However, a review of the literature introduced the concept of traditional and additional (subtle) signs of infection (Cutting and Harding, 1994) in an attempt to provide a more comprehensive approach to the clinical identification of wound infection (*Table 17.2*).

Table 17.2: Traditional and subtle signs of infection	
Traditional	Additional (subtle)
Abscess	Delayed healing
Cellulitis	Discolouration
Discharge: • serous exudate/inflammation • seropurulent • haemopurulent • pus	Friable granulation tissue/bleeds easily Pain/tenderness Pocketing at base of wound Bridging of epithelium/soft tissue Malodour Wound breakdown

The above criteria have been subjected to two validation studies (Cutting 1998; Gardner *et al* 2001) with both investigations demonstrating supportive results. They have been incorporated into many wound assessment forms both at home and abroad but have yet to achieve significant recognition within the surgical wound healing community.

The consideration that signs of infection may be closely associated with wound type has resulted in the development of core criteria and criteria specific to wound type (Cutting *et al*, 2005). The core criteria may be seen in *Figure 17.1* and those specific to venous ulcers, arterial and diabetic foot ulcers may be seen in *Figures 17.2, 17.3* and *17.4*.

Wound type				
Acute/surgical 1	Cellulitis	Pus	Malodour	Exudate chng vol/vis
Acute/surgical 2	Cellulitis	Pus	Malodour	Exudate chng vol/vis
Arterial	Cellulitis	Pus	Malodour	Exudate chng vol/vis
Burns (partial)	Cellulitis	Pus	Malodour	Exudate chng vol/vis
Burn (full)	Cellulitis	Pus	Malodour	Exudate chng vol/vis
Diabetic foot ulcer	Cellulitis	Pus	Malodour	Exudate chng vol/vis
Pressure ulcer	Cellulitis	Pus	Malodour	Exudate chng vol/vis
Venous ulcer	Cellulitis	Pus	Malodour	Exudate chng vol/vis

score 8 or 9	score 6 or 7	score 4 or 5

Wound type				
Acute/surgical 1	Erythema	Breakdown/size increase	Pain	Delayed healing
Acute/surgical 2	Erythema	Breakdown/size increase	Pain	Delayed healing
Arterial	Erythema	Breakdown/size increase	Pain	
Burns (partial)	Erythema	Breakdown/size increase	Pain	
Burn (full)	Erythema	Breakdown/size increase	Pain	
Diabetic foot ulcer	Erythema	Breakdown/size increase	Pain	Delayed healing
Pressure ulcer	Erythema	Breakdown/size increase	Pain	Delayed healing
Venous ulcer		Breakdown/size increase	Pain	Delayed healing

score 8 or 9	score 6 or 7	score 4 or 5

Wound type			
Acute/surgical 1		Oedema	
Acute/surgical 2	Discolouration	Oedema	Friable/bleed
Arterial	Discolouration	Oedema	
Burns (partial)	Discolouration	Oedema	Friable/bleed
Burn (full)	Discolouration	Oedema	Friable/bleed
Diabetic foot ulcer	Discolouration	Oedema	Friable/bleed
Pressure ulcer	Discolouration	Oedema	Friable/bleed
Venous ulcer	Discolouration		Friable/bleed

score 8 or 9	score 6 or 7	score 4 or 5

Figure 17.1: Core criteria

score 8 or 9	score 6 or 7	score 4 or 5
		New onset dusky wound hue
	Increase in local skin temperature	Discolouration, eg. dull, dark brick red
	Newly formed ulcers within inflamed margins of pre-existing ulcer	Friable granulation tissue that bleeds easily
	Delayed healing despite appropriate compression therapy	Increase in exudate viscosity
	Wound bed extension within inflamed margins	Increase in exudate volume
Cellulitis	Increase in ulcer pain	Malodour

Figure 17.2: Venous leg ulcers

score 8 or 9	score 6 or 7	score 4 or 5
	Change in colour/viscosity of exudate	
	Change in wound bed colour	
	Crepitus	Erythema
	Deterioration of wound	Erythema +/- persists with elevation
	Dry necrosis turning wet	Fluctuation
	Increase in local skin temperature	Increase in exudate volume
	Lymphangitis	Increase in size in a previously healing ulcer
Cellulitis	Malodour	Increased pain
Pus/abscess	Necrosis, new or spreading	Ulcer breakdown

Figure 17.3: Arterial ulcers

210

	Crepitus in the joint	Blue-black discolouration and haemorrhage
	Erythema	Bone or tendon becomes exposed at base of layer
	Fluctuation	Delayed/arrested wound healing despite offloading and debridement
	Increase in exudate volume	Deterioration of the wound
	Induration	Friable granulation tissue that bleeds easily
Cellulitis	Localised pain in a normally asensate foot	Local oedema
Pus/abscess	Malodour	Sinuses developed in an ulcer
Lymphangitis	Probes to bone	Spreading necrosis/ gangrene
Phlegmon	Unexpected pain/ tenderness	Ulcer base changes from healthy pink to yellow/ grey
score 8 or 9	score 6 or 7	score 4 or 5

Figure 17.4: Diabetic foot ulcers

The signs of infection identified in the above tables have been generated from collating expert opinion via an orthodox research method, the Delphi approach. These signs are of practical benefit in the clinical situation as they are specific to wound type. Validation of these criteria should be carried out following feedback derived from empirical testing. The scores or rankings allocated to the criteria were generated as a result of statistical process following the responses by the experts. The rankings indicate their importance as signs of infection as viewed by the expert panels. Those criteria scoring 8–9 were considered as diagnostic of infection and may be viewed as sole or discrete indicators of infection, whereas those achieving lower scores should be used in combination, ie. clusters of signs of infection.

The significance of delayed healing as a sign of infection should not be underestimated. Although other causes of delayed healing (eg. smoking, nutrition, use of steroids/non-steroidal anti-inflammatory drugs [NSAIDS], etc) need to be ruled out, the presence of infection, particularly where visual signs of infection are absent, should be considered. This approach has important clinical significance as a means of promptly reducing morbidity and of lowering the risk of cross-contamination. Recently published comment (White and Cutting, 2006) suggests that there are at least three currently known modes of action where bacteria may delay healing without inducing a host response. These are:

- the ability to evade detection by the immune system
- suppression of the cellular wound healing response
- the formation of biofilm.

These mechanisms may be viewed as being integral to our understanding of what constitutes critical colonisation.

The Wound Infection Continuum (Kingsley, 2001) has served to rationalise our thoughts in respect of potential progression to the state of infection. In light of recent findings, perhaps it is now time to give consideration to modifying the current model to enhance our understanding of the relationship of bioburden and delayed healing. Where others (Edwards and Harding, 2004) have stipulated that critical colonisation and infection share common signs of infection, White and Cutting (2006) have indicated otherwise. The significant difference being that although critical colonisation is not a benign state, it does not necessarily demonstrate its presence with visible signs. Rather, this is a state where the anticipated host response has been suppressed or avoided.

Definition of terms:

Apoptosis:	programmed cell death
Critical colonisation:	The inability of the wound to maintain a balance between an altered bioburden and an effective immune system, denoted by a delay in healing but not necessarily accompanied by obvious deterioration in the wound or other overt signs of infection
Polymorphonuclear neutrophils (PMNs):	most abundant type of white blood cell that migrate towards a site of inflammation/infection forming an integral component of the immune system

---

Ulcers of the lower limb, in particular those that are predominantly venous in origin, may present with an erythematous margin that is regularly considered a sign accompanying chronic (histological) inflammation. This cause of erythema may require reconsideration. It has been found that a Morganella species commonly found in wounds (*M. morganii*), expresses histamine (Cooper *et al*, 2004). It is therefore possible that peri-wound erythema could result from colonisation with *M. morganii*. Microbiological samples from wounds are not usually screened for this Gram-negative bacillus, but Hansson *et al* (1995) found *M. morganii* in 23% of venous leg ulcers (n = 58) and Bowler and Davis (1999) found this bacterium in infected leg ulcers. These findings emphasise the need to reconsider how we identify the presence of infection in clinical practice, and the vulnerability of relying on microbiology laboratory reports. It also indicates that within our current knowledge, the state of critical colonisation is more easily understood from a microbiological rather than a clinical perspective.

Although wound biofilms (Percival, 2006) and their implications for delayed healing have received increasing attention in recent years, the problem exists in respect of acquiring an accurate diagnosis. In the chronic wound, it is pertinent to consider that a wound is chronic because of (undiagnosed) biofilm (Wound Care Center, 2006). If this is found to be the case, then application of a diagnostic test would be unnecessary. The Wound Care Center (2006) also states that slough is more than just devitalised tissue and that it behaves like a living growing organism. Slough should therefore be considered as manifestation of a biofilm. The Delphi study (Cutting *et al*, 2005) referred to above produced some interesting results that support these arguments relating to slough and biofilm formation. This is illustrated in *Table 17.3* that collates criteria from four wound types.

Pseudomonas aeruginosa (Gram-negative aerobe) is commonly found in chronic wounds and is known to regularly form biofilms (Costerton, 2001). *P. aeruginosa* is also known to secrete immuno-evasive factors, eg. phenazine (Usher *et al*, 2002) which is thought to induce apoptosis in PMNs. Pseudomonal infections of leg ulcers are known to persist and can be difficult to resolve. Although relatively easy to diagnose, clinically, they can resist treatment with systemic antibiotics yet may respond to topical antiseptic therapy. The same applies to the different bacterial species that may form biofilms in wounds. If wound chronicity is the key to diagnosis of (biofilm) infection, in the absence of other cause(s), this has implications for management. The Wound Care Center (2006) has developed an approach called 'biofilm-based wound care' and indicate that anti-bacterial biofilm agents have a long industrial history in food preparation, manufacturing, dentistry and meatpacking among others. It is also claimed that many of these agents may be of use in medicine. The agents that may be useful in wound care have recently been summarised by Cutting (2006) (*Table 17.4*).

Agents that have been regularly used in daily clinical practice as topical antiseptics include iodine, silver and more recently honey. Although there is ample evidence of anti-bacterial efficacy of these agents this is predominantly derived from in vitro investigations. It is important to remember that although *in vitro* evidence is of value, it does not possess the capacity to replicate what occurs in the *in vivo* situation. Corroborative evidence from rigorously conducted *in vivo* studies are required to substantiate anti-infective efficacy.

Table 17.3: Consensus criteria for wound infection identified in four wound types	
Wound type	Indication
Diabetic foot ulcers	Ulcer base changes from pink to yellow/grey
Venous leg ulcers	Sudden appearance or increase in amount of slough
Pressure ulcers	Viable tissue becomes sloughy
Arterial ulcers	Dry necrosis turns wet

Iodine is a useful antibacterial agent effective against a wide range of pathogens including multi-resistant strains. It is generally regarded nowadays as safe to use on wounds due to the modern formulations that provide a slow release mechanism, such as povidone-iodine and cadexomer iodine. Currently there is no *in vivo* evidence in respect of iodine's effectiveness against biofilm. However, cadexomer iodine is regularly used for its desloughing properties and retrospective assessment has demonstrated improvement in healing in chronic wounds.

Silver is also recognised as being generally safe while possessing a broad spectrum of antibacterial activity. Debate continues on the optimal level of silver ions that are required in a wound, although the oligodynamic approach appears to be favoured. Chaw *et al* (2005) have demonstrated *in vitro* the capacity of silver to partially disrupt the outer structures of the biofilm.

Table 17.4: Outcome measures

Biofilm-based wound care	Explanatory notes/examples
Antibacterial biofilm agents	For example, lactoferrin, a naturally occurring agent sequesters iron and has a bacteriostatic impact on planktonic bacteria. Lactoferrin acts as a serine protease and can degrade proteins required for attachment. Lactoferrin works synergistically with PMNs and has bactericidal activity
Quorum sensing inhibitors	These are agents that would prevent/interrupt the biochemical 'crosstalk' between organisms and could inhibit the production of virulence factors that enhance the ability on microbes to delay healing or cause deterioration in the wound by invasion
Biocides	Non specific biocides, eg. acetic acid, bleach, alcohol, carbolic acid are bactericidal but also cytotoxic to host cells. Specific agents, eg. silver, have a proven planktonic antibacterial effect but their impact on biofilm remains unclear.
Debridement	Carefully cutting out the bed of the wound removes the biofilm along with any remaining sloughy or necrotic tissue and the biochemically dysfunctional tissue in the chronic wound, in effect, returning it to an acute wound that should be more able to progress towards healing
Antibiotics	These kill or stop bacterial cell division of vegetative organisms that emerge from the protective biofilm preventing invasion into the deep compartment of the wound
Antibiofilm dressings	Clinicians need to determine which dressings will maintain a moist environment yet will not support biofilm formation. Wet to dry gauze supports biofilm formation. Presumably, those dressings that debride are antibiofilm
Bacteriophages	These are viruses that attack bacteria disrupting their normal lifecycle, thus preventing progression of bacterial communities to biofilm systems
Advanced technologies	Hyperbaric oxygen therapy may be antibiofilm

Honey is receiving increasing recognition as a wound management therapy and, in particular, as a topical treatment for infection. Honey is relatively easy to apply and there are no known side-effects. Some patients have reported stinging on first application, although this generally subsides over the next few dressing changes.

Biofilm disruption by manuka honey has been demonstrated by Okhiria *et al* (2004) in an *in vitro* study. This implies an increasing potential for honey, especially in chronic wound management.

Application of topical antimicrobials should not be discussed without reference to the carrier dressing. The production of exudate is usually increased in the presence of wound infection. It is, therefore, reasonable to assume that dressings with a high absorbent capacity are best suited to manage infection in a wet environment.

Debridement as a management strategy for wound infection should not be ignored. Debridement is particularly relevant when considering the observations made by the Wound Care Center (2006) that slough behaves as a living, growing organism. Debridement should be carried out on a regular basis and would need to be accompanied by topical antimicrobial therapy, as biofilms are readily able to re-establish adherence and growth patterns.

In most instances, local infection can be managed through local measures. If the infection has invaded the soft tissues and is spreading, systemic therapy may be required.

References

Bowler PG, Davies BJ (1999) The microbiology of infected and non-infected leg ulcers. *Int J Dermatol* **38**: 101–6

Chaw KC, Manimaran M, Tay FEH (2005) Role of silver ions in destabilization of intermolecular adhesion forces measured by atomic force microscopy in *Staphylococcus epidermidis* biofilms. *Antimicrob Agents Chemother* **49**(12): 4853–59

Cooper RA , Morwood S, Burton N (2004) Histamine production by bacteria isolated from wounds. *J Infect* **49**: 39

Costerton JW (2001) Cystic fibrosis pathogenesis and the role of biofilms in persistent infection. *Trends Microbiol* **9**(2): 50–2

Cutting KF, Harding KG (1994) Criteria for identifying wound infection. *J Wound Care* **3**(4): 198–201

Cutting KF (1998) The identification of infection in granulating wounds by registered nurses. *J Clin Nurs* 7: 539–46

Cutting KF, White RJ, Mahoney P, Harding K (2005) Clinical identification of wound infection: a Delphi approach. In: EWMA Position document. *Identifying criteria for wound Infection.* London: MEP Ltd, 2005

Cutting KF (2006) *Wound infection — understanding, assessment and control.* Wound Care Society Booklet, Huntingdon

Edwards R, Harding KG (2004) Bacteria and wound healing. *Curr Opin Infect Dis* 17: 91–6

Gardner SE, Frantz RA, Doebbeling BN (2001) The validity of the clinical signs and symptoms used to identify localized chronic wound infection. *Wound Rep Regen* 9(3): 178–86

Graham ID, Harrison MB, Nelson EA, *et al* (2003) Prevalence of lower limb ulceration: A systematic review of prevalence studies. *Adv Skin Wound Care* 16(6): 305–16

Hansson C, Hoborn J, Möller A, Swanbeck G (1995) The microbial flora in venous leg ulcers without clinical signs of infection. *Acta Derm Venereol (Stockh)* 75(1): 24–30

Kingsley A (2001) A proactive approach to wound infection. *Nurs Standard* 15(30): 50–8

Okhiria O, Henriques A, Burton N, Peters A, Cooper R (2004) The potential of manuka honey for the disruption of biofilms produced by strains of *Pseudomonas aeruginosa* isolated from wounds (Poster presentation). 155th meeting of the Society for General Microbiology, Dublin 6–9th September

Percival S (2004) *Understanding the effects of bacterial communities and biofilms on wound healing.* Available online at: www.worldwidewounds. com/2004/july/Percival/Community-Interactions-Wounds.html (last accessed 10 December 2006)

Usher LR, Lawson RA, *et al* (2002) Induction of neutrophil apoptosis by *Pseudomonas aeruginosa* exotoxin pyocyanin; a potential mechanism of persistent infection. *J Immunol* 168: 1861–68

White RJ, Cutting KF (2006) Critical colonisation; the concept under scrutiny. *Ostomy/Wound Management* 52(11): 50–6

Wound Care Center (2006) *Biofilm-based wound management.* Available online at: www.woundcarecenter.net/CHAPTERTEXT.pdf (last accessed 20 December 2006)

CHAPTER 18

INFECTION CONTROL WITHIN A SOCIAL ENVIRONMENT

Andrew Kingsley

There has been a major increase in the public perception of infection with the global threats of severe acute respiratory syndrome (SARS), bird flu, pandemic flu, the fear of bioterrorism and the formation of the Government's Health Protection Agency which incorporates control of infection as part of public health. In particular, healthcare acquired infection (HCAI) in the last few years has hit the headlines with stories on methicillin-resistant *Stapylocccus aureus* (MRSA), *Clostridium difficile* and *Norovirus*, as well as dirty hospitals and poor compliance of healthcare workers with hand hygiene. Patient environment action teams (PEAT) have had a strong infection control aspect to their work on improving standards of cleanliness and patient and public involvement forums (PPI) have also targeted infection control issues in many hospitals. The prevalence of hospital-acquired infections in the UK is approximately 9% and these infections are considered to cost around £1 billion annually (Department of Health [DoH], 2005). The Chief Medical Officer (CMO) published *Getting Ahead of the Curve* in 2002 (DoH, 2002), which was a strategy for control of infectious disease to combat the low profile of this aspect of care in the NHS. This was shortly followed by the release of a practical action plan, *Winning Ways: Working together to reduce healthcare acquired infections* (DoH, 2003) containing seven action areas including reducing risk from instrumentation, reducing resevoirs of infection and instituting high standards of hygiene in clinical practice. The DoH has continued to put the control of infection in the spotlight with MRSA bacteraemia featuring in the star rating system, which was superceded in 2005/06 by self-evaluation under the Standards for Better Health programme, which is used by the Healthcare Commission (HC) to produce ratings under its annual health checks system, covering issues such as safety, the outcomes of treatment for patients, and the standard of the environment in which care is provided. A Code of Practice for the Prevention and Control of HCAI (DoH, 2006a) was released in October 2006 under the Health Act 2006 and will be used as a basis for subsequent HC inspections. In January 2007, the DoH made available a sum of £300 000 which each acute NHS hospital trust can bid for to improve infection control. This was a non-recurring, 'spend it or lose it' sum for infection control teams to use creatively for raising standards; examples might include e-learning packages, replacing ward furniture such as footstools, waste bins and commodes, installing new bedpan macerators, removing carpets in clinical areas, upgrading mattresses and so on.

Beyond the NHS, the Commission for Social Care Inspection (CSCI) has a remit to, ' ...inspect and report on care services and councils to improve social care and stamp out bad practice' (CSCI, 2006a) in among other institutions/agencies, care homes for older people, nurses agencies and domicillary care services. Infection control for care homes (CSCI, 2006b) utilises the document *Infection Control Guidance for Care Homes* (DoH, 2006b) and the improvement tool, *Essential steps to safe, clean care* (DoH, 2006c) will be integrated into regulations and national minimum standards. The section of this tool on 'preventing the spread of infection' aims to:

> *Reduce the risk of microbial contamination in everyday practice and to ensure there is a managed environment that minimises the risk of infection to patients, clients, staff and visitors.*

It concentrates on hand hygiene, use of personal protective equipment, aseptic technique and safe disposal of sharps (mirrored in the hospital oriented *Saving Lives' package — High Impact Intervention No 1 Preventing the risk of microbial contamination*). In the introduction to this document, the Chief Medical Officer and Chief Nursing Officer acknowledge that HCAIs not only cost significant sums but, more importantly, cause our patients unnecessary suffering and anxiety, which is why they have set the direction of travel towards 'no avoidable infections'. The HC and CSCI are set to merge in the near future. Both healthcare staff and organisations have a duty of care to provide safe care, so it is within this context that we need to consider the unique set up of Leg Clubs delivering healthcare in social communal settings. At present, it is the HC that has jurisdiction to inspect a Leg Club (personal communication – F Goodall HC Inspector Bristol Office – phone conversation 11.1.07) because the clinical input is provided by NHS nurses using NHS equipment and supplies. If the HC inspectors had a concern about infection rates within an NHS trust they could choose to investigate aspects of clinical work both in traditional clinical environments as well as that provided in patient's own homes or in an outreach situation like the Leg Club. The inspectors would use the *Standards for Better Health* as their starting point. Further infection control focus in the wider healthcare setting beyond acute hospitals will continue to feature with the National Patient Safety Agency's 'cleanyourhands' campaign in 2007, as stakeholder consultation events are taking place across England and Wales in January to February (NPSA, 2007).

Infection control guidelines

The guidance provided to each Leg Club is based on the standard infection control precautions concept of infection control which is a 'work safe at all times' system, irrespective of knowledge of carriage of pathogens by the patient.

Leg ulcers are bacterially-colonised wounds, often heavily so, with mixed flora from all parts of the patient's body. To avoid harm to the patient being treated, the principle is not to introduce any microbe with known wound pathogenicity that was not already there. To do this a clean, non-sterile procedure is acceptable rather than a full sterile/aseptic theatre procedure which is neither achievable nor warranted. 'Clean' then becomes the consistent theme from non-sterile gloves to the use of tap water in leg-washing buckets. Unless all elements of a procedure are sterile, asepsis will be compromised and this is inevitable in the care of leg ulcers in both routine clinical and non-clinical environments, so clean is adopted as the appropriate level of approach for the procedure. Clean means free of visible soil, dust and moisture.

To prevent the spread of microbes from one patient to another through the intermediary of the environment and communal equipment, choosing a suitable environment in which to function, strict control of the clinical procedure, decontamination and waste management are all necessary (Khan, 2003). The following table (*Table 18.1*) explores the immediate environment where the clinical work will be carried out (work station), the equipment and products required for the leg ulcer care and a plan of the procedure itself as well as decontamination and waste control. Both infection control (column B) and general nursing rationales (column C) are given to aid understanding.

Table 18.1: Leg Club infection control guideline

Process point, column A	Infection control nursing rationale, column B	General nursing rationale, column C
Work station		
1. 100% plastic rigid smooth garden chairs with arms and high backs	1.1 Easy to clean between patients. Surfaces can be decontaminated 1.2 Tolerant to chemical disinfection following body fluid contamination 1.3 100% surfaces capable of decontamination	1.1 Lightweight for safe lifting 1.2 Can be stacked for ease of storage/transportation 1.3 Comfort from back support 1.4 Sitting and standing stability for patient
2. Plastic matting under and in front of chair	2.1 Prevent contamination of Club venue's flooring from water, exudate and skin scales 2.2 As B1.1, B1.2, B1.3	2.1 Psychological reassurance of cleanliness 2.2 Long-lasting work surface 2.3 As C1.1 2.4 Can be rolled up for ease of storage
3. Blue or white paper towel over plastic matting	3.1 To collect gross contamination of skin scales and exudate which can be 'fixed' to plastic by cleaning processes and particularly by alcohol wipes. Scales are sometimes sticky and translucent, making them difficult to spot 3.2 Clean, dry single patient use surface appropriate for resting scissors and other equipment that is being used	3.1 Increased comfort for resting bare feet over plastic surface alone 3.2 Assists in the complete drying of the soles of the feet after washing
Equipment		
4. 100% plastic buckets lined with plastic bags	4.1 As B1.1, B1.2, B1.3, B3.1 4.2 To reduce risk of splash contamination of the environment and personnel when emptying buckets, as waste water can be poured away in a specific direction	4.1 As C2.1
5. Stainless steel dressing trolley on wheels with two open shelves (no drawers)	5.1 As B1.1, B1.2, B1.3 5.2 Absence of drawers prevents continued storage of product, which would otherwise discourage complete decontamination of trolley	5.1 To hold sufficient supplies for the day's Leg Club. One shelf maximises convenience and time efficiency for nurse 5.2 Provides convenient work surface for preparing dressings, bandages and emollients for each case 5.3 Wheels allow for easy movement

Table 18.1: cont		
Process point, column A	Infection control nursing rationale, column B	General nursing rationale, column C
6. Dopplers with surfaces that can be disinfected to enable units to be cleaned of ultrasound gel and wiped over with alcohol wipes after each patient use	6.1 To prevent hand-held dopplers being a source of cross-contamination between patients, either by contaminated probe heads that touch the patient or via the hands of nurses who are using them	
7. Sphygmomanometers with cuffs that can be cleaned with detergent wipes between patients and be laundered at NHS time/temp combinations in case of visible contamination during use. 'Cling film/food wrap' or plastic should be used under the cuffs on all legs as contamination of skin with wound pathogens in the proximity of the ulcer is more likely than on the arms	7.1 Nylon style cuffs can be wiped over to remove loose skin scales or ultrasound gel that might contribute to cross-contamination 7.2 Laundry cleaning at 71°C /3 minutes or 68°C/10 minutes in the washing cycle will disinfect any cuff with visible contamination by blood/ body fluids 7.3 'Cling film' reduces the contamination of cuffs without compromising readings	
8. Gloves should be powder-free, made preferably of latex and be low in extractable proteins (<50mcg/g) and residual chemicals. If latex sensitivity/ allergy is a problem for patient or nurse, nitrile (acrylonitrile) vinyl or similar robust examination glove products can be used (thin clear plastic gloves presented on backing paper are not considered suitably robust but may be used to line other glove types)	8.1 Powders can induce starch granuloma and act as foci for infection/inflammation	8.1 Latex gloves are the most conformable and easy to work in, cramping the hands less than other materials 8.2 Good quality latex gloves with low residual manufacturing chemicals and proteins reduce risk of contact dermatitis/allergy for the nurse 8.3 Nitrile or other non-latex gloves need to be available for staff and patients who have latex allergy
9. Scissors should be made of stainless steel without serrations and with one protected end and sufficiently robust to cut through disposable bandages. Alternatively, a supply of single-use disposable scissors (can be serrated) or a single patient use reusable Sterile Services supply can be used if available.	9.1 To prevent cross-contamination by enabling effective cleaning and disinfection between uses or providing a sterile supply 9.2 Removal of bandages by scissors reduces linting to the environment	9.1 Suitably robust and sized scissors will make the cutting process possible and less arduous for the nurse 9.2 A protected end designed for cutting bandages allows the process to occur without the threat of skin trauma

Table 18.1: cont		
Process point, column A	Infection control nursing rationale, column B	General nursing rationale, column C
10. A new plastic apron is used for each episode of patient care and for cleaning activities	10.1 To prevent gross contamination of nurse 10.2 To prevent patient to patient transmission of pathogens from contaminated clothing	
11. Stools or kneeling pads if used should be able to be cleaned with detergent wipes after each patient use, and disinfection with a chlorine releasing agent at 1000 ppm if visibly soiled with contaminated wash water, blood or body fluids	11.1 To prevent cross-contamination of subsequent clean work station	
Products		
12. Pump action emollients in multi-dose containers	12.1 To prevent contamination of product reservoir	12.1 Dispensing convenience preventing need for auxiliary container such as a gallipot per person 12.2 Cost-effectiveness of multi-dose over single dose emollient pack presentations
13. Prescribed steroid preparations brought in by and returned to patient after redressing	13.1 Single patient use tubes prevent cross-contamination in use	13.1 Proper control of POM category products
14. Bandages and dressings removed from packets, or cut using disinfected or sterile scissors (see A9 above) from boxed multi-portion rolls at start of each treatment	14.1 To reduce risk of contamination of open product 14.2 To prevent cross-contamination of multi-portion rolls by contaminated scissors and gloves mid-procedure after handling contaminated dressings and wash water	14.1 Individual preparation for each patient to make the redressing process time-efficient. Also convenient for the nurse and inspires confidence in the patient from the professional task delivery
Leg care procedure		
15. First procedure of day alcohol wipe trolley, allow to dry and stock with product sufficient for the day/session	15.1 To remove dust accumulated during storage and decontaminate work surfaces	15.1 Prepare for the day/session
16. Wash hands using soap and water or use an alcohol hand-gel if hands are free of visible	16.1 To prevent cross-contamination via healthcare worker's hands	

223

Table 18.1: cont		
Process point, column A	Infection control nursing rationale, column B	General nursing rationale, column C
contamination (the hand hygiene at this point in the procedure is necessary on the first case of the Leg Club, thereafter at point A38 (see below) final hand and arm wash also serves as the pre-procedure hand hygiene step		
17. With the plastic matting and paper towel rolled back out of the way, sit Leg Club member in chair and aid in removal of shoes. Roll back the work surface and place bandaged leg(s) onto the clean area	17.1 To prevent contamination of clean working surface with outside shoes	17.1 To prepare patient for procedure 17.2 Self-care where possible to encourage/maintain independence and personal involvement in process
18. Apply single patient use disposable plastic apron	18.1 To prevent contamination of uniform during leg care to prevent production of reservoir of contamination for indirect transmission of pathogens between patients 18.2 To prevent gross contamination of nurse	18.1 To demonstrate application of infection control to Leg Club member and thus allay any fears of cross-contamination
19. Listen to Club member's symptoms and experiences since last attendance and observe for strikethrough of exudate amount and odour while preparing dressings and bandages onto trolley surface	19.1 Be alert to the possibility of deterioration through critical colonisation or infection 19.2 Clean trolley surface acceptable, as this is a 'clean' procedure rather than a full 'sterile/aseptic' one	19.1 Active listening improves interpersonal relationship 19.2 Interpretation of clinical signs and symptoms may lead to modification of treatment procedure
20. Apply gloves (see A8 above)	20.1 To prepare for procedure in which contamination of hands will occur	20.1 As C 18.1
21. Place bandaged leg into plastic waste bag (preferably orange) and using specialist bandage scissors (see A9 above) cut off bandages and remove dressings, unless adhered, directly into bag	21.1 Cutting rather than unwinding reduces linting of contaminated fibres to environment (non-cohesive short-stretch bandages which need to be unwound are low-linting products) 21.2 Immediate containment of contaminated materials reduces cross-contamination of work station	21.1 Time efficient removal and disposal 21.2 Prevention of iatrogenic skin damage through use of protected end bandage scissors

Table 18.1: cont		
Process point, column A	Infection control nursing rationale, column B	General nursing rationale, column C
22. Place leg in bucket of water — remove loosened dressings, skin scales, wash off exudate from skin	22.1 Removal of dressings and scales in water reduces aerosolisation of dried exudate and contaminated skin scales	22.1 To reduce pain at dressing removal 22.2 To remove exudate from skin that can cause skin irritation/excoriation 22.3 To reduce odour 22.4 To promote feelings of cleanliness for patient
23. Remove leg from bucket and support by placing foot on bucket edge and 'pat' dry with disposable paper towel	23.1 Drain majority of contaminated water back into bucket, preventing excessive contamination of work station	23.1 Patting dry rather than rubbing prevents abrasive skin damage
24. Place bucket in a convenient position on workstation plastic mat for later disposal	24.1 To prevent contamination of the work station from drips of water	24.1 To prevent interruption of redressing procedure that might lead to drying of ulcer surface and unnecessary pain
25. Further remove skin scales and wound edge fibrin deposits with gloved finger and sterilised metal forceps, or size 15 scalpel blade attached to handle	25.1 Forceps/scalpel need to be sterile following last use to prevent cross-contamination. They should be clean, dry and dust-free at the point of use, so that they can be placed on non-sterile surface trolley or work station surface 25.1 Removal of scales, etc reduces harbouring points for micro-organisms	25.1 Loose scales can be removed atraumatically with gloved fingers but many adherent scales can be better removed by careful separation, with appropriate instrument reducing likelihood of damage to underlying delicate skin 25.2 The use of metal instruments and scalpel blades attached to handles allows for greater dexterity in the procedure, thus reducing the risk of harm 25.3 The use of the scalpel is for separation, not cutting, so is not sharp debridement. It is still a skilful procedure and must be performed by a competent and accountable practitioner
26. Dispose of fully disposable scalpel into a CE marked orange-lidded sharps bin immediately at end of use, or if using a reusable handle, employ a proprietary blade remover	26.1 To prevent contaminated sharps injury	26.1 Comply with HTM07-01 Safe management of healthcare waste

Table 18.1: cont		
Process point, column A	Infection control nursing rationale, column B	General nursing rationale, column C
27. Dispense chosen emollient into gloved hand using the forearm to depress the plunger and without touching nozzle end	27.1 To prevent contamination of product reservoir that would facilitate transmission of micro-organisms between patients	
28. Apply emollient to leg in downward strokes	28.1 Reduces probability of inducing folliculitis	
29. If required, apply topical steroids from patients own supply	29.1 To avoid potential for cross-contamination	29.1 As C13.1 29.2 Treat eczema/dermatitis to increase comfort and reduce chronic inflammation that can contribute to non-healing
30. Apply dressing of choice relevant to needs of the ulcer, in particular, use of antimicrobial slow-release dressing products are suited for the control of odour and the state of critical colonisation	30.1 Reduction of bioburden in wounds where healing is delayed may return wound to healing progress 30.2 Use of slow-release antimicrobial products in ulcers that are wet and have tendency to strikethrough on outer surface of bandages between dressing changes may contribute to reducing shed of microbes to the general environment of the Leg Club	30.1 While simple non-adherent dressings are often advocated for venous ulcer bandages, there will be times when other dressings, including fully occlusive products, may be more suitable, for example, occlusive foam products in combination with hosiery or in mixed aetiology ulcers
31. Apply chosen bandage system to venous ulcers or post healing legs with venous pathology (in absence of arterial disease of note) at relevant compression according to assessment	31.1 Reduction of oedema by compression removes one of the risk factors for infection	31.1 Reversal of underlying venous hypertension is the mainstay of ulcer healing and prevention of occurrence/recurrence
32. Fold up the paper towel work surface to contain loose skin flakes and dispose into orange waste bag	32.1 To prevent contamination of the Leg Club environment	32.1 As C18.1
33. Assist as necessary with replacing shoes/clothing		33.1 As C17.2
34. Control the disposal of waste water to toilet by grasping the neck of the bucket liner. Discard liner, work station paper towel, apron and gloves	34.1 All items contaminated by blood/body fluids (and skin) until recently were classed as clinical waste. However the new HTM07 allows	34.1 Capture any soaked off dressings to prevent drain blockages

Table 18.1: cont		
Process point, column A	Infection control nursing rationale, column B	General nursing rationale, column C
to orange basket, wash and disinfect hands	soiled dressings to be classed as infectious waste which can be disposed of in the orange sack waste stream. It is essential that local NHS trust procedures are followed for transportation and final disposal of all waste associated with the Leg Club in accordance with HTM07-01: http://www.dh.gov.uk/assetRoot/04/14/08/93/04140893.pdf.	
35. Dispose of recognisable healthcare waste that is neither infectious nor hazardous into yellow/black coded bags (such as dressing packaging). (Waste which is not identifiable as healthcare associated waste can go to the domestic waste stream — black bag waste)	35.1 Waste is not contaminated so can go to landfill at suitably licensed facilities. However, it is essential that local NHS trust procedures are followed for packaging, transportation and final disposal of all waste associated with the Leg Club in accordance with HTM07-01 http://www.dh.gov.uk/assetRoot/04/14/08/93/04140893.pdf)	35.1 To reduce cost of disposal
36. Apply a clean pair of gloves and using detergent wipes clean trolley dressing surface, chair, plastic matting and bucket. Dispose (unless going on to do item A37) of the gloves and used wipes to orange bag, unless instructed otherwise by local NHS trust arrangements	36.1 As B34.1 36.2 Physical removal of any soilage or dust will remove the vast majority of micro-organisms that may have collected during the procedure 36.3 The wipe may be soiled with minor amounts of blood/body fluid (or skin scales) so is infectious waste	36.1 As C18.1 36.2 Use of gloves for occupational health and safety to prevent skin damage from active agents
37. For any areas that had visible contamination with blood/body fluids (including exudate) disinfect previously cleaned surface (see A36) by wiping with alcohol wipes and allow to air dry before next use. Dispose of gloves	37.1 Ensure disinfection of surfaces (chlorine-releasing agents are considered the first line choice for blood spillage disinfection, but with repeated exposure stainless steel surfaces will rust so the use of alcohol hard surface disinfection wipes,	

Table 18.1: cont		
Process point, column A	Infection control nursing rationale, column B	General nursing rationale, column C
and apron to orange bag waste, unless instructed otherwise by local NHS trust.	following pre-cleaning of the contaminated surface with detergent, is an acceptable alternative) 37.2 Wipe will have been in contact with areas previously soiled with blood/body fluids so would be best regarded as infectious waste (orange bag) for disposal purposes 37.3 As B34.1	
38. Wash hands and forearms with soap and water to remove micro-contamination of skin occurring throughout procedure. Dispose of paper towels to black or yellow/black waste sacks	38.1 To remove any transient organisms on skin from procedure to reduce risk of staff carriage and subsequent cross-contamination	38.1 To remove any residual proteins or glove-manufacturing chemicals on skin that might be a potential sensitiser to nurse
Clearing up at the end of a Leg Club clinical session		
39. Use detergent wipes to thoroughly clean the toilet (cistern [if modern low flush box design], seat, rim and outside of the bowl) used for waste water disposal, and discard used wipes to orange waste sacks	39.1 To remove any vestige of microbial contamination generated from the waste water disposal process	39.1 To ensure the owners of the centre housing the Leg Club are confident that it will be safe for the next users
40. Clean the toilet bowl using a proprietary toilet cleaner and toilet brush provided by the centre housing the Leg Club, or products approved for this purpose by the domestic department of the local NHS trust	40.1 As B39.1	40.1 As C39.1
41. Secure all waste bags firmly either by knotting or by sealing tags	41.1 To prevent contamination of environment by accidental spillage of contents	41.1 To ensure the centre housing the Leg Club is completely ready to facilitate its next users without hindrance or concern for hygiene
42. Write date and address of Leg Club (eg. Leg Club, Debenham) on the outside of each orange and yellow/black	42.1 Comply with waste regulations (HTM07-01 Safe Management of Healthcare Waste:	42.1 Comply with regulations, avoid prosecution

Table 18.1: cont		
Process point, column A	Infection control nursing rationale, column B	General nursing rationale, column C
bag using an indelible felt tip pen	http://www.dh.gov.uk/assetRoot/04/14/08/93/04140893.pdf	42.1 Comply with regulations, avoid prosecution
43. Transportation of waste can be done by the community nurse (called option 1 in the guidance), providing waste is contained in rigid, leak-proof containers, but interpretations of the HTM07-01 may vary locally, so each Club will need to verify the process with the NHS trust waste manager. The alternative process (option 2) will involve collection direct from the Leg Club venue. The community infection control nurse and the district council environment department may also be sources of advice	43.1 As B42.1 In particular, the section on community nursing pages 62–67 govern this area of practice — note options 1 on page 66 and option 2 on page 67	43.1 As C42.1

Conclusion

Keeling *et al* (1997) found that elderly patients with chronic wounds generally experienced low levels of social and emotional support. According to Moffatt *et al* (2006) 'chronic leg ulceration is associated with poorer socioeconomic status, and factors which relate to social isolation'. They were unable to ascertain whether relative poverty and isolation were causative or consequential to the ulceration phenomenon. Franks and Moffatt (2006) were able to produce some evidence to support that patients treated in nurse-led ulcer clinics had better health-related quality of life scores for pain and sleep than those individuals treated in their own homes. Flanagan *et al* (2001) explored the feasibility of a collaborative model of care utilising social service home carers and community nurses. They concluded that there is a need to improve carers' and patients' understanding of ulcer recurrence factors and to facilitate the development of a more balanced professional–patient relationship. These few papers raise issues of isolation and patient empowerment, both of which the social setting of the Leg Club model may go some way to addressing. The increasing popularity of the model will require more organisations to confront issues of how to achieve infection control outside the normal settings of health care. In the UK, there is help in the form of the community infection control nurse, who may be linked to the acute or primary healthcare trust, or be part of the health protection agency (HPA) team. The HPA infection control team also incorporates the consultant in communicable disease control who has a remit to run a district infection control committee (DICC). The DICC brings together the hospital and community infection control teams and other related professionals, such as environmental health officers and may, for example, co-opt members of water companies to discuss matters of community infection control. This might be a suitable forum at which to raise the proposal for a new Leg Club so that matters of relevance such as surveillance of infection, environmental audit, the management of swab specimens, waste control and disposal of liquid wastes to drain can be raised and resolved in advance of the first session at the new venue.

References

Commission for Social Care Inspection (2006a) *Making social care better for people*. CSCI, London, Newcastle and Leeds. Available online at: www. csci.org.uk/ (last accessed 8 November 2006)

Commission for Social Care Inspection (2006b) Website for social care professionals, available online at: www.csci.org.uk/professional/ (last accessed 15 October 2007)

Department of Health (2002) *Getting ahead of the curve: a strategy for combating infectious diseases (including other aspects of health protection). A report by the Chief Medical Officer*. DoH, London

Department of Health (2003) *Winning Ways: Working together to reduce healthcare acquired infections*. DoH, London. Available online at: www. dh.gov.uk/PublicationsAndStatistics/Publications/PublicationsPolicyAn dGuidance/PublicationsPAmpGBrowsableDocument/fs/en?CONTENT_ ID=4095070&chk=J9Gyqw (last accessed 11 January 2007)

Department of Health (2005) *Saving Lives: a delivery programme to reduce Healthcare Associated Infection including MRSA*. DoH, London. Available online at: www.dh.gov.uk/publications

Department of Health (2006a) *A Code of Practice for the Prevention and Control of HCAI*. DoH, London. Available online at: www.dh.gov.uk/asse tRoot/04/13/93/37/04139337.pdf (last accessed 8 November 2006)

Department of Health (2006b) *Infection Control Guidance for Care Homes*. DoH, London. Available online at: www.dh.gov.uk/assetRoot/04/13/63/84/04136384.pdf (last accessed 11 January 2007)

Department of Health (2006c) *Essential steps to safe, clean care: Reducing healthcare-associated infections*. DoH, London. Available online at: www.dh.gov.uk/PublicationsAndStatistics/Publications/PublicationsPolicyAndGuidance/PublicationsPolicyAndGuidanceArticle/fs/en?CONTENT_ID=4136212&chk=fyaZ0R (last accessed 11 January 2007)

Flanagan M, Rotchell L, Fletcher J, Schofield J (2001) Community nurses', home carers', and patients' perceptions of factors affecting venous leg ulcer recurrence and management of services. *J Nurs Management* 9(3): 153–9

Franks P, Moffatt C (2006) Do clinical and social factors predict quality of life in leg ulceration? *Int J Lower Extremity Wounds* 5(4): 236–43

Keeling D, Price P, Jones E, Harding K (1997) Social support for elderly patients with chronic wounds. *J Wound Care* 6(8): 389–91

Khan D (2003) Health centres. In: Lawrence J, May D, eds. *Infection Control in the Community*. Churchill Livingstone, Edinburgh

Moffatt C, Franks P, Doherty D, Smithdale R, Martin R (2006) Sociodemographic factors in chronic leg ulceration. *Br J Dermatol* 155(2): 307–12

National Patient Safety Agency (2007) *Clean your hands campaign*. National Patient Safety Agency, London. Available online at: www.npsa.nhs.uk/cleanyourhands (last accessed 11 January 2007)

Chapter 19

Allergies and leg ulceration

Janice Cameron

Management of peri-ulcer skin can be complex and challenging involving the use of a wide range of topical treatments. Nurses play a key role in the decision-making process of leg ulcer management and care of the peri-ulcer skin and, as such, require a good working knowledge of the appropriate and timely use of topical products such as dressings, emollients, skin protectants, topical steroids and bandages. Allergic contact dermatitis is a common complication of venous ulceration and it is possible for a patient to become allergic to any part of their topical treatment (Tavadia *et al*, 2003; Saap *et al*, 2004; Machet *et al*, 2004). An allergic response may unfavourably influence the healing outcome by leading to breakdown of the surrounding skin and increased serous fluid loss. This can be distressing for the patient who may complain of burning, stinging and itching of the affected area resulting from increased sensory stimulus to the skin (Cameron, 2006). Treatment is directed at controlling any eczema present and identifying the responsible allergen. This is established by patch testing and requires referral to a dermatologist. Changing the treatment alone is not enough, as this could re-expose the patient to the same allergen, which may be present in several different topical preparations (Cameron and Powell, 1992).

Eczema

The terms eczema and dermatitis are now used synonymously. Eczema is an inflammatory reaction in the skin due to different causes. Endogenous eczema is the type of eczema that is related to constitutional factors such as atopic eczema. Exogenous eczema describes the type of eczema that is related to contact with external substances. Allergic contact dermatitis and irritant contact dermatitis fall into this second group. Varicose eczema is coincident to underlying venous dysfunction, although how the eczema develops and its relation to venous dysfunction remains unclear (Monk and Graham-Brown, 1992). Varicose eczema usually first develops around the medial malleolus but can spread over the lower leg. Itchy skin is often a predominant symptom of eczema. If the patient then scratches the eczematous area there is a risk of further loss of epithelium, causing increased discomfort to the patient and delaying healing (Cameron, 1995a). Eczema is seen clinically in the acute phase as erythematous skin, with some skin scale, exudation and vesiculation. In the chronic phase the skin tends to be dry with more skin scale and little or no exudate.

Allergic contact dermatitis (contact sensitivity)

Allergic contact dermatitis, also known as contact sensitivity, is a delayed, type IV, hypersensitivity response activated by T-lymphocytes (Sibbald and Cameron, 2001). When an allergen comes into contact with the skin, allergen-bearing Langerhans cells from the skin, travel via the lymphatics to the draining lymph nodes, where they present the allergen to T-lymphocytes of the immune system. Specific T-cells proliferate to establish immunological memory. The memory T-cells mediate allergic contact dermatitis (Friedman, 1998). The activated (sensitised) lymphocytes produce mediators (eg. lymphokines), which enter the peripheral tissues and skin. On renewed contact with the allergen, these lymphocytes are reactivated via the skin and circulation, where they produce a response. This is seen clinically as inflamed skin, characterised by erythema, weeping, scaling and itching (allergic contact dermatitis) (Scheper *et al*, 1992). This reaction is usually seen in the area of direct contact with the responsible allergen.

The stratum corneum is the most superficial layer of the epidermis and provides the epidermal barrier to water loss from the skin. Cutaneous changes resulting from varicose eczema or maceration impair the skin's natural barrier function. It has been suggested that the occlusive nature of leg ulcer applications on skin where the barrier function has been disturbed in this way, creates the perfect environment for developing allergic contact dermatitis (Wilson *et al*, 1991). Sensitisation requires at least 10–14 days of exposure to the allergen. It is possible, however, for a substance to be used for several years before resulting in an allergic reaction. If a contact allergy is suspected, the patient should be referred to a dermatologist for investigations as to the cause.

Patch testing

Patch testing is an established method of investigating contact dermatitis. The procedure involves the application of prepared test strips applied to healthy skin on the patient's upper back. After two days the test strips are removed and the back examined. A further examination is undertaken two days later. At each examination the degree of erythema, oedema, induration and vesicle formation is recorded and responses graded. The patch testing procedure is undertaken according to guidelines set by the International Contact Dermatitis Group.

Documentation of patch test results

Contact sensitivity to topical applications is particularly common in patients who have chronic venous leg ulcers and many patients have multiple sensitivities, complicating local therapy considerably (Tavadia et al, 2003; Saap et al, 2004; Machet et al, 2004).

Once an allergy has been identified, it is essential that the healthcare team and the patient themselves are aware of the allergy and its potential sources (Table 19.1). The information needs to be clear and concise, in language that can be easily understood by someone who is not familiar with the names of allergens. Just giving a list of allergens to avoid is not enough to prevent re-exposure. The information needs to be well documented and accessible to both the patients and their carers. This should also include guidelines on how to avoid identified sensitisers in clinical practice. Failure to keep this information readily available may result in the patient being re-exposed to the same responsible allergens. This was found to be the case in one study where 72% (n = 50) patients had positive patch tests to allergens relative to leg ulcer treatment, and 47% of these patients had identified sensitisers used in their subsequent treatment (Cameron and Powell, 1996). Patients were often treated repeatedly with products containing the same responsible allergen for up to three months with no improvement before being referred for expert advice. The costs of exposing patients to many weeks of inappropriate treatment like this are enormous, and there is much discomfort for the patient.

Table 19.1: Leg ulcer allergens and potential sources		
Name of allergen	Type	Potential sources
Thiuram/carba/mix	Rubber accelerator	Elastic tubular supports, bandages, elastic stockings, latex gloves worn by carer
Balsam of Peru/ fragrance mix	Perfume	Bath oils, over-the-counter preparations, such as moisturisers and baby products
Wool alcohols	Lanolin	Bath additives, creams, emollients, skin barriers and some baby products
Neomycin, framycetin, bacitracin, gentamicin	Antibiotics	Antibiotic creams and ointments
Parabens (hydroxybenzoates)	Preservatives	Medicaments, creams and paste bandages
Cetylstearyl alcohol, stearyl alcohol, cetyl alcohol	Vehicle (emulsifier)	Most creams, including aqueous cream and corticosteroid creams, and also in emulsifying ointments
Colophony/ester of rosin/ester gum resin	Adhesives	Adhesive-backed bandages and dressings
Tixocortol pivalate	Steroids	Hydrocortisone preparations

Adapted from Cameron, 1995b

Patient information

Information on avoidance of identified sensitisers should be given to the patient in a form that is acceptable to them. Cameron (1998) describes how an allergen alert card was developed containing relevant information regarding what the patient is allergic to and the products that should be avoided in the patient's treatment. Elderly patients find it difficult to remember what they are allergic to and, even if they do, remember few patients would challenge a nurse's or doctor's treatment decision. The allergen alert cards are designed for the patients to carry themselves and can fit easily into a pocket or handbag. The cards are then readily available for the patient to present to the primary health care team for consultation, before instigating a change in treatment.

Main leg ulcer allergens

Rubber accelerators (thiuram mix, carba mix)

Clinical relevance: There appears to be a steady increase in allergic reactions to rubber chemicals (Gooptu and Powell, 1999). This appears to coincide with changes in nursing practice over the years to increased use of rubber latex gloves. Other possible sources of rubber exposure include some elastic bandages and some compression stockings.
Recommendation: It is advisable to wear vinyl gloves, instead of rubber latex to treat leg ulcer patients. If a patient has a confirmed rubber allergy, you should check with the relevant manufacturers that any stockings of choice do not contain rubber latex before prescribing these.

Topical antibiotics (neomycin; framycetin; gentamicin, bacitracin)

Clinical relevance: Neomycin and gentamicin remain high sensitisers in leg ulcer patients. A number of sensitivities to topical antibiotics have been found to correspond to increased use locally (Saap *et al*, 2004).
Recommendation: It is best to avoid using topical antibiotics around leg ulcers as they may sensitise.

Fragrances (Balsam of Peru/fragrance mix)

Clinical relevance: Balsam of Peru and fragrance mix are both markers of fragrance allergy and continue to be main sensitisers in leg ulcer patients. Fragrances can be found in creams, barrier preparations and bath additives (Machet *et al*, 2004; Tavadia *et al*, 2003).
Recommendation: Avoid products containing fragrances on leg ulcer patients. Advise patients not to use over-the-counter moisturisers on their legs themselves.

Lanolin (wool alcohols)

Clinical relevance: Although lanolin is not a potent sensitiser on normal skin, it remains a significant sensitiser in patients with varicose eczema and leg ulcers (Renna and Wollina, 2002; Machet *et al*, 2004). Lanolin is present in some barrier preparations, creams, bath additives and emollients used in the management of leg ulcers. It is also present in some over-the-counter products, including baby products, which may be used by the patients themselves.

Recommendation: Lanolin is often listed in the product ingredient labelling as wool alcohols and healthcare teams and patients may not always recognise this as being lanolin. The newer lanolins may still have a potential to sensitise and, as the aim of treatment is to avoid potential sensitisers, they are best avoided on this group of patients (Cameron, 2006). An efficient and cost-effective emollient is a mixture of 50% white soft paraffin in 50% liquid paraffin (50/50).

Emulsifier (cetylstearyl alcohol, cetyl and stearyl alcohol, cetearyl alcohol)

Clinical relevance: Cetylstearyl alcohol is used in creams, ointments and other topical preparations as a stiffening agent and emulsion stabiliser. It is found in emollients such as aqueous cream and emulsifying ointment and in most creams, including those used as direct ulcer applications. It is also present in some paste bandages and in steroid creams (Cameron and Powell, 1992).

Recommendation: Creams should be avoided where possible on leg ulcers and on the peri-ulcer skin. This includes topical steroid creams. Where possible, ointments in a white soft paraffin base should be used instead.

Other leg ulcer allergens of relevance

Preservatives — parabens (hydroxybenzoates)

The parabens group of preservatives are widely used in topical preparations and possess antibacterial and antifungal properties.

Hydrogels

Sensitisation to hydrogels is becoming increasingly reported (Dawes, 2000; Tavadia *et al*, 2003; Lee and Kim, 2004). This is thought to be due to the ingredient propylene glycol, which is found in some hydrogels.

Topical corticosteroids

It is possible for a patient to become allergic to topical steroids used to treat their eczema (Gonul and Gul, 2005, Reichart *et al*, 1999). Therefore, patients who are exhibiting a poor response to treatment with topical steroids should be referred for patch testing.

Adhesives (colophony/ester of rosin/ester gum resin)

Colophony is a widespread, naturally occurring material, which is obtained from tree rosin. Colophony and its derivatives can be found in the adhesive backing of some tapes, plasters, bandages and dressings. Skin reactions to adhesive dressings are not always due to an allergy however. Continual repeated application and removal of adhesive dressings may lead to an inflammatory skin reaction in some individuals (Zillmer *et al*, 2006; Dykes *et al*, 2001). Without the benefit of patch testing, it is difficult to determine whether the resulting skin reaction is an allergic or irritant reaction, as the clinical appearance is often indistinguishable. A further potential complication of adhesive-backed tapes and dressings is blistering of the skin at the dressing edges. This occurs when the epidermis becomes separated from the dermis due to excessive shear forces at the epidermis/dermis interface (Cosker *et al*, 2005). A barrier preparation that leaves a protective film on the skin surface may be applied under adhesive dressings to aid adhesion and prevent trauma on removal.

Frequency of allergic contact dermatitis in leg ulcer patients is summarised in *Table 19.2*.

Treatment

Treatment of allergic contact dermatitis is directed at controlling any eczema present and identifying the responsible allergen. Topical steroids are the mainstay of treatment for eczema and classified according to their potency as follows; weak, moderate, potent and very potent. The choice of potency will be dependent on the severity of the eczema (*Table 19.3*). Topical steroids are available in lotions, creams and ointments. Where possible, an ointment in a white soft paraffin base should be used around a leg ulcer. Ointments are generally free of potential sensitisers, have moisturising properties and an occlusive effect that enhances penetration of the steroid into the skin (Monk and Graham-Brown, 1992).

The amount of steroid to apply is measured in fingertip units (FTU) (*Box 19.1*). A patient with an acute eczema over the lower leg would require approximately three FTUs of a potent topical steroid ointment for a few days. The steroid ointment should be applied in a thin layer to the eczematous area and not rubbed into the skin. When the eczema resolves, the amount of topical steroid should be gradually reduced and replaced with an emollient such as 50/50 over several days (Sibbald and Cameron, 2001). If the steroid ointment is stopped suddenly, there may be a rebound effect where the inflammatory process takes hold again.

Table 19.2: Allergic contact dermatitis in leg ulcer patients			
Reference	Number of patients patch tested	Frequency of contact sensitivity	Most frequent sensitisers
Wilson *et al*, 1991	81	67%	lanolin, neomycin, framycetin, cetylstearyl alcohol, parabens, balsam of Peru, rubber accelerators, ester gum resin, gentamicin
Zaki *et al*, 1994	85	81%	bacitracin, neomycin, framycetin, lanolin, balsam of Peru, cetylstearyl alcohol
Gallemkemper *et al*, 1998	36	78%	lanolin, balsam of Peru, colophony, fragrances, cetearyl alcohol, neomycin, propylene glycol
Reichert-Penetrat *et al*, 1999	359	82.5%	Balsam of Peru, lanolin, neomycin
Tavadia *et al*, 2003	200	68%	balsam of Peru, fragrances, neomycin, metronidazole, lanolin, cetyl/stearyl alcohol, rubber accelerators, topical corticosteroids
Machet *et al*, 2004	106	75%	balsam of Peru, fragrances, lanolin, colophony, neomycin, topical corticosteroids
Saap *et al*, 2004	54	63%	balsam of Peru, bacitracin, fragrances, propylene glycol, neomycin, rubber accelerators

> ### Box 19.1: Measuring a finger tip unit
>
> One figure tip unit (FTU) is the amount of ointment expressed from a tube (with a 5mm diameter), along the distance from the tip of the adult index finger to the first crease.
>
> 1 FTU = 0.5 g
>
> (Long and Finlay, 1991)

When a topical steroid is required long term on a patient with chronic eczema, a moderately potent steroid would be appropriate (*Table 19.3*).

Dressings

It is best to avoid using adhesive dressings, or those with an adhesive border, on eczematous skin. Once the eczema has resolved following application of a topical steroid for a few days, an adhesive dressing may be applied unless, of course, the patient has been found to be allergic to that particular dressing.

Inappropriate choice of a dressing on a heavily exuding ulcer or unrealistic expectations of wear time may result in excessive wound exudate coming into contact with the skin. Chronic wound exudate contains raised levels of proteolytic enzymes that can damage healthy tissue (Trengove *et al*, 1999). Erythematous maceration may occur where the peri-wound skin is red and inflamed and may be moist or weeping. The patient may complain of burning, stinging and itching of the affected area. The inflammatory response can appear similar to an allergic reaction and the dressing being used at the time can be mistakenly attributed to causing an allergic reaction. The use of a suitable skin protectant applied to the peri-wound skin can prevent skin damage from wound exudate and reduce the risk of further loss of epithelium (Cameron *et al*, 2005). Before using a skin protectant, a topical steroid preparation may be applied for a few days to reduce the local inflammation.

Avoidance of identified allergens

Before changes to the patient's wound and skin care treatment are instigated, any documentation regarding allergies should be consulted and relevant sensitivities noted. The ingredient labelling on the packaging can then be checked to identify if the relevant allergen is present before the treatment is applied to the patient. Where there is doubt as to the suitability of the product on a patient with known sensitivities, the company should be contacted for advice.

Identification and subsequent avoidance of any responsible allergens will reduce the complications associated with an allergic contact dermatitis. The effect on the patient is an improvement in the condition and comfort of their skin and sometimes healing of the wound (Cameron, 2006).

Guidelines for avoiding leg ulcer allergens, include:

- avoid wearing latex gloves. Use vinyl gloves instead
- avoid using topical antibiotics around leg ulcers
- avoid products containing fragrance
- avoid creams and use ointments in a white soft paraffin base instead

Table 19.3: Topical steroids		
Potency	Steroid preparation	Indications for use
Very potent	Dermovate™ (Glaxo SmithKline) (clobetasol propionate)	Severe inflammatory skin conditions not responding to a less potent topical steroid. For short-term use only. Reduce to a lower potency preparation after one week
Potent	Betnovate™ (Glaxo SmithKline) (betamethasone) Elocon™ (Schering Plough) (mometasone furoate)	Severe inflammatory skin conditions
Moderately potent	Eumovate™ (Glaxo SmithKline) (clobetasone butyrate)	Inflammatory skin disorders. Suitable for use on patients with chronic eczema when treatment is required for longer periods of time
Mild	Hydrocortisone	For mild inflammatory skin disorders. Suitable for the face and flexural areas

- apply 50/50 white soft paraffin mix as a regular emollient
- patients exhibiting an inflammatory response to treatment should be referred for patch testing.

Allergen avoidance in leg ulcer treatment could prevent the incidence of contact sensitivity, improve patient care and reduce health service costs associated with inappropriate treatment.

Definition of terms:

Allergens:	substances causing an allergic reaction
Corticosteroids:	steroids
Eczema:	itchy, inflammatory disorder of the skin.
Erythematous:	reddened
Lymphocytes:	specific white blood cells important in immunity and allergy
Sensitisers:	substances that provokes an allergic reaction on re-exposure

---

References

Cameron J, Powell S (1992) Contact dermatitis: its importance in leg ulcer patients. *Wound Management* 2(3): 12–13

Cameron J (1995a) Contact sensitivity and eczema in leg ulcer patients. In: Cullum N, Roe B, eds. *Leg ulcers: Nursing management*. Scutari Press, London

Cameron J (1995b) The importance of contact dermatitis in the management of leg ulcers. *J Tissue Viability* 5(2): 52–5

Cameron J, Powell S (1996) *Contact sensitivity in relation to allergen exposure in leg ulcer patients*. Poster presentation at 6th European Conference on Advances in Wound Management, Amsterdam

Cameron J (1998) Red card for allergies. *Nursing Standard* 13(3): 22–4

Cameron J (2006) Allergic reactions to treatment. In: White R, Harding K, eds. *Trauma and Pain in Wound Care*. Wounds UK Ltd, Aberdeen

Cameron J, Hofman D, Wilson J, Cherry G (2005) Comparison of two peri-wound skin protectants in venous leg ulcers; a randomised controlled trial. *J Wound Care* 14(5): 233–6

Cosker T, Elsayed S, Gupta S, *et al* (2005) Choice of dressing has a major impact on blistering and healing outcomes in orthopaedic patients. *J Wound Care* 14(1): 27–30

Dawe RS, Bianchi J, Douglas MB (2000) Allergic reactions to hydrogels. *J Wound Care* **8**(4): 179 (letters)

Dykes P, Heggle R, Hill SA (2001) Effects of adhesive dressings on the stratum corneum. *J Wound Care* **10**(2): 7–10

Friedman PS (1998) Allergy and the skin. II — Contact and atopic eczema. In: Durham SR, ed. *ABC of Allergies*. BMJ Books, London

Gallenkemper G, Rabe E, Bauer R (1998) Contact sensitisation in chronic venous insufficiency: modern wound dressings. *Contact Dermatitis* **38**: 274–8

Gonul M, Gul U (2005) Detection of contact hypersensitivity to corticosteroids in allergic contact dermatitis patients who do not respond to topical corticosteroids. *Contact Dermatitis* **53**: 67–70

Gooptu C, Powell SM (1999) The problems of rubber hypersensitivity (Types I and IV) in chronic leg and stasis eczema patients. *Contact Dermatitis* **41**: 89–93

Lee JE, Kim SC (2004) Allergic contact dermatitis from a hydrogel dressing (Intrasite gel) in a patient with scleroderma. *Contact Dermatitis* **50**: 376–7

Long CC, Finlay AY (1991) The finger-tip unit — a new practical measure. *Clin Exp Dermatol* **16**: 444–7

Machet L, Couhe C, Perrinaud A, *et al* (2004) A high prevalence of sensitisation still persists in leg ulcer patients: a retrospective series of 106 patients tested between 2001 and 2002 and a meta-analysis of 1975–2003 data. *Br J Dermatol* **150**(5): 929–35

Monk BE, Graham-Brown RAC (1992): Eczema. In: Graham-Brown RAC, Monk BE, eds. *Skin Disorders of the Elderly*. Blackwell Scientific Publications, Oxford

Reichert-Penetrat S, Barbaud A, Weber M, Schmutz JL (1999) Leg ulcers. Allergologic studies of 359 cases. *Ann Dermatol Venereol* **126**(2): 131–5

Renna R, Wollina U (2002) Contact sensitization in patients with leg ulcers and/or leg eczema: comparison between centers. *Lower Extremity Wounds* **1**(4): 251–5

Saap L, Fahim S, Arsenault E, *et al* (2004) Contact sensitivity in patients with leg ulcerations: a North American study. *Arch Dermatol* **140**(10): 1241–6

Scheper RJ, von Blomberg M (1992) Cellular mechanisms in allergic contact dermatitis. In: Rycroft RGJ, Menné T, Frosch PJ, Benezra C, eds. *Textbook of Contact Dermatitis*. Springer-Verlag, Berlin

Sibbald RG, Cameron J (2001) Dermatological aspects of wound care. In: Krasner DL, Rodeheaver GT, Sibbald RG, eds. *Chronic Wound Care: A clinical source book for healthcare professionals*. 3rd edn. Wayne, PA, HMP Communications: 273–85

Tavadia S, Bianchi J, Dawe RS, *et al* (2003) Allergic contact dermatitis in venous leg ulcer patients. *Contact Dermatitis* **48**: 261–5

Trengove NJ, Stacey MC, MacAuley S, *et al* (1999) Analysis of the acute and chronic wound environments: the role of proteases and their inhibitors. *Wound Rep Regen* **7**: 42–52

Wilson CL, Cameron J, Powell SM, *et al* (1991) High incidence of contact dermatitis in leg ulcer patients — implications for management. *Clin Exp Dermatol* **16**: 250–3

Zaki I, Shall L, Dalziel KL (1994) Bacitracin: a significant sensitiser in leg ulcer patients? *Contact Dermatitis* **31**: 92–4

Zillmer R, Agren MS, Gottrup F, Karlsmark T (2006) Biophysical effects of repetitive removal of adhesive dressings on peri-ulcer skin. *J Wound Care* **15**(5): 187–91

Chapter 20

Wound pain and dressings

Deborah Hofman

Patients with wounds, whether acute or chronic, are likely to suffer associated pain. For many patients, the worst aspect of their wound is the pain that it causes, rather than other factors which may affect quality of life such as exudate, odour, and restricted mobility. The presence of unrelieved pain may delay healing, leading to a vicious circle of pain, emotional debilitation, poor concordance, and slow healing (*Figure 20.1*).

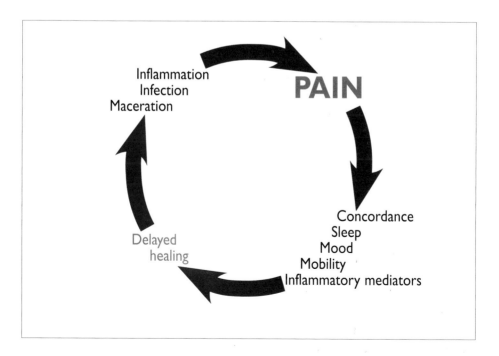

Figure 20.1: Vicious circle of pain

It has become widely recognised that the problem of pain associated with chronic wounds is often ignored and/or poorly managed, resulting in prolonged suffering (Dallam, 1995; Hofman, 1997; Noonan and Burge, 1998; Moffatt, 2002). Persistent pain is often marginalised or ignored because it can be a difficult problem to resolve. Moreover, older patients with chronic wounds are often reluctant to take medication, either because they are already taking multiple medicines, or because they are concerned about the side-effects, eg. confusion, constipation, nausea and nightmares. Ways of managing wound pain that reduce the need for systemic analgesia should therefore be considered. Over the last decade, industry and wound care practitioners have been paying more attention to the role of dressings in reducing wound pain (Thomas, 1994; Dallam *et al*, 1995; Briggs, 1996; Hofman and Cooper, 2005; Hollinworth, 2005).

This chapter concentrates on leg ulceration, although much of what is discussed is relevant to other types of chronic wounds where pain is a problem.

Wound assessment

Before considering dressing choice for a patient, a full assessment should be undertaken to determine the aetiology of the wound and the possible cause(s) of wound pain. It is important to establish the cause of a wound to instigate correct treatment which may, of itself, bring pain relief. The practitioner must be clear as to what is causing the ulcer in addition to what is causing the pain.

Leg ulceration assessment is a complex process and, with an increasingly elderly and frail population, it is common to see multiple pathologies which may have an impact on healing and pain. An accurate diagnosis must be established, although it may be necessary to address the problem of pain in the first instance. This may mean systemic analgesia, soothing dressings, and withholding compression (if indicated) until the pain has been resolved.

All leg ulcers may be painful, and the pain may result from one or more causes. For example, leg pain may be related to the damage to the surrounding skin or underlying vascular structures, or arise from the wound itself. Patients may also have underlying arthritic and/or muscle pain. In addition, there may well be an emotional component (*Table 20.1*). Not all types of pain are amenable to relief by dressings alone and a multidisciplinary approach is often required.

Dressings helpful in controlling pain, may be beneficial in patients suffering from hypersensitivity and wind-up pain. However, dressings are unlikely to have any beneficial effect on some of the other causes of pain listed in *Table 20.1*, eg. allodynia, phlebitis, arthritis, or claudication. Involving the patient in dressing choice and dressing removal may help to reduce the negative psychological aspects.

Table 20.1: Leg ulcer pain	
Skin	Maceration, dermatitis, infection, inflammation, oedema, lipodermatosclerosis, atrophie blanche
Vascular	Phlebitis, ischaemia, deep vein thrombosis (DVT)
Muscular	Cramp, claudication
Skeletal	Arthritis, gout
Nerve	Neuropathy (allodynia, hypersensitivity, wind-up)
Wound	Infection, inflammation, injury, poor exudate management
Psychological	Depression, anger, fear

Useful pain

Pain is the body's alarm signal for tissue damage and pain assessment should be given the same priority as assessment of temperature, pulse, respiration and blood pressure (Turk and Melzack, 2001). In wounds, further tissue damage may be caused by infection, inflammation, or ischaemia. It may also be iatrogenic, being caused by bandaging or inappropriate dressings. It is necessary to establish the cause of the pain before considering dressing choice (*Table 20.2*).

Infection

High bacterial load will increase pain levels even before frank infection is apparent. Wound infection without cellulitis can also be identified by signs such as change of granulation tissue, increased exudate and odour, as well as an increase of pain. Many patients report immediate pain relief when systemic antibiotics are prescribed, even when there are no signs of cellulitis. It would, therefore, be reasonable to suppose that dressings which reduce the bacterial bioburden of the wound will also relieve pain. Unfortunately, some of these dressings can cause increased pain on application (eg. iodine and honey dressings).

For the last ten to fifteen years, most topical antimicrobials have been out of vogue with wound care practitioners, although cadexomer iodine dressings have retained a role, especially with the emergence of methicillin-resistant *Staphylococcus aureus* (MRSA). However, iodine dressings may be painful and many patients cannot tolerate them. Honey dressings have recently become popular in the management of heavily colonised/infected wounds (Cooper *et al*, 1999; Cooper and Molan, 1999), although many patients report a drawing sensation when these dressings are applied. This can be intolerable so they are not the first choice for very painful wounds (Hollinworth, 2005).

Table 20.2: Useful pain (the four Is)	
Causes of pain	Dressings/treatments to consider
Infection	• systemic antibiotics • antimicrobial dressings (iodine, silver, honey dressings — iodine and honey may cause increased pain – and metronidazole gel) • Prontosan® antibiotic creams (B. Braun)
Inflammation	• new generation hydrogels, eg. ActiFormCool® (Activa) • topical anti-inflammatory treatment, eg. Biatain Ibu® (Coloplast), topical corticosteroids
Ischaemia	• check Doppler reading (refer to vascular unit if appropriate) • avoid pressure on area • choose dressings that promote angiogenesis, eg. hydrocolloids, lipidocolloids, second-generation hydrogels
Iatrogenic	• check dressings and bandaging are not causing tissue damage • allow more time at dressing change • consider analgesia prior to dressing change and/or Entonox® • consider patch testing

In the author's experience, silver sulfadiazine cream (SSD cream) is often soothing on painful wounds, but it is unclear whether this is because it is a cool cream or because its antibacterial action is analgesic. SSD cream can be used in conjunction with a non-adherent or soft silicone dressing, but is not appropriate in heavily exuding wounds. A lipidocolloid impregnated with silver sulfadiazine is useful in managing wet wounds where application of a cream is not appropriate (Carsin *et al*, 2004). Pseudomonas thrives in wet wounds and causes increased exudate, maceration, and soreness of the surrounding skin, as well as producing proteases which trigger inflammation and pain (see below).

Recent case reports have shown that Prontosan®, (B Braun) (a wound irrigation liquid and gel), is effective at reducing bacterial load in chronic wounds and has an impact on pain levels. It also has the additional benefit that it is not painful on application (Horrocks, 2006).

Over the last few years, there has been much interest in the role of dressings containing silver in the management of bacteria (Thomas, 2003; Bowler, 2004; Lansdown, 2005). Absorbent silver dressings have been developed which absorb exudate as well as releasing silver into the wound. These are particularly beneficial in wet, heavily colonised wounds. Dressings which hold exudate next to the skin increase skin damage and pain and this is true of some foam dressings (*Figure 20.2*). Dressings which draw exudate away from the skin surface should, therefore, be selected.

Chronic wounds are often heavily colonised with anaerobic bacteria which can be treated by metronidazole gel. Caution,

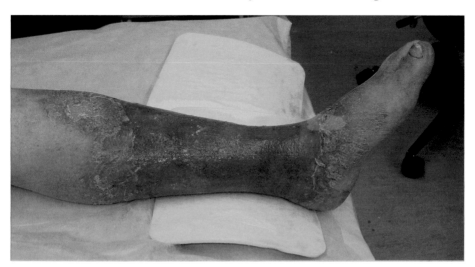

Figure 20.2: Patient whose eczema has been exacerbated by a foam dressing keeping exudate in contact with the skin

however, should be used in patients taking warfarin as metronidazole enhances the anticoagulant effect.

Wounds where there is necrotic tissue or slough will have a heavy bioburden (Bellingeri and Hofman, 2006), and consequent inflammation and pain. Once the necrotic tissue is removed the wound may be less painful, although the process itself, be it sharp debridement or larval therapy, may cause pain. Topical anaesthesia is effective when applied to the wound prior to sharp debridement, although it is not licensed for this purpose (Hansson *et al*, 1993). Moist dressings which enhance autolysis are a gentler approach than sharp debridement, although the process will take longer. However, new generation hydrogel sheets appear to have a much faster debriding action than hydrogels (Armitage and Roberts, 2004).

Inflammation

Chronic inflammation in the wound is considered to be one of the major factors in delayed healing (Agren *et al*, 2000). The inflammatory mediators that modulate wound healing can also induce pain by triggering nociceptors, and add to the heightened perception of pain by lowering the triggering threshold of nociceptors (Cunha *et al*, 2005). Inflammation is associated with infection, but can be present in a wound that is otherwise showing no signs of infection (Agren *et al*, 2000). Inflammation would, therefore, appear to be an important feature of persistent pain in patients with chronic wounds. In wounds where inflammation is a problem, there is a growing interest in some specialist centres in the role of topical corticosteroids (Hofman *et al*, 2007), but their use remains controversial and they should not be applied by the non-specialist as there are increased risks of infection, contact sensitivity, and reduced vascularisation of the wound. Dressings which have been impregnated with non-steroidal anti-inflammatory agents may prove a useful tool in the management of the painful wound (Biatain Ibu®, Coloplast) (Flanagan *et al*, 2006). Clinical experience has shown that new generation hydrogel sheets (Actiform Cool®, Activa) appear to reduce inflammation and are beneficial in the management of persistent wound pain (Armitage and Roberts, 2004).

A wound that is inflamed will be sensitive and non-adhesive silicone dressings may be helpful. Such dressings can be invaluable in the management of patients with wounds associated with auto-immune disorders, such as systemic lupus erythematosus or scleroderma, where the surrounding skin tends to be painful, as well as in the management of children with hereditary fragile skin (epidermolysis bullosa). Adhesive soft silicone dressings (Safetac technology) are especially useful on fragile/tender skin.

Ischaemia

Patients with ischaemic wounds should, where appropriate, be reviewed by a vascular surgeon. In some cases, little can be done surgically to enhance the vascularisation of the wound. In others, the large vessels may be adequate (normal ankle brachial pressure index [ABPI]), but the microcirculation is impaired, eg. in patients with diabetes, patients who smoke, or in patients with microcirculatory disorders, such as sickle cell anaemia, Raynaud's phenomenon). These wounds are normally very painful. Dressings which keep the wound moist and encourage angiogenesis may help to relieve the pain, such as soft silicone dressings, hydrocolloids, hydrogels, and hydrogel sheets.

Iatrogenic-induced pain

All too often, it is the person changing the dressing who causes or exacerbates pain. Pain at dressing change is sometimes difficult to avoid and has been extensively covered in two consensus documents (European Wound Management Association [EWMA], 2002; World Union of Wound Healing Societies [WUWHS], 2004).

When pain at dressing change is anticipated to be severe, or when the patient is afraid of potential pain, systemic analgesia or Entonox® (50% nitrous oxide and 50% oxygen gas) may be given. Fentanyl lozenges given prior to dressing change are also effective (MacIntyre *et al*, 2007).

However, in most cases, selection of a genuinely non-adherent dressing is sufficient. Where there is insufficient exudate, alginates or cellulose dressings will adhere and be difficult to remove. Hydrogels with a non-adherent dressing and pad may also adhere badly (*Figure 20.3*). Traditional dressings, such as gauze and paraffin gauze, often cause trauma and pain on removal and should be avoided (WUWHS, 2004). More modern, adhesive-backed dressings can also cause trauma to fragile skin around the wound and to the wound bed (Hollinworth, 2005); whereas soft silicone or lipidocolloid dressings do not adhere to the wound bed or surrounding skin, and can remain in place for several days so that only the cover dressing is removed. This is of great benefit to a patient who has come to dread dressing changes.

If a patient complains of increased pain following dressing application or bandaging, it may be an indication of tissue injury and the dressing should be removed and the wound re-assessed. The problem of contact sensitivity, and the implications of applying a dressing to which the patient has become sensitised, is dealt with in *Chapter 19*.

Applying a moist dressing to a heavily exudating wound will increase pain and tissue damage. Although it is well-established that a moist environment enhances epithelialisation (Bishop *et al*, 2003), it is also the case that wound exudate is a corrosive biological fluid rich in enzymes which destroys epithelial cells and causes maceration of the surrounding skin (Trengrove *et al*, 1999; Cutting and White, 2002). Moisture balance is crucial not only for patient comfort, but also to provide a good healing environment. The practitioner must become expert at assessing exudate quantity and in choosing dressings which will hydrate, but not over-hydrate a wound and absorb excess exudate.

Bandage injury is unfortunately common and, in a patient with normal sensation, will be preceded by pain. A patient should always be asked whether he is comfortable with the dressing and bandage applied. Nurses should anticipate problems in cases where ulceration occurs over bony prominences, or in sites where bandage creasing will exacerbate a wound (*Figure 20.4*). Cushioning dressings, such as hydrocolloids or foams, can reduce pressure and tissue injury.

Useless pain

Pain caused by damaged nerves (neuropathic pain) performs no useful function in terms of prevention of tissue damage, but can be severely debilitating for the patient.

Neuropathic pain

Careful assessment of wound pain will enable an alert practitioner to identify neuropathic pain, which is common in patients with long-standing wounds. Some neuropathic pain has a different quality from nociceptive pain and is often described as shooting, burning, stabbing or electric shock-like in quality (Cooper and Hofman,

2003). Patients may experience allodynia, where the wound is more or less insensate but the adjacent tissues are hypersensitive and even stroking is unbearable, or hyperalgesia, where the wound has become over a period of time exquisitely painful, and the lightest touch is

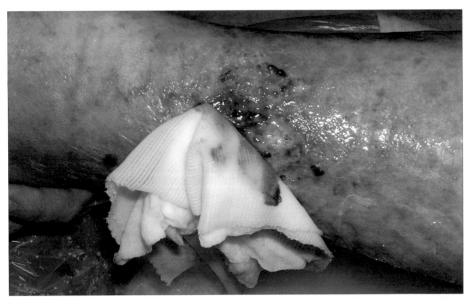

Figure 20.3: Hydrogel and gauze dressing adhering to the wound bed, causing pain and trauma on removal

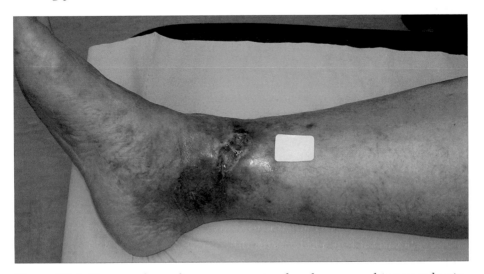

Figure 20.4: Venous ulcer where compression bandage caused increased pain and trauma. Resolved by a hydrocolloid dressing and compression hosiery

unbearable. Wind-up pain, associated with long-standing tissue damage, results in an increase in the perceived intensity of pain. Neuropathic pain normally responds well to oral medication, but dressing choice also has an important part to play. Patients with neuropathic pain will often benefit from a completely non-adherent dressing (eg. a soft silicone or lipidocolloid dressing). In the case of patients suffering from hyperalgesia, a soothing dressing such as a hydrogel or hydrogel sheet may be beneficial. In cases of severe persistent pain, topical morphine or diamorphine mixed with a hydrogel has been shown to be beneficial (Back and Finlay, 1995; Twillman *et al*, 1999; Grocott, 2000; Ashfield, 2005). Topical application, as opposed to systemic administration, has the advantage of minimising the side-effects of opioids (Ashfield, 2005). Patients suffering from wind-up pain or hyperalgesia will need extra care and time during dressing and wound interventions, to allow for reassurance and ensure good communication between the patient and practitioner. It is important to educate practitioners dealing with patients suffering from these types of pain, so that the unusual sensations that these patients report are clearly understood and not dismissed.

Conclusion

There are as yet no randomised control trials (RCTs) listed in the Cochrane database that prove that any dressing has superior pain-relieving qualities over another. However, there is a wealth of expert evidence in the form of published case studies, which can guide practitioners dealing with painful wounds to make sensible and informed choices. The ultimate choice should, of course, rest with the patient who, alone, can make a pronouncement on the pain — relieving qualities or comfort of a dressing. What works for one patient may well not work for another. The best qualities a practitioner working in the field of wound care can have are to actively listen, and to use experience and knowledge effectively to make informed choices in the attempt to alleviate persistent wound pain and promote healing.

References

Agren MS, Eaglstein WH, Ferguson MW, Harding KG, Moore K, Saarialhokere UK, Schultz GS (2000) Causes and effects of the chronic inflammation in venous leg ulcers. *Acta Derm Venereol Suppl* (Stock) **210**: 3–17

Armitage M, Roberts J (2004) Caring for patients with leg ulcers and an underlying vasculitic condition. *Br J Community Nurs* Dec Suppl: S16–S21

Ashfield T (2005) The use of topical opioids to relieve pressure ulcer pain. *Nurs Standard* **19**(45): 90–2

Back IN, Finlay I (1995) Analgesic effect of topical opioids on painful skin ulcers. *J Pain Symptom Manage* **10**(7): 493

Bellingeri A, Hofman D (2006) Debridement of pressure ulcers. In: Romanelli M, Clark M, Cherry G, Colin D, Defloor T, eds. *Science Practice of Pressure Ulcer Management*. Springer, London: 131

Bishop SM, Walker M, Rogers AA, Chen WY (2003) Importance of moisture balance at the wound dressing interface. *J Wound Care* **12**(4): 125–8

Briggs M (1996) Surgical wound pain: a trial of two treatments. *J Wound Care* **5**(10): 456–60

Bowler PG (2004) *Infection: the role of bacterial communities in wound healing*. Paper presented at 2nd World Union of Wound Healing Societies meeting, Paris

Carsin H, Wasserman D, Pannier M, Dumas R, Bohbot S (2004) A silver sulphadiazine-impregnated lipidocolloid wound dressing to treat second-degree burns. *J Wound Care* **13**(4): 145–8

Cooper S, Hofman D (2003) Leg ulcers and pain: A review. *Int J Lower Extremity Wounds* **2**(4): 198–207

Cooper RA, Molan PC (1999) The use of honey as an antiseptic in managing Pseudomonas infection. *J Wound Care* **8**(4): 161–4

Cooper RA, Molan PC, Harding KG (1999) Antibacterial activity of honey against strains of *Staphylococcus aureus* from infected wounds. *J R Soc Med* **92**: 283–5

Cunha TM, Verri WA, Silva JS, *et al* (2005) A cascade of cytokines mediates mechanical inflammatory hypernociception in mice. *PNAS* **102**(5): 1755–60

Cutting KF, White RJ (2002) Maceration of the wound bed 1, its nature and causes. *J Wound Care* **11**: 275–8

Dallam L, Smythe C, *et al* (1995) Pressure ulcer pain: assessment and quantification. *JWOCN* **22**(5): 211–17

European Wound Management Association (EWMA) (2002) *Position Document: Pain at wound dressing changes*. Medical Education Partnership Ltd, London

Flanagan M, Vogensen H, Haase L (2006) *Case series investigating the experience of pain in patients with chronic venous leg ulcers treated with foam dressing releasing ibuprofen*. World wide Wounds, April. Available online at: www.worldwidewounds.com/2006/april/Flanagan/Ibuprfen-Foam-Dressiong.html (last accessed 3 November 2006)

Grocott P (2000) The management of malignant wounds. *Eur J Palliative Nurs* **8**(5): 214–21

Hansson C, Holm J, Lillieborg S, Syren A (1993) Repeated treatment with lidocaine/prilocaine cream (EMLA) as a topical anaesthetic for the cleansing of venous leg ulcers. *Acta Derma Venereal* (Stock) **73**: 231–3

Hofman D, Lindholm C, Arnold F, *et al* (1997) Pain in venous leg ulcers. *J Wound Care* **6**: 222–4

Hofman D, Cooper S (2005) Towards understanding and managing pain in leg ulcers. *Dermatol Practice* **13**(1): 10–12

Hofman D, Moore K, Cooper R, Eagle M, Cooper S (2007) Use of topical corticosteroids on chronic leg ulcers. *J Wound Care* **16**(5): 227–30

Hollinworth H (2005) The management of patients' pain in wound care. *Nurs Standard* **20**(7): 65–73

Horrocks A (2006) Prontosan wound irrigation and gel:management of chronic wounds. *Br J Nurs* **15**: 1222–28

Lansdown ABG, Williams A, *et al* (2005) Silver absorption and antibacterial efficacy of silver dressings. *J Wound Care* **14**(4): 155–60

MacIntyre PA, Margetts L, Larsen D, Barker L (2007) Oral transmucosal fentanyl citrate versus placebo for painful dressing changes: a crossover trial. *J Wound Care* **16**(3): 118–21

Moffatt CJ, Franks PJ, Hollinworth H (2002) Understanding wound pain and trauma: an international perspective. EWMA Position Document (2002) *Pain at Wound Dressing Changes*. Medical Education Partnership, London

Noonan L, Burge SM (1998) Venous leg ulcers: is pain a problem? *Phlebology* **13**: 14–19

Thomas S (1994) Low-adherence dressings. *J Wound Care* **3**(1): 27–30

Thomas S (2003) A comparison of the antimicrobial effects of four silver-containing dressings on three organisms. *J Wound Care* **12**(3): 101–7

Trengrove NJ, Stacey MC, MacAuley S, *et al* (1999) Analysis of the acute and chronic wound environments: the role of proteases and their inhibitors. *Wound Rep Regen* **7**: 442–52

Turk DC, Melzack R (2001) Preface. In: Turk D, Melzack R, eds. *Handbook of Pain Asssessment*. The Guildford Press, New York: viii

Twillman RK, Long TD, Cathers TA, Mueller DW (1999) Treatment of painful skin ulcers with topical opioids. *J Pain Symptom Manage* **17**(4): 288–92

World Union of Wound Healing Societies (2004) *Principles of Best Practice: Minimising pain at wound dressing-related procedures. A consensus document*. Medical Education Partnership Ltd, London. Available online at: www.wuwhs.org/pdf/consensus_eng.pdf

INDEX